The Handbook of Practical Low-Salt Living

(or How to Follow Doctor's Orders without Really Suffering)

THIRD EDITION

Coleen Balch, MSN, RN-BC, ANP, AACC

Grindstone
Press & Graphics

NOURISH YOUR MIND

GrindstonePress.com

Contents

Acknowledgments

*I would like to express my sincere appreciation
for the efforts of several persons and entities.*

To **Saint Rita**, patron saint of desperate cases and the impossible, which only goes to show that with Saint Rita's help, nothing really is impossible.

To **Cathleen Berry**, publisher, Grindstone Press and Graphics, without whom I never would have attempted this project.

To my partner **Anne Milewski-Craner, NP**, for her unwavering dedication, support and encouragement throughout the development and production of this cookbook.

To my mother **Elenor Berry**, for daring to allow me into her kitchen and cookbooks during my formative years.

To my husband **David** and sons **Nathan** and **Jason**, for being guinea pigs on several of the recipes.

To **James Longo, MD, Catherine Wolf, RN**, and **Linda Donnelly, RD**, for their valuable input in the development of this book.

Introduction

"You are the salt of the earth."
"She really earned her salt today."
"That guy's just not worth his salt."

"Bam!" Quick, what image came to your mind? Of course it was one of many TV cooks and chefs tossing salt, sometimes by the handful, into the dish they're preparing. Fun aside, do you really need all that salt? From a culinary perspective that may incite a heated discussion, but from a health perspective, the answer is a resounding "No!" **In fact, for many Americans salt is poison.**

Sodium, the active component of salt, is found naturally in many foods. The human body requires tiny amounts to regulate body fluids and blood pressure and to keep muscles and nerves working smoothly. It does not, however, require the oftentimes mega-doses people make part of their daily diet. In fact, studies have demonstrated that Americans easily consume in excess of 4 grams, even 6 grams (4000–6000 mg.), of sodium per day and too frequently as much as 9 or 10 grams. Does that make you pucker up with thirst? Mmm-hmm. Hold that thought.

Salt is a part of our culture. Not so long ago, before we had freezers and refrigerators, salt was absolutely necessary for preservation of meats, fish, and poultry. Even my hometown of Syracuse, New York, is known as the "Salt City." Salt is part of our lives. It's in our language and in our food. Unfortunately, the American diet is laden with many times the amount of salt we

humans need. Salt shakers are on our tables at home and in our restaurants. If the fry guy forgets to shake it on, we remind him.

The snack aisle in the supermarket shouts salt at us. It's in most canned foods, and commercially frozen foods are not immune. Even some baby foods still have added salt. One place it hides and gets away with it is in our water supply! Stand at the bottled water shelves in your grocery store and compare labels for a real shock. Do you have a water softener at home? Water is "softened" by a process that adds sodium to it. Salt also shows up in additives our government stirs into the reservoirs. Twenty-first-century Americans have a strong taste for salt. We were raised on salt, and that makes it a hard habit to break.

After nearly forty years as a nurse, most of it in the care of heart patients in hospital cardiac and critical care units, I have developed a serious respect for salt. The way something seemingly so insignificant can have such a huge impact, even a life-and-death effect, on people amazes me. I have spent nearly two decades as a hospital nurse practitioner (NP), admitting and managing patients with heart failure, various heart diseases, high blood pressure, and many other cardiac and non-cardiac conditions, all of whom could have reaped serious benefits from a low-sodium lifestyle.

All too often these folks are "repeat offenders" or "frequent flyers" who have never heard about the dark side of sodium (not if they were my patients, of course), didn't appreciate the influence of sodium consumption on their health, or never really understood how to manage it. Possibly they were influenced negatively by the "healthy diet" cookbooks they read, their high-salt-consuming friends and families, those cooking shows that seem to support the salt industry adding salt to recipes by the fistfuls, or the lack of media coverage on the dangers of sodium, unlike the public awareness campaigns against fat and cholesterol.

Do I hear you thinking, "Sodium dangerous? Can't be. It's as common as air and water." It's common all right. Therein lies the problem. It's everywhere, and we are much too complacent about its use. Don't kid yourself any longer. If the millions of people who could benefit from low-salt living would do so, my cardiologist colleagues and I would be looking for new specialties, and our hospitals would solve their overcrowding problems. Most importantly, there would be a positive impact on health care overall. Is that a gauntlet being thrown?

Studies have demonstrated that a serious reduction in our sodium intake as a nation could reduce the number of Americans who develop new heart disease, strokes, or heart attacks by tens of thousands every year, and deaths by nearly 100,000 annually as well. Of course, health care costs are staggering in our country, so what would you think if they went down by 24 million dollars every year? They could—easily—if we would get serious about taking salt out of the places we've been putting it for decades.

How much should we eat? It's not a matter of should, because all the sodium we need is available from unseasoned, naturally occurring sources—how do you think the cavemen did it? No, it's a matter of how much sodium we can tolerate without undesired side effects. Not so long ago, science thought 2.3 grams or 2300 mg. of sodium was a reasonable daily limit; that idea has been amended. (OK, hold on here for just a minute. Time for a bit of clarification. Think back to your high school chemistry. Salt is sodium chloride: $NaCl$, but those food labels—yeah, the ones I know you're reading—report the sodium content, not sodium chloride content. For clarity, 5.8 grams or 5800 mg. of salt contain 2.3 grams or 2300 mg. of sodium. Just stay focused on sodium).

The Centers for Disease Control (CDC) have a wing devoted to heart disease and stroke. They've studied this whole issue and recommend that anyone with the diagnosis of high blood pressure, controlled on medication or not, and everyone over age 40, healthy or not, reduce their sodium intake to 1500 mg. per day. This is also true for all African-Americans no matter age or blood pressure because of a gene-based increased sensitivity to sodium's effects. Two thirds of Americans fit into one or more of those three groups.

The results from the DASH-Sodium Trial showed that a reduction in sodium intake from 2300 mg. to 1500 mg. per day made the most significant impact on lowering blood pressure. At present, less than 10% of Americans meet the old 2300 mg. restriction, never mind the new 1500 mg. recommendation!

The American Heart Association has also recommended that all Americans reduce their sodium intake to 1500 mgs. per day. They are working with federal agencies to reduce the amount of sodium in our food. In fact, they are encouraging restaurants, and food processors and producers to decrease the sodium in our food supply by half over the next decade. Have you noticed the apples available at one fast food restaurant? Even the Centers for Disease Control are in agreement, and they want to start young—no waiting till you're old. The CDC wants everyone, including the

young and healthy, to stay under that 1500 mg. line. The American Society of Hypertension, the American Dietetic Association, and even the American Academy of Pediatrics also stand behind the restriction of sodium intake to under 1,500 mg per day for everyone.

People with no medical problems appear to handle a salt intake much higher than those who do have problems. But that doesn't make it healthy for anybody. There are over five million people in this country living with heart failure. One in every four Americans has high blood pressure. In fact, inadequately controlled high blood pressure is one of the leading causes of heart failure. All heart failure patients and many high blood pressure patients would feel better and be healthier if they controlled their salt intake. For folks with heart problems or blood pressure to control, a diet containing amounts of salt above minimal levels can contribute to their illness, decrease their quality of life, and shorten their lives.

What can reducing your intake of sodium be expected to accomplish? Astonishing and life-saving things, that's what. For example, decreasing our daily sodium intake by as little as 1200 mg. (from whatever level a person has been consuming sodium) will decrease blood pressure enough to reduce new cases of coronary artery disease (the disease that leads to heart attacks) by as many as 120,000 per year, actual heart attacks by as many as 99,000, and strokes by up to 66,000 per year. In fact, decreasing sodium intake may reduce the annual number of deaths from any cause by 44,000. The reduction in mortality from decreased stroke and heart disease due to sodium intake reduction alone may be greater than that achieved by medication. Imagine putting the pharmaceutical industry out of business! All this translates to a national health care cost reduction of as much as $24 billion per year. Imagine the impact of dietary sodium reduction on the economy, on hospitals' bottom lines, on taxes to pay for health care, and so on. This simple, small change can result in big-dollar benefits, not to mention a healthier new you.

So where should we begin to fix this problem? Since an estimated 70 to 80 percent of sodium in the average American diet comes from processed foods, that seems like a good place to start. The salt shaker is the source of only 10% of our daily sodium intake. It's a common misconception that not using a salt shaker means one's sodium intake is minimal, but in reality we get most of our daily dose from food in cans and at the deli, bakery, and frozen food sections. Did you notice the food label on your holiday turkey? Many are injected with sodium-containing solutions to enhance juiciness and flavor, but at what cost? Whatever happened to herbs, spices, and a little creativity?

Eating out is another very large source of dietary sodium, especially in fast food restaurants. A few of these are beginning to get the message and reduce some of the sodium in their menus. In fact there is a national initiative intended to cut salt in packaged and restaurant foods across the United States by 25 percent in five years. Some, such as Taco Bell, have been quietly testing a reduction in overall sodium content and so far have not received complaints. This is a great goal, but do be aware, it is in no way an accomplished one yet—eater beware.

A study sponsored by the National Heart, Lung and Blood Institute found that reducing dietary sodium decreases the blood pressure of both hypertensive patients and healthy patients with normal blood pressures. Everyone benefits. A high-sodium intake also contributes to osteoporosis, especially worrisome for women, but men are not immune. Salt causes the process of calcium loss from bone to speed up, and it encourages the kidneys to excrete the calcium instead of selectively filtering it out and returning it to the body.

Other effects of elevated sodium intake, aside from cardiac, include increased platelet reactivity (think clots, strokes), hardening of the arteries (medical professionals call it decreased arterial compliance), and increased asthma, especially in children.

Heart attack and stroke, commonly a direct result of high blood pressure, are this nation's leading causes of death. Recognizing and reducing the sodium content of our food will go a long way to a healthier nation and a healthier you. The Institute of Medicine recently recommended mandatory national standards for the sodium content of foods. Let's not wait for them to be implemented. Let's get our sodium intake under control now. The health of our hearts is in our hands; I'm not willing to wait until the government gets around to telling me what to eat. Good heavens, they'll probably tell us we have to eat broccoli . . . just kidding, broccoli is good, really.

History 101

Let's explore a little of the history of salt on planet earth to put it into perspective. Going waaayyy back, it seems that Homer (the ancient philosopher, not Simpson) called salt divine, and his buddy Plato referred to it as especially dear to the gods. It had worldwide significance in religious ceremonies and as part of magical charms.

Salt is mentioned in the Torah, or Old Testament, a few times as a symbol of God's promise. In the book called Chronicles, for example, He says: "The Lord God of Israel gave the kingdom over Israel to David forever, even to him, and to his sons, by a covenant of salt." Salt was used in the early practices of Judaism and Islam to symbolize an indisputable agreement. In the Middle Ages, it was tradition to bring bread and salt to the new homes of friends and family as a form of blessing. It was in that era that salt as a preservative began to come into use. Grain was soaked in salty water to overcome a fungal infection called ergot that was poison to the people and animals who ate it. Salt has been used to shield newborns from evil, to protect from the evil eye, and to break the spell on zombies in Haiti. For centuries, salt was hoarded as a symbol of prosperity. In many lands over the history of the world, salt was taxed heavily. In fact, it was often used as payment for work performed.

Soy sauce had its origins in salt use in China. Initially, salt was used to ferment fish, which eventually included soybeans, and finally the fish was dropped and soy sauce was invented. You may have heard of 1000-year old Chinese eggs. They were soaked in a salt solution for months. Egyptians, long before mummy making began, managed to preserve bodies in the salty desert sand such that discoveries today still have flesh and skin after 5000 years. They were also the first, or among the first, to recognize the usefulness of salt in food preservation brining vegetables, fish, fowl, and meat for the long, dry years. The extensive skills and knowledge on preservation of food may have been what set them onto preservation of cadavers.

The Celts, now thought of as settlers of the British Isles, were actually much better traveled than that. Perhaps as long ago as the Bronze Age, they traded throughout Europe and perhaps as far as China. But one of the things they traded most was the salt they actually mined. Bodies of salt-preserved Celts have been found at (and an unlucky few *in*) the salt mine in Austria at Halstatt (from the Celt word for salt, hal). Well outfitted and tooled, they were clearly salt miners giving a distinct indication of the importance of the salt trades and its use in everyday life several millennia ago.

In the seventh century BC, the Roman Empire was a fledgling city, but it was propelled by its proximity to a salt works. The Via Salaria or Salt Road, was an ancient road built for salt trade that contributed immensely to the building of Rome. Roman soldiers were paid at times in salt, hence the term salary and the phrase "worth his salt." Salted greens in the Roman diet led to the term "salad." Salt was a highly taxed item in the Empire.

"Irish" corned beef most likely has its origins in the Middle Ages when they traded for salt that was used for fish, leathering, and beef. The salted beef became known in Europe for its long shelf life. The English are believed to have given corned beef its name in the 17th century but they did a poor job imitating the carefully made Irish product. Fish salting, especially of cod, provided sustenance for Europeans for centuries.

Ever watch cooking shows when the chef tells his audience to work an anchovy or two into a sauce? You aren't supposed to taste fishiness, but it is supposed to enhance the flavor. The practice started hundreds of years ago in . . . wait for it . . . France! French cooking, of course! In the 18th century, the English used salted anchovies in a sauce made with vinegar, wine, and shallots, and numerous spices that they called, uh, ketchup. Yup. It didn't include tomatoes, because they were still waiting for discovery in America. But try to convince the Greeks and Italians of that.

On the American side of the world, it is said that the Mayans not only rose to such a high civilization because of its control of salt three thousand years ago, but they also fell as its salt trade declined. Or perhaps it was the fact that salt, combined with a selection of herbs, was used for birth control (kids, don't try this at home). Trying to debunk the theory that they were all taken by aliens is beyond the scope of this book.

So important was salt all through history that whole civilizations depended on whether they could get or trade enough. Salt was even vital in naming towns and cities around the world.

In America, animal trails led to local salt licks. Because of the need of salt by the new settlers in the 17th and 18th centuries, animal trails became people roads and salt lick sites became settlements, emphasizing the importance of salt in the success of the new settlers. Evidently, villages, towns, and eventually cities, were named for the animals that led the settlers to the salt source where the settlers then, well, settled and named the settlement after the animal that led them to the salt source. An example of this is a town down the road from me: Buffalo, New York.

One of the main purposes for digging "Clinton's Ditch," or the Erie Canal, was to provide a waterway to New York City from the Upstate New York salt works, of which my hometown, Syracuse, was a centerpiece. Salt potatoes—new potatoes boiled in a salty brine, then well buttered—were a creation of some of my Irish ancestors who came to escape the homeland potato famine and work on the canal. Today these sodium-laden spuds remain a local traditional favorite found in all the grocery stores and summer festivals, proving once again that the salt habit is hard to shake (and that humans will follow any trail to a salt lick).

It was the industrious 19th- and 20th-century Americans who began to turn to cold for food preservation, eventually allowing the food industry to rise as refrigeration, and ultimately, long-term freezing became available. While it deflated the salt market, it flamed industry and made millionaires like Clarence Birdseye.

Of course the development of new technologies improved salt operations just as the need for access to salt inspired more technology. Inventions of engines and development of transportation methods improved the ability to move salt around the country. Drilling apparatus advanced, making it easier to mine salt, and coincidentally, oil in the process. By the 1920s in America, The Diamond Crystal Salt Company published a booklet entitled "One Hundred and One Uses for Diamond Crystal Salt." It included ways to use salt to whip cream rapidly, remove rust, kill poison ivy (imagine, salt is a poison to a poison; ironic, huh?), and many other helpful hints. They must have had marketing people with good foresight who saw the coming decline in use of salt for food. After all, eating salt is no longer necessary, or healthy (yep, I snuck that line in—wanted to be sure you kept your focus).

In 2002, the nations producing the greatest amount of all types of salt were, in descending order: United States, China, Germany, India, and Canada. In 2010, a group in New York City began the National Salt Reduction Initiative that called for voluntary compliance of the food industry in a reduction of sodium content by 25% in the next couple years. Some major food producers have announced plans to make some changes in some of their products . . . next it will be a tax on salt and history will repeat itself.

Biology 101

So what is the biological connection between humans and salt? Glad you asked. Understanding how that all works may help you beat the addiction.

Sodium is one of the three main electrolytes in our bodies; the others are potassium and chloride. Sodium is the electrolyte that is primarily on the outside of our cells, and has a positive charge. (In case you were wondering—extra points if you were—potassium is the main electrolyte inside the cells. It also has a positive electrical charge.) It's all part of, and essential for, the way our cells work. If not for these electrolytes, the movement of essential nutrients and fluids in and out of the body's cells would not happen, and nerve cell conduction, or muscle cell contraction, for just a couple examples, wouldn't happen properly.

Sodium is essential for normal bodily functions. It is used to balance the fluids in your body and does this well if you don't have heart or kidney problems. It's part of the chemical process of making the nerves transmit impulses around your body and brain and plays a role in the contraction and relaxation of your muscles.

Normal kidneys are supposed to hold on to sodium when the levels in your body are low. And they are supposed to eliminate excess sodium when the level in your system is too high. But if your kidneys have a problem eliminating enough sodium, they start the fluid-retention ball rolling. Because sodium attracts and holds water, your blood volume increases. Increased blood volume makes your heart work harder to move more blood through your blood vessels, which increases pressure in your arteries. It all backs up, and it may not be very long until you gain fluid weight, get swelling in your ankles, then gradually up your legs and other places. Your lungs get into the act and start soaking up fluid, too. This may or may not happen right along with the edema in your feet and legs.

It can all become just too overwhelming for the kidneys, and they can start to squawk at you—but that isn't something you'll really know until you have blood drawn. The sample taken to the lab will tell the provider if your kidneys are losing the battle or not. When they can't manage anymore, there are changes in the chemistry of your body because waste products begin to back up. This is something that your doctor and the team will watch closely as they adjust medications to get rid of the fluid and improve the heart function.

Some people's bodies are even more sensitive to the effects of sodium than others. If you're sodium sensitive, you retain sodium more easily, leading to fluid retention and increased blood pressure. If this becomes chronic, it can lead to heart disease, stroke, kidney disease, and congestive heart failure. Depending on the degree this reaches, you may need medications to reduce your blood pressure and the excess fluid, before damage happens.

If you don't yet have high blood pressure, heart failure, heart disease, or kidney disease, you may be able to prevent a great deal of future trouble by cutting your sodium intake now. Think of it as preventive medicine (and it's free!) instead of, well, essentially closing the barn door after the horse is out. Once the pressure starts up, you can still make a good offensive move by cutting sodium and taking your medicines. But once the heart and/or kidney failure starts, it becomes imperative that sodium is reduced and managed without exception. It's as important as the medicines.

By the way, there are other, oh, let's call them side benefits, of reducing your sodium intake. For example, reducing salt consumption will reduce the amount of calcium you lose in your urine—yup, that can mean reduced risk of calcium-based kidney stones, and, ladies, it can also mean reduced risk of osteoporosis, a killer of women (and yes, men can have it too). Patients with kidney disease, especially diabetics with decreased kidney function, who decrease their sodium intake, can expect a better kidney-protective effect from medicines of the angiotensin inhibitor class (a group of medicines shown especially useful in both protecting diabetic kidneys, and strengthening the heart).

Platelets, those factors in our bloodstream that ordinarily clump together to make blood form a clot, are affected by sodium intake. They are more reactive in people with high-sodium diets; you may remember that clot is what we fight against in acute heart attack and stroke patients.

There is evidence that high salt intake has a direct effect on the stiffness of our arteries, another factor in hypertension. And, as I mentioned briefly before, there is even a link between ordinary high (I'm not talking really high, just typical high) sodium diets and childhood asthma!

Now here's some interesting insights I didn't know. Those taste buds, or papillae, we have all over our tongues vary from person to person in their number.

Say we put a magnifying glass in front of our tongues in a mirror and studied an area of just a few millimeters in diameter, let's say an area the size of your pupil in moderate light. (Go ahead, go to the bathroom mirror. Look at your pupil. Tiny, huh? Now look at your tongue. Try to imagine a section of your tongue the same size as the pupil you see.) The number of taste buds in that area can be as few as 10 or as many as 40! The more you have, the more you taste. Sounds simple right? Not.

The people with lots of taste buds need less sugar and less fat to satisfy their taste needs, but here's the surprise, they are the people who can't get enough salt! They seem to need many times the amount of salt as those of us with fewer taste buds in order to gain taste satisfaction. More tongue salt sensors equals more salt seeking! So there is a wide range of sensitivity to the taste of salt and that may help explain why some people have so much trouble cutting their salt intake. No, you'll never get disability for being a salt-aholic.

Even more interesting is something I recently learned from an executive chef I know. It seems that those salt-sensitive taste buds happen to live in the same neighborhood as the ones for tasting sour flavors. So the key here is to ramp up what you offer the little sour guys so they help minimize what the salt-tasting buds sense. How? My chef friend says "reach for acids like lemon, lime, and the various vinegars when cooking" to fool the salty guys and reduce that craving. Live and learn!

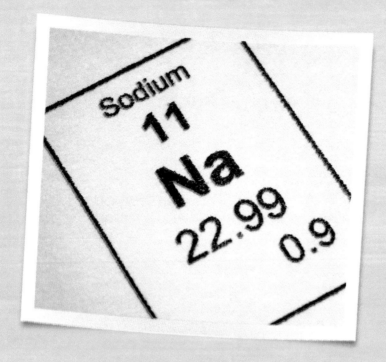

Chemistry 101

What exactly is salt, anyway? The salt we eat is a chemical combination of sodium and chloride. It is the chemical created from the interaction of the acid (sodium) and the base (chloride). Sodium is actually an unstable metal capable of spontaneous combustion. Chloride is a poisonous gas, which in its liquefied chemistry, is bleach. Combined they are NaCl in chemical-speak, or sodium chloride, more commonly known as salt. Most often when care providers say "salt" they mean "sodium" and vice versa. There are different kinds of salts, however. For example, there's a salt made from calcium that we put on our icy driveways in the winter but certainly not in our food. Other edible salts (read your food labels and be amazed) include magnesium chloride and potassium chloride. The potassium salt is often sold as a salt substitute for people on a salt-restricted diet. (Are you thinking, hmm, I'll just use that instead? Maybe, maybe not. We'll talk more on this one.)

Now, there is a faction of people we may refer to as salt snobs who insist that salt is healthy and define several dozen "different" salts. Okay, I will grant that there are a few salts with differing tastes, but healthy? really? Let's investigate.

There are some minor mineral variations in salts mined or produced from different areas of the world which provide a slightly different taste and result in pitting the countries or producers against each other in a silly competition of which is best, or, oh horrors, which is healthiest. Unrefined salts, such as rock salt, are used in the natural state for example, in ice melting and bath salts. In fact most salt is used in non-food industries. Refined salt is cleaned up a bit, purifying it for consumption and improved storage.

Some salt is obtained from mines, such as the Austrian Dürnberg Mountain mine where pre-history Celt miners' bodies were once found, almost completely preserved. Salt is also obtained by evaporation of sea water and is usually referred to as sea salt or sometimes solar salt. Purification involves dissolving the salt into a brine solution, then adding magnesium and calcium salts followed by variable evaporation methods resulting in recrystallization of the salt.

To become fine crystals of table salt, so when it rains it pours, involves more additives (and there are a number of possible chemicals that can be chosen including, yes, aluminum! Hello, where was the FDA on this one? They approved it!) to prevent caking. Since 1924, iodine in one form or another has been added to American salt and is also commonly added in several other countries. Some countries add fluoride where water is not fluoridated; even folic acid and iron are often added for anemia and birth defect prevention in infants of the developing world. The sodium part of salt is the chemical that actually causes all this havoc, so we'll concentrate on that.

I often hear patients or their families say that they have solved their salt problem by switching to sea salt. Salt is salt. And sea salt will do the same harm to a heart failure patient as salt from any other source.

Those salt snobs I mentioned will argue that "artisan salt" is actually good for you (as compared to the sea, kosher, and table salts we commoners use), and then they will cite such forms as "fine flakes" of Maldon sea salt with its "oceanic flavor," or the "mystical crystals" of *fleur de sel*, or the "grassy warmth" of Hawaiian bamboo leaf salt, or the "sweetness" (huh?) of Celtic sea salt. Oh heaven, run the other way!

And then the salt snobs try to convince you that you ought to sprinkle this one or that on your fried eels, or sea snails, or tea-smoked duck, or (for us commoners) your ice cream, uh-huh, or, oh yes--and I found this in print--in your baby formula! Stop the insanity! They should be ashamed! No matter how expensive your salt is, these fancy salts contain as much sodium as any other salt, and they need to be avoided in the

same way. Sodium is the real culprit here, though, so for our purposes we'll use the terms "salt" and "sodium" interchangeably.

There's another change people make and think they've done all they need to do. I hear this all the time: "Oh, don't worry, I already swore off salt. I never touch that salt shaker," or, "I don't add salt when I cook, and I don't put the shaker on the table, even though my husband isn't happy about it." My first reaction is to congratulate them on shaking the shaker; it has to be done. But that can't be the end. There's so much more to do.

Salt added during cooking or at the table usually accounts for only 10–20% of the sodium we consume. You read that right; it's not a typo. The rest comes from the sodium already in the foods we choose to eat. Giving up the shaker is a vital first step, but not the last step in our journey to low-salt-living, by any means. As the Chinese philosopher Lao-tzu warns: "a journey of a thousand miles begins with a single step." You think he ate a low-sodium diet??

Hypertension and the Salt Connection

Sodium intake control is a vital part of managing hypertension and heart failure. We define hypertension, or high blood pressure, as a blood pressure of 140 or more in the top number (systolic) or 90 or greater in the bottom number (diastolic). There is also a category called prehypertension that is just kindergarten for hypertension. The numbers there are between 120 and 139 on the top or between 80 and 89 on the bottom.

Hypertension among Americans is the starting point to coronary heart disease (blockages in the heart's arteries that can lead to heart attacks) and stroke (the first and third most common causes of death in this country) as well as heart failure and renal (kidney) disease. Hypertension can lead directly to heart failure or first to heart damage and then to heart failure.

High blood pressure is not something we see in cultures where freely added salt is uncommon. Places in the world where sodium intake is around one gram (1000 mg) or less just don't have this deadly problem. It's societies like ours that have daily sodium intakes twice that or more, that have to deal with hypertension and all its consequences. And this seems to be independent of such risk factors as family history or being overweight, which also contribute to develop-

ment of high blood pressure. So sodium intake alone can be a major player in high blood pressure.

And to make matters worse, some people are just more sensitive to the effects of salt than others. Sodium sensitivity seems to be especially great in older people and in African-Americans. Eating more sodium than a bare minimum over the years also plays a role in the development of high blood pressure. You may not have high blood pressure to begin with, but after a few decades of high sodium intake, you may become much more sensitive to its effects than if you had controlled the consumption of sodium all that time. Now you have hypertension that you weren't programmed to have. And you have to deal with all its nasty effects.

Studies have clearly demonstrated that reducing sodium intake has a significant impact on the reduction in blood pressure, in those with prehypertension and those who already have high blood pressure, as well as those with normal blood pressures who would like to keep it that way. All is not lost if you have been given the diagnosis of hypertension, providing you get serious about managing it in a way that truly controls it: take your medicine and cut your sodium intake every single day.

Heart Failure and the Salt Connection

If you've been told you have heart failure, it's important that you understand the effect salt can have on your health. Your heart has lost a lot of its pumping power. For whatever the reason, and there are many causes of heart failure, your heart is weaker than it used to be.

You may have noticed swelling, or perhaps shortness of breath has been occurring lately. Are your rings or shoes tighter than the other day? It can happen quickly, or it can sneak up on you gradually until you finally notice you're in lots of trouble. Maybe your eyes look puffy or your belt is too tight in its usual notch. These are signs of too much fluid in your system.

It can take several quarts of extra water in your body to puff your ankles just a little. More retained fluid means more puff and more work for your heart. Extra fluid gets stored everywhere, not just in your ankles. It can also go to your lungs and take up space where air belongs. When the air sacks in your lungs fill with fluid, oxygen can't get through. That's a large part of why you get short of breath. The extra fluid increases the pressure in your body. Your heart has to overcome that pressure in order to push blood out of your heart and around your body. But as you have just learned, your heart is weaker not stronger, so this is not a time to make the workload tougher for it.

Salt is like a sponge. It loves to soak up lots of fluid. The more salt there is in your system, the more fluid it will make your body hold. And as you've just learned, the more fluid in your system, the harder your heart has to work. The harder your heart works, the sicker you feel, and the sicker you get. It's a little like dominoes and every bit as hard to stop. The best way to manage the problem is to keep your salt intake at a bare minimum. Studies have shown that one of the biggest reasons heart failure patients end up in the hospital is because they don't adequately control their salt intake. There have been many, many times I've admitted folks to the hospital who ended up in bad trouble with their heart failure just because they got into some salt they should have avoided. Human nature being what it is, we all think we can cheat once in a while and not get caught. Reality is that there is always a price. For you, and millions of Americans like you, salt is poison.

What Are You Trying To Tell Me?

In a sentence, I'm trying to tell you that salt is great for de-icing. It chills an ice cream churn very nicely, and it makes a beautiful candle holder (I have one), but that's about it. Only one in every ten Americans meets the recommended daily sodium intake. I want to see that number improve, and I want to start with you.

This book is meant to help high blood pressure and heart failure patients understand how sodium can be harmful and to provide some ideas on ways to stay out of trouble because of it, or in spite of it. I am not going to harp on low-fat, low-cholesterol diets. Not every heart failure patient needs a drastic reduction in these, and the media has flooded us with information about how to avoid high-cholesterol, high-fat foods, anyway.

This is also not a health food cookbook so don't expect any lectures on the benefits of brown rice or tofu (even if they are good for you). It's not all-inclusive, either. There are some excellent books in the bookstores that will tell you the sodium content of every food known to man along with the cholesterol, fat, calorie, protein, and vitamin content of it all.

I most definitely want you to become adept at re-working the ingredients in all your own favorite recipes, so you can enjoy them again. While this book will get you started, it isn't meant to be your only resource for low-salt recipes. Just learn from here, and take that knowledge to other recipes, so you can re-invent them and make them fit your current need. I know you can do this.

Use this guide to get you started, as an assistant for meal planning, a reference, a resource, and maybe a little bit of a crutch until you get the hang of low-sodium eating and realize that it's not so hard to do. What I hope to do is to help you find the places where evil sodium is lurking, trying to trip you up and trick you into losing control of your low-sodium diet. And maybe you'll even find some foods and ideas that you like better than salt.

Salting is an ingrained habit in cooking and eating, but by the time you finish reading this book, it will be crystal clear that it's a habit that needs to be shaken. Do we dare call this an adventure?

Shake the Shaker

Okay, so now you know that sodium is a demon. And you've resolved to shake the habit. Great! Because it's amazing how much sodium is in the refrigerators, pantries, and cupboards of our kitchens, not to mention the fast-food and not-so-fast-food restaurants we frequent. Sodium is measured in grams or milligrams, one gram containing 1000 milligrams. (Don't panic, this isn't going to turn into a lecture on the metric system or that modern math stuff.) The average diet in this country contains 4 to 10 grams of sodium each day (4,000 to 10,000 milligrams). The American Dietetic Association and the American Heart Association recommend keeping our sodium intake under 1500 milligrams (1.5 grams) per day even for people with healthy hearts. Some sodium is needed in our diets, but it's vital to realize that all the sodium any human needs is provided completely naturally in our foods without any help from man.

Typically, 2000 milligrams is the maximum recommendation we, as care providers, ask our heart failure patients to follow. It's clearly not a restriction when you look at the national recommendations. Rather we are prescribing a maximum safe sodium intake. This provides a generous target that just seems like a severe restriction because of the lifestyles we have developed. The first thing most people think when they hear us say, "you have to cut down on salt" is "oh no, twigs and berries for the rest of my life!" Not true! With a little planning and some time to adjust, you'll find a low-sodium diet isn't so terrible after all. In fact many of my patients, once they try in earnest for a while, find they actually prefer it. They can really taste the food at last, not the salt. And if they accidentally get into something high in sodium, they know right away because the taste is so SALTY! Yuck. It's important to note, however, that you can't tell how much sodium is contained in any food item by how salty it does or does not taste. So don't be lulled.

Flavor isn't sensed only in the tongue. The tongue does its job differentiating tastes like sweet, salty, bitter, and sour. But those have to be further refined, and our sense of smell has a lot to do with that. In fact, aroma is responsible for most of our discernment of flavor, and that happens primarily after the food is in our mouths. The aroma chemicals interact with receptors in the nose and the mouth, which send a signal to the brain where we perceive flavor. So while we may be led to the kitchen by the aroma of Grandma's signature spaghetti sauce, it's not fully experienced until our nose and tongue work together to define the taste. Cook to this knowledge and introduce new flavors to help beat that same old taste of salt.

The Many Faces of Sodium

Okay, so we know salt is really sodium, and it's out there in all our favorite foods, luring us into doing something very unhealthy. How do we recognize it in its many disguises? That's easier than you may think. Sodium comes in four main forms when we talk about food. The obvious one is table salt, which you're learning how to recognize even when it's not in the shaker.

But a source of sodium that is easy to forget, or ignore, is in the baking powder and baking soda we use in cakes, biscuits, muffins, and most any baked goods. It's possible to get a far greater load of sodium from one biscuit at dinner than the entire rest of the meal! The hidden source here is not just the salt that is used in the recipe, but the baking powder in it, too. One homemade biscuit can give you a whopping 600 milligrams of sodium. And who ever stops at just one? (Come on, be honest.) Two homemade biscuits, without adding butter or margarine, add up to over half your entire day's allowance of sodium. Whoops! That makes eating for the rest of the day pretty tough. And remember, that was from a homemade recipe.

The cost goes up much more for the kind you buy in the dairy section and bake at home. You guessed it; the ones you eat in a restaurant are even higher—they are usually twice as big, too. Unavoidable baking powder, which is needed in the recipe, accounts for a large part of the problem. There are, however, "low-sodium" baking powders on the market that you can look for and experiment with carefully.

Baking soda hides in a similar way. It's used in many recipes and in store-bought baked goods along with baking powder and salt. One teaspoon of baking soda contains 821 milligrams of sodium. The same amount of baking powder holds 400 milligrams of the nasty stuff, and one teaspoon of salt will cost you way more than an entire day's allowance: 2400 milligrams of sodium. Ugh.

This is an excellent reason never to treat an upset stomach with "bicarbonate of soda." That's just baking soda stirred into water, and you know what that means. For the same reason, it's important to avoid plop-plop-fizz-fizz type medicines, too. They make your stomach feel better by neutralizing acid with baking soda. Some other drugs contain high amounts of sodium. Carefully read the labels on all over-the-counter drugs. Look at the ingredient list and warning statement to see if the product has sodium. A statement of sodium content must be on labels of antacids that have 5 mg or more per dosage unit (tablet, teaspoon, etc.). Some companies are now producing low-sodium over-the-counter products. If in doubt, ask your provider or pharmacist if the drug is OK for you.

It lurks in those baking mixes, too. One-third cup of Bisquick contains 490 milligrams. One cup of self-rising flour will set you back 1587 milligrams. Baked goods are not evil, but they do warrant caution. If you do most of your own baking, you can make adjustments that will help minimize the impact of sodium on your diet. For example, I've found that most cakes, breads, cookies, and other baked goods made from scratch can have the salt called for in the recipe reduced by at least half, if not eliminated altogether, without changing the outcome or ruining the taste. Later you'll see some recipes I've provided to help you deal with this problem. Some low-sodium baked goods are available in grocery stores, but use caution and become a label reader.

The fourth and probably best-disguised form of sodium comes in the many sodium-containing additives used in processed food to preserve it. Most of them have names that start with sodium, disodium, or mono-sodium. That famous "taste enhancer" monosodium glutamate (MSG) is a name to look for on the label. It's the one that, for people who are sensitive, can cause a strong flushing reaction especially noted in Chinese restaurant foods; but it's actually used in many restaurants of all types (see "The Spice of Your Life" chapter).

Similarly, you will find most meat tenderizers are mainly salt. All of these also contribute to the total sodium content of each food item and should be accounted for in the sodium labeling on the package. Read those labels!

Check Out the Labels on Everything

Focusing on reading labels provides a big advantage. As long as the serving size we eat is the same as the serving size on the label (don't underestimate the ease with which we underestimate portions), we can add up the milligrams of sodium we consume and reduce that number to a safer range. We can also look for low-sodium options such as canned tomatoes with no salt added and fresh vegetables instead of canned or frozen in salty sauces. Switching to unsalted versions of butter or peanut butter, using garlic powder and onion powder instead of garlic salt and onion salt, and skipping packaged foods like potato and pasta mixes in favor of homemade will have a big impact.

As long as we're on the subject, let's look more closely at those labels. The government did us a favor by requiring all the food we buy in packages to carry nutritional labeling. This is where we look to learn the breakdown and percentages of the components of our food. This is where we will find how much the manufacturer considers one serving to be and how much sodium that one serving contains. That makes it simple and keeps us honest.

Listed are the amount for sodium, in milligrams (mg), and the "% daily value." Also be sure to review the ingredient list for hints of other sources of sodium in the product such as "soda" or "sodium bicarbonate", also known as baking soda; the additives used for preservatives, such as disodium guanylate; of course

the flavor enhancer, monosodium glutamate; or even the chemical symbol, Na, as another sneaky way to comply with the mandate to list all sodium but still try to hide it from the unsuspecting public!

Take a look at the nutrition information reproduced on the opposite page from a box of popular cereal. Up near the top you'll see that one serving is described as one cup. This is important because so often we just pour it into the bowl and don't think about how much we're eating. It's easy to assume that our bowlful is one serving when it may be much more. If the sodium content is to be calculated accurately, the amount of cereal in our bowl needs to be measured carefully. Use a measuring cup the first several times you do this until you know exactly where in the bowl one cup comes to. Then do it once in a while as time goes on just to be sure you don't lose your accuracy. Do it with everything—milk, butter, applesauce, noodles, gravy, corn—measure everything you put in your mouth.

Look down the listing a little further on the nutrition guide and see the sodium content of that one serving. It's 220 milligrams. That's more than 10% of your daily total intake of sodium. That's why it's so important to be accurate in the measuring process. It's not unlike counting calories, and who hasn't done that? Look on the package, measure the food, and keep a running tab of the sodium you eat over the course of each day. Stop at 2000 milligrams. Every nutrition guide on every package of food you buy will tell you these two very important things. This is how you can keep your sodium intake under control.

Look a little further yet down the guide. It divides out the total amounts of fat, cholesterol, sodium, potassium, carbohydrate, and fiber individuals should have according to the number of calories they should be eating. Of significance here is the fact that it doesn't matter if you're big or little, eating high-calorie or low-calorie diets; the sodium intake for everyone should be less than 2000 milligrams. They don't distinguish between those with healthy hearts and those fighting heart failure. Keeping sodium intake down is a matter of extreme importance for you, but it is a diet your family can and should get behind, too. It's a healthy road for all of us to go down, with or without heart failure. You may be doing your family members a great service helping them bring their sodium intake down right along with yours. Become a member of the Sodium Patrol. Read labels. It will be an eye-opening experience, guaranteed.

And in case you wondered about vague and hard-to-quantify terms on some labels, here's what the Food and Drug Administration (FDA) says they mean:

Sodium free
One serving contains less than 5 milligrams of sodium

Very low sodium
There's 35 milligrams or less in one serving

Low sodium
Each serving has no more than 140 milligrams

Reduced sodium
Must be reduced by 25% from usual sodium content

Unsalted, no salt added, or without added salt
Must be made without the usually added salt, but still contains any sodium always in the product itself naturally

Now, these major sources of sodium are also listed in the section called Sodium Content Listing for milligram amounts of sodium per serving of food, but it warrants review here (and yes, I do mean LEVEL teaspoons):

1 teaspoon baking soda	821 mg sodium
1 teaspoon baking powder	400 mg sodium
1 teaspoon salt	2,360 mg sodium

Nutrition Facts

Serving Size 1 cup (30g)
Servings Per Container About 17

Amount Per Serving	Wheaties	with ½ cup skim milk
Calories	110	150
Calories from Fat	10	10
	% Daily Value**
Total Fat 1g*	**1**%	**2**%
Saturated Fat 0g	**0**%	**0**%
Polyunsaturated Fat 0g		
Monounsaturated Fat 0g		
Cholesterol 0mg	**0**%	**1**%
Sodium 220mg	**9**%	**12**%
Potassium 110mg	**3**%	**9**%
Total Carbohydrate 24g	**8**%	**10**%
Dietary Fiber 0g	**12**%	**12**%
Sugars 4g		
Other Carbohydrate 17g		
Protein 3g		
Vitamin A	10%	15%
Vitamin C	10%	10%
Calcium	0%	15%
Iron	45%	45%
Vitamin D	10%	25%
Thiamin (Vitamin B$_1$)	50%	50%
Riboflavin (Vitamin B$_2$)	50%	60%
Niacin (Vitamin B$_3$)	50%	50%
Vitamin B$_6$	50%	50%
Folic Acid	50%	50%
Vitamin B$_{12}$	50%	60%
Phosphorus	10%	20%
Magnesium	8%	10%
Zinc	50%	50%
Copper	4%	4%

* Amount in Cereal. A serving of cereal plus skim milk provides 1g total fat, less than 5mg cholesterol, 280mg sodium, 310mg potassium, 30g total carbohydrate (10g sugars) and 7g protein.

** Percent Daily Values are based on a 2,000 calorie diet. Your daily values may be higher or lower depending on your calorie needs:

	Calories:	2,000	2,500
Total Fat	Less than	65g	80g
Sat Fat	Less than	20g	25g
Cholesterol	Less than	300mg	300mg
Sodium	Less than	2,400mg	2,400mg
Potassium		3,500mg	3,500mg
Total Carbohydrate		300g	375g
Dietary Fiber		25g	30g

Sacrifice?

Giving up the goodies we grew up on, love, and are constantly tempted by may seem like the supreme sacrifice. But along with taking all those pills, it's the best way a patient with heart failure, active or inactive, has to control his health. For those truly addicted to salt and salty foods, it will seem like torture at first. No sense kidding you, it will be hard. But not as hard as the effort to breathe if you allow salt to get you into trouble.

Remember, water follows salt. Too much salt in your body is an engraved invitation for fluid to start the trouble. Water in the lungs makes it hard to get air in and makes it hard work to breathe. Once that water gets in there, it can be tough to get out. That's why heart failure patients should never be encouraged to drink lots of fluids. You've heard all your life that when you're sick, you should drink more, even up to eight glasses of water a day. But what they didn't tell you was to do that only if you are otherwise healthy. Fluids help flush out the flu, but heart failure and high blood pressure patients who try to flush out too much salt intake will retain that fluid because water follows salt. It often means a trip to the doctor, but it can mean a stay in the hospital, and even a breathing tube and life-

support machine in severe enough cases. Sure makes skipping the potato chips less of a sacrifice once you've experienced that one.

Of course the whole idea is to avoid the problem in the first place by avoiding the poison: salt. Once your taste buds get used to not being "a-salt-ed" by the sodium that passes over them, they will be delighted at all the new flavors they will enjoy. Salt doesn't enhance flavor, it masks it. Let the natural taste escape, and your taste buds will thank you, but more importantly, your heart will thank you. Salt may preserve ham and bacon, but it won't preserve your heart. The health of your heart is in your hands. What you do to make its workload easier may seem like sacrifice at first, but it could make the biggest impact on your heart of anything you do. I wish I could show you how hard it is to tell a patient who just couldn't get these lifestyle changes into his or her life, that his or her life is now severely shortened because this is yet another in a series of hospital admissions for worsening heart failure that we just can't fix. It's a slippery slope when patients think that a little cheating here and there won't hurt. It breaks my heart to have to tell families and patients that it's time for hospice and time is short.

Pinch Hitters

Okay, you've resolved to give up the habit and live the clean life. Does that mean the end of life as you knew it? Yes! But it doesn't mean chewing on cardboard. And there are many ways to flavor food without adding salt. Someone should mention this to the food processing industry.

First, let's talk about those commercial salt substitutes. They require caution, because they're actually a potassium salt. So what, you ask? After all, our bodies need potassium. True, and if you have been prescribed a diuretic (or water pill), you may also have been asked to take potassium pills. This is because, as the diuretic removes excess water from your body, it also takes potassium with it. We can replace it with pills because we know exactly how much potassium you will be getting. It's important to get enough, but it's not something you should have too much of, either. And this is especially important if your kidneys aren't working perfectly.

There are some medications called angiotensin converting enzyme (ACE) inhibitors and aldosterone antagonists that are excellent medications for heart failure patients. They can promote retention of potassium in the process of their action to support your heart, an action we capitalize on in many cases. But, you could end up with way too much potassium if you take one of these (or a potassium supplement) and add salt substitute to your diet. Too much potassium could be dangerous. When we prescribe these medications we know how they work and adjust the dosing for all the contingencies that we introduce and that your condition presents. We also test your blood from time to time to determine its potassium level. That makes all those medications perfectly safe and health promoting. Throwing salt substitute into the mix may be like throwing a monkey wrench into a well-running machine. Being able to take all the medications is much more important than using potassium-containing salt substitutes, so we generally discourage their use. The fact is, many patients don't like the bitter aftertaste of potassium salt-substitutes and avoid them anyway.

There are also combinations of potassium salt and sodium salt often labeled as "light" salt. Bad idea anytime you shake something containing sodium onto your food. Enough said.

Herbs, on the other hand, are a great substitute. They taste good and are low in sodium. We'll talk at length about herbs and spices in another chapter.

Calculate Before You Eat

Now you know why salt is poison for hearts like yours and what you have to do about it. Next I want to give you the tools to assess the amounts of sodium in the things you eat, or used to eat. Salt is everywhere, even in cake! And it occurs naturally in many foods, too. The next several pages will chart many of them with their serving sizes and sodium content for each in milligrams. This will be the ruler you can use to plan your meals and snacks each day. You can buy books that will expand greatly on this list and tell you fat and calories if you want to know those, too.

A word of caution if you get the bug to search out "healthy cooking" cookbooks; just like with foods labeled "healthy," that's not always the case. As I did the research for this book, I discovered there are many books out there that claim to be full of recipes for things that are good for you, but as I read the fine print I was struck by the fact that while they may be low in calories or fat or cholesterol, often they make up for what's missing with salt.

In fact, the incredible lack of good resources for my patients was the real motivation for the decision to write this book. So be careful not to get lured in by the "healthy" cookbook titles. Read the fine print on every recipe you want to try for the actual sodium content per serving, and take note of how big each serving is. Some recipes will be delicious and low salt; some won't. And as you learn more about the process, you'll find ways to "downshift" the sodium content of many recipes you'd like to try. Others won't be so easy.

For the tables that follow, I stuck to brand names, but store brands run along the same lines and sodium content will be on their labels, too. These tables will get you started with a good basis to work from. I've tried to include the most commonly used fresh, canned, and frozen foods, some of the offensive stuff and lots of the good. You need all the ammunition you can get. Use the tables to add up the sodium content of your own recipes and maybe find ways to cut or avoid sodium as a result. Before we look at those tables, let's break down a typical recipe.

Warning: This may shock you. I know I was quite surprised at the sodium content of several items myself. That cake I mentioned a moment ago is a good example. Yes, I know, not even the hard-core users shake salt on their cake. But, it contains plenty on its own:

Two cups flour	2 milligrams
One cup brown sugar, packed	86 milligrams
One-half cup granulated sugar	0 milligrams
Three teaspoons baking powder	1200 milligrams
One teaspoon salt	2360 milligrams
One-half teaspoon baking soda	410 milligrams
One-half cup shortening	0 milligrams
One and one-quarter cups milk	150 milligrams
Three eggs	189 milligrams
One-half cup chocolate chips	0 milligrams
One and one-half teaspoons vanilla	0 milligrams
	Total: 4397 milligrams

Okay, let's divide that cake among friends, say 10 all together. Your share is 440 milligrams, and I haven't yet accounted for the filling or frosting—forget the scoop of ice cream on the side (yes, they even add salt to ice cream). YIKES! That can sure put you on a tightrope for the rest of the day. And who eats just one-tenth of a birthday cake? But you get the idea on how to break down a recipe and the harmful way total sodium content can sneak up on you.

Butter and margarine are two big pitfalls. You won't believe all the salt they add. If you're baking with it, putting just a stick (one-half cup) of either one into a cookie recipe adds 1000 milligrams of sodium. Unsalted butter and margarine can make a huge differ-ence in the total sodium content of foods you cook. It doesn't cost any more, either. I use unsalted butter in baking and anytime I need a little in the frying pan. I've never felt the need to add salt to make up for it. It just doesn't leave you with the sense that something is missing.

About the only place I really notice a flat taste is on plain bread or rolls. Even melted on vegetables and anywhere there is another flavor to compensate, you won't miss what's missing in unsalted butter or margarine. And here's a handy hint I stumbled on by accident, well maybe thanks to my Irish heritage: unsalted, imported Irish butter (yes, Virginia, there is such a thing) has no sodium, but great taste!

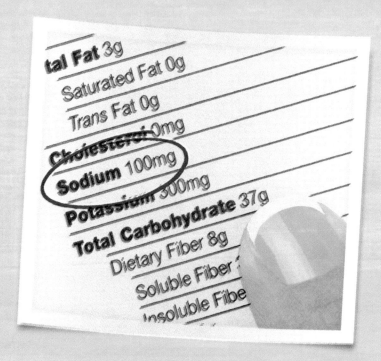

Sodium Content Listing

Let's look at some other common foods and their sodium content. Measure carefully . . .
you're going for a day's maximum of 2000 milligrams!

Food Item and Serving Size	Mg. of Sodium
Baking	
Baking chocolate, 1/2 ounce	
Hershey's semisweet chips	0
Nestle semisweet chips	0
Baking mix, Bisquick, 1/3 cup	490
Baking powder, 1 teaspoon	400
Baking soda, 1 teaspoon	821
Bread crumbs, 1/4 cup	
Contadina plain	525
Progresso plain	210
Butter-flavored cooking spray	0
Cocoa, unsweetened, 1 tablespoon	0
Cocoa, unsweetened, 2 tablespoons	2
Coconut	
Milk, 1/4 cup	7
Shredded, sweetened, 1 ounce	74
Shredded, unsweetened, 1 ounce	10
Cornmeal, whole grain, yellow, 1 cup	43
Cornstarch, 1 tablespoon	0
Flour, all purpose, whole wheat, unbleached, or rye, 1 cup	2
Flour, self rising, 1 cup (it's loaded with salt, baking powder and soda)	1587
Graham cracker crumbs, 1/4 cup	200

Food Item and Serving Size	Mg. of Sodium
Milk, evaporated, 2 tablespoons	
Carnation	35
Pet	30
Milk, sweetened condensed, 2 tablespoons	
Carnation	45
Borden	40
Molasses, 1 tablespoon	
Br'er Rabbit	15
Gramma's Gold	0
Gramma's Green	10
Nuts, 1 ounce (2 tablespoons) salted, dry-roasted peanuts	250
Almonds	
Planter's	0
Honey-roasted	190
Walnuts, 1/3 cup	
Planter's	0
Pie crust, purchased	
Graham, Honey Maid, 1/6 crust	125
Nilla Cookie, 1/6 crust	65
Oreo, 1/6 crust	180
Pillsbury, frozen, 1/8 crust	140
Sugar, 1 cup	
Brown, packed	86
Granulated	1
Powdered	1

Beverages

Apple Juice, 8 ounces
    Minute Maid 30
    Mott's 20
    Musselman's Premium Natural 15
    Veryfine 35
Bloody Mary Mixer, Mr. & Mrs. T, 8 ounces . . 1350
Chocolate milk, 8 ounces made with:
    Nestle's Quik 120
    Hershey's Syrup 130
Coffee, nothing added
    Brewed, 6 ounces 4
    Instant 1 teaspoon mix 1
Coffeemate nondairy creamer, 1 tablespoon 0
Cranberry juice, 8 ounces
    Ocean Spray 35
    After The Fall 25
Grapefruit juice, Dole, 8 ounces 20
Hot chocolate mix
    Carnation, 3 tablespoons 95
    Carnation with mini marshmallows,
        3 tablespoons 170
    Hershey's Goodnight Kisses, 1 envelope . . 160
    Ovaltine, rich chocolate, 4 tablespoons . . . 140
    Swiss Miss, 1 packet 140
Juicy Juice, all flavors, 8 ounces 15
Lemonade, Minute Maid, 8 ounces 25
Milkshakes, dietary supplement
    Boost, 8 oz. can 130
    Carnation Instant Breakfast, all flavors,
        1 packet 100
    Ensure, 8 oz. can 200
    Slimfast, 11 ounce can 220
Orange juice, Tropicana Pure Premium,
8 ounces 0
Pineapple juice, 8 ounces
    DelMonte 10
    Dole 20
Soft drinks, 8 ounces
    Canada Dry Ginger Ale 10
    Coca-Cola Classic 35
    Pepsi 35
    Root beer
        A&W 35
        Hires 110
        Schweppes tonic water 45
Tea, bag, instant or iced tea mix, nothing
    added, any size 0
Tomato juice, 8 ounces
    Campbell's 860
    DelMonte 760
    Hunt's 690
    Hunt's No Salt (yes, they can do it if
        they want to) 10

V-8, 8 ounces 620
Wine, 1 ounce
    Table 1
    Cooking (it's supposed to keep the
        cook from nipping!) 190-230
Yoo Hoo, 9-ounce bottle. 200

Breads

Bagel, Lenders, frozen plain 320
Bagel, plain, large (4 ounce) 700
Biscuits (just one can ruin your day)
    Grands! Homestyle, 1 600
    Hungry Jack, 1 600
Bread, one slice, varies by brands (reading labels
    pays off well here)
    Italian 140-260
    Low Sodium 5
    Oatmeal 135-200
    Pita, 1 ounce 115-300
    Pumpernickel 150-230
    Raisin 75-160
    Rye 125-180
    Sourdough 220-260
    Wheat 110-210
    White 140-200
    Crumbs, 1/4 cup, seasoned 590
Muffins, English, Thomas' 200
Pita
    Arnold's Pocket Bread, 2 ounce 230
Rolls, Pepperidge Farm Brown and Serve, 1 . . 100
    Arnold Dinner, 1 140
    Arnold Hamburger, 1 250
    Arnold New England Style Hot Dog, 1 210
Thomas' Toast-r-Cakes 220
Tortillas
    Corn 0
    Flour 340

Breakfast Cereals

One cup except where noted, and for the most part, very reasonable. Do measure carefully.

Apple Jacks 135
Cheerios 280
Cinnamon Toast Crunch 275
Cocoa Crispies 263
Cracklin' Oat Bran, 3/4 cup 180
Fruit Loops 150
Grapenuts Flakes, 3/4 cup 140
Grapenuts, 1/2 cup 350
Healthy Choice Flakes 210
Kellogg's All Bran, 1/2 cup 280
Kellogg's Corn Flakes 330
Kellogg's Frosted Mini Wheats (go Kellogg's!) . . . 0

Nabisco Shredded Wheat, 2 pieces (way to
    go Nabisco!) 0
Post Raisin Bran 300
Puffed Rice 0
Quaker instant oatmeal, cinnamon spice,
    1 envelope 290
Quaker instant oatmeal, plain, 1 envelope
    (add your own goodies) 80
Quaker quick or old fashioned, 1/2 cup 140
Rice Crispies, 3/4 cup 160
Total 157
Total, whole grains 256
Wheaties, 1 cup 220

Convenience Foods

Frozen and canned foods may save time,
but ... the numbers tell it all.

Beef pot roast TV dinner
    Healthy Choice 460
    Swanson Hungry Man 910
Chicken a la King, Swanson, canned, 1 cup .. 1080
Chicken hot dog, 2 ounce link 465
Chicken TV dinner
    Swanson Hungry Man 1390
    Banquet Extra Helping 1820
    Mary Callender's 1680
    Healthy Choice 340
    Swanson nuggets 980
Chili with beans, Hormel, 1 cup 1200
Dinty Moore Stew, 10-ounce can 730
Hormel Chili one 7 3/4 ounce can 1050
Lasagna, frozen
    Banquet 900
    Healthy Choice 580
"Lunchables"
    Bologna and American cheese 1580
    Ham and Swiss 1790
    Turkey and Monterey Jack 1700
Kraft Macaroni and Cheese, 2 1/2 ounces 560
Mary Kitchen Corned Beef Hash, 1/2 of
    15-ounce can 1000
Noodle mixes
    Lipton Noodles and Sauce, Alfredo,
        1/2 package 940
    Noodle Roni, Parmesan, 1 cup 950
Onion rings, frozen
    Mrs. Paul's Old Fashioned, 7 rings 450
    Ore-Ida Classic, 8 rings 1020
Pancake, 3 pieces, frozen
    Aunt Jemima 700
    Downy Flake 700
    Hungry Jack Microwave Original 550
Pie, frozen, 1/6 of Mrs. Smith's pie (most
    brands run similarly; check labels)

    Apple 300
    Blueberry 320
    Pecan 450
    Pumpkin 320
Pizza, frozen
    Celeste For One, cheese 1090
    Pepperoni, 1/4 of large pie 990
    Tombstone Deluxe, 1/4 of 12-inch pie 640
Pizza pockets, 1 piece
    Hot Pockets, pepperoni 780
    Sausage 690
Rice mixes, 1 cup prepared
    Chicken
        Country Inn 750
        Rice-a-Roni Less Salt
        (uh, define "less") 690
    Spanish
        Country Inn 750
        Lipton Rice and Sauce 940
Sausage, breakfast
    Perdue, turkey, 2 links 450
    Brown and Serve, pork, 3 links 670
    Louis Rich, turkey, 2 ounces smoked, ... 500
Soup
    Broth, canned, 1 cup
        Beef, Swanson 820
        Chicken, College Inn 1050
        Chicken, College Inn Less Sodium ... 640
    Campbell's condensed, canned, 1 cup pre-
        pared (other brands run similarly)
        Beef noodle 920
        Chicken noodle 980
        Healthy Request 480
        Clam Chowder, New England 980
        Minestrone 960
        Tomato 730
        Vegetable 920
        Healthy Request 480
Soup, dehydrated
    Maruchan Ramen Noodle, 1/2 of
        3-ounce package 820
    Mrs. Manischewitz Instant Matzo Ball
        Soup, 0.5 ounces 960
Spaghetti, canned, 1 cup
    Franco-American (most people I know
        eat the whole can, like my
        husband, for example) 1020
Spam, 2 ounces 750
    "Less Salt," 2 ounces 560
Stuffing Mix, 1/6 of box
    Stove Top 440
Poptart, 1 170
Turkey TV dinners
    Lean Cuisine 590
    Swanson 1040

Velveeta Shells, 4 ounces (my kids would eat the whole box if I'd let them!) 1030
Waffle, frozen, 2 pieces (did you check out the syrups below?)
    Aunt Jemima 410
    Downyflake, buttermilk 480
    Eggo, homestyle 480

Dairy

If you decide to cut down on dairy intake to cut down on sodium, you should ask your care provider about a calcium and vitamin D supplement. Low calcium intake can be a risk factor in the development of osteoporosis.

Butter, 1 tablespoon 115
Butter, unsalted, 1 tablespoon 1
Cheese (one ounce of regular cheese is a cube about 1 inch on all sides)
    American processed, 3/4-ounce slice
        Borden 260
        Kraft Singles 290
    Bleu, 1 ounce 380
    Cheddar, 1 ounce 200
    Cheez Whiz, 2 tablespoons 560
    Cottage, 1/2 cup 400
    Cream, Philadelphia Brand, 1 ounce 90
    Feta, 1 ounce 316
    Goat, 1 ounce 104
    Monterey Jack, 1 ounce 190
    Mozzarella, whole milk, 1/4 cup shredded . 210
    Muenster, 1 ounce 180
    Parmesan, 1 tablespoon, grated 93
    Provolone, 1 ounce 248
    Ricotta, 1/4 cup
        Breakstone's 90
        Sargento 52
    Romano, 1 tablespoon 100
    Swiss, 1 tablespoon 50
    Velveeta 1 ounce 420
Cream, whipped, 2 level tablespoons
    Cool Whip Non-Dairy 0
    Kraft, real 0
    Rich's, pressurized can 5
Egg, large 63
Margarine 1 tablespoon
    Kraft 110
    Mazola Light 130
    Parkay 120
    Promise, Take Control 110
    Smart Beat 90
Milk, 8 ounces
    Skim 126
    Whole 120
Onion dip, Heluva Good, 2 tablespoons 160

Sour cream, regular, 2 tablespoons 15
Sour cream, fat free, 2 tablespoons 40
Yogurt, whole milk, plain, 8 ounces 114
Yogurt, fat free, 8 ounces 187

Desserts and Snacks

Cakes
    Angelfood 1/6 of cake 220
    Chocolate layer, Sara Lee, 1/8 of cake 180
    Cupcake, Hostess, 1 260
    Pound, Pepperidge Farm, 1/5 of cake 280
Cookies
    Animal, Barnum's, 1.1 ounce 160
    Chips Ahoy, 3 125
    Fig Newtons, 2 120
    Honey Maid Grahams, 8 pieces, (that's the little pieces) 180
    Nilla Wafers, 8 115
    Oreo, 3 220
    Pepperidge Farm, Nantucket, 3 75
Corn chips, 1 ounce Frito's (ever try to eat one ounce?) 150
Crackers
    Town House, 5 150
    Ritz, 5 135
Ice Cream, Breyer's, varies with flavor, 1/2 cup 30-50
    Perry's, peanut butter fudge, 1/2 cup 130
Jell-O, 1/2 cup, varies by flavor 35-75
Saltines, 5
    Krispy 180
    Premium 180
    Premium Low Salt 35
Potato chips, 1 ounce, (bet you can't eat just one!)
    Lay's 120
    Ruffles 120
    Wise 220
Pretzels, 1 ounce
    Bachman sticks (wow) 1460
Toppings
    Caramel, 2 tablespoons 90
    Kraft, chocolate, 2 tablespoons 30
    Smucker's, hot fudge, 2 tablespoons 60

Fast Foods

You really didn't think I'd leave this one out, did you?

Arby's regular roast beef sandwich 1009
    Roast beef sub (oh, brother) 2034
    Barbecuc sauce, 1 packet 113
Baskin-Robbins, 1/2 cup vanilla ice cream (wish this was calories?) 40

Burger King, breakfast biscuit with bacon,
    egg, and cheese 1530
    Big Fish 980
    Chocolate shake (can you believe this?) ... 230
    Small onion rings 210
    Regular cheeseburger 770
    Whopper (think they'll make it your way,
        salt free?) 870
    Whopper with cheese 1350
Dairy Queen, double cheeseburger 1130
    Regular chocolate shake (there it
        is again) 420
Domino's Pizza, 2 slices deep dish cheese ... 1184
    Thin crust, sausage and mushroom,
        2 slices 1240
Kentucky Fried Chicken, original recipe
    Breast, 1 (yes, just one) 870
    Biscuit 564
    Drumstick 210
    Potatoes and gravy 386
    Potpie (no wonder drink refills are free;
        you'll be thirsty quickly) 2050
    Thigh (just one of these, too) 570
    Wing (and these) 380
Little Caesar's, Pizza! Pizza! 2 pieces cheese .. 562
    Pepperoni, 2 pieces (Salty! Salty!) 716
McDonald's, Big Mac 1040
    Chicken McNuggets, 6 pieces 510
    Egg McMuffin, plain 730
    Fries, large 290
    Hamburger, regular 530
    Quarter Pounder with Cheese
        (and salt) 1160
    Side salad 10
    Newman's Own Low-Fat Italian
        Dressing (ridiculous!) 740
    Sausage and Egg breakfast biscuit 1220
    Shake, chocolate (unbelievable!) 300
Pizza Hut, hand-tossed, supreme, 1 slice,
        medium pie 884
    Pan pizza, Meatlover's, 1 slice 838
    Personal Pan Pizza, pepperoni (the salt
        is personally yours, too) 1340
Subway, 6 inch sub, ham 1291
    Meatball 1014
Taco Bell, beef burrito (only one!) 1303
    Chicken burrito 854
    Soft Taco Supreme 551
    Taco salad (muy salado) 1132
Wendy's bacon cheeseburger 910
    Baked potato, plain, nothing on it
        (who eats it plain?) 25
    Baked potato with bacon and cheese 1430
    Biggie fries 150
    Chili, small (8 ounces) 800

    Double with everything and cheese 1440
    Frosty, large (there's more salt here
        than in the french fries!) 330
    Single with everything 810

Fruits

*This is the only place that canned does not
mean salted! Eat to your heart's content.*

Apple, 1 fresh 1
Applesauce, 1/2 cup 15
Banana, 1 medium 1
Blackberries, 1/2 cup 1
Blueberries, 1/2 cup 5
Cantaloupe, 1/2 of a 5-inch melon 23
Cherries, fresh, sweet, 10 medium 1
Grapes, 10 fresh 1
Honeydew, 1/10 of a melon 13
Mango, 1/2 cup sliced 2
Orange, 3 inch navel 1
Peaches, 2 1/2 inch fresh 0
Peaches, 1/2 cup canned 10
Pears, fresh, 1 medium 4
Pears, 1/2 cup canned 10
Pineapple, fresh, 2 slices 10
Pineapple, canned, 4 ounces 10
Plum, 2 inch fresh 1
Raisins, 1/4 cup
    Sunmaid Golden 10
    Sunmaid Seedless 10
Rhubarb, 1/2 cup fresh 2
Strawberries, 1 pint 4

Herbs and Spices

Allspice, 1 teaspoon 1
Basil, 1 tablespoon chopped fresh 0
Celery salt, 1 teaspoon (unbelievable) 1584
Chili powder, 1 teaspoon 26
Chives, 1 tablespoon chopped fresh 1
Cinnamon, 1 teaspoon ground 0
Cloves, 1 teaspoon ground 0
Curry powder, 1 teaspoon 3
Dillweed, 1 teaspoon dried 2
Garlic, 1 clove 1
Garlic powder, 1 teaspoon 1
Garlic salt, 1 teaspoon (isn't this
    outrageous?) 2233
Mustard, dry, 1 teaspoon 1
Onion powder, 1 teaspoon 2
Onion salt, 1 teaspoon (that's why they call
    it salt!) 1599
Oregano, 1 teaspoon dried 0
Paprika, 1 teaspoon 1
Parsley, 1 teaspoon dried 1

Rosemary, 1 teaspoon dried, crumbled 1
Sage, 1 teaspoon dried 0
Tarragon, 1 teaspoon dried 0
Thyme, 1 teaspoon dried 0

Meat, Fish, and Poultry

Four ounces is about the size of a deck of cards.

Bacon, 2 slices
    Oscar Mayer 250
    Oscar Mayer, low sodium 170
Bass, freshwater, 4 ounces, raw 79
Beef, 4 ounces
    Lean, raw 75
    Regular ground, raw 77
    Sirloin, raw 75
    Corned (I'll bet you knew this one) 1286
    Dried, 1 ounce (but did you guess
        this one?) 1240
Bologna, 2 ounces
    Boar's Head 530
    Oscar Mayer Light 620
Bratwurst
    Boar's Head, 4 ounces 650
    Pork, 1 (and only one) ounce 158
Catfish, 4 ounces, raw
    Farm raised 15
    Wild 66
Chicken, plain, unseasoned, roasted
    1/2 chicken, 1 pound including bone 244
    Diced, 1 cup, meat only 120
    Skin only, 1 ounce (not to be confused
        with fat content) 18
    Breast, 8 ounces with skin and bone 69
    Thigh, 3 ounces with skin and bone 52
    Canned in water, Swanson, 5-ounce can . . 575
Cod, 4 ounces
    Raw 62
    Canned, 4 ounces 247
Crab, Alaskan King, steamed, 4 ounces 948
Flounder, 4 ounces 105
Haddock, 4 ounces raw 78
Ham, 4 ounces (I knew ham was bad, but
    this surprised even me) 1456
Hot Dog, 1 link
    Boar's Head 460
    Hoffmann, Skinless Wiener 390
    Hoffmann, Snappy Griller (I didn't
        expect this) 780
    Oscar Mayer 450
Lamb, 4 ounces 75
Liver
    Beef, 4 ounces, pan-fried 120
    Chicken, 4 ounces, raw 65
Lobster, 4 ounces, steamed 431

Orange Roughy, 4 ounces, raw 72
Perch, 4 ounces, broiled 90
Polish sausage (kielbasa) 4 ounces, beef 680
Pork loin, 4 ounces, roasted 85
    Chop, 4 ounces 41
Red Snapper, 3 ounces 57
Salmon
    Canned, drained, King, 1/4 cup 270
    Fresh baked, 4 ounces 69
Shrimp, 4 ounces, raw, shelled 168
Sole, 4 ounces, raw 125
Swordfish, 4 ounces, raw 102
Trout, Rainbow, 4 ounces, raw
    Farm raised 40
    Wild 35
Tuna, fresh, 4 ounces, raw 44
    Canned, 1/4 cup in oil or water
        (2 little ounces)
        Bumble Bee 250
        Chicken of the Sea 250
        Star Kist 250
        Star Kist Low Salt (why can't all
          canned foods be like this?) 35
Turkey, fresh, unseasoned, (this means
    unsalted, unpre-basted) 4 ounces 79
    Frozen basted, 4 ounces 270-490
    Smoked, 4 ounces, widely variable
        by brand 70-1050
Veal, loin, 4 ounces, raw 91
    Shoulder 108
Venison, 3 ounces 77

Pantry

Barbecue sauce, 2 tablespoons (you'll want
    to make your own, I bet)
    Hunts Original 400
    KC Masterpiece 640
    Kraft Honey 320
Bouillon, 1 teaspoon or cube (scare you?)
    Herbox, varies with flavor 700-1040
    Herbox, low-sodium variety, any flavor 5
    Knorr, varies with flavor 1200-1290
Broth concentrate, Knorr, 2 teaspoons 800
Browning sauce, Gravy Master, 1/4 teaspoon . . 110
Campbell's Pork and Beans, 1/2 cup
    (be sure to measure this) 420
Capers, Progresso, 1 teaspoon 105
Chili sauce, 1 tablespoon (brands do matter)
    Del Monte 480
    Nance's 75
Chili seasoning mix
    Durkee, 1/5 package 660
    Old El Paso, 1 tablespoon 770
Couscous, 1/2 cup cooked 4

Gravy, 1/4 cup (save those meat juices from
the next roast for homemade)
  Brown
      Durkee, prepared from mix 250
      French's, prepared from mix 250
      Heinz, jarred 360
  Chicken
      Durkee, prepared from mix 350
      Franco-American, canned 270
      French's, prepared from mix 250
      Heinz, jarred 350
  Homestyle
  Durkee, prepared from mix 240
  French's, prepared from mix 230

Horseradish, prepared, 1 teaspoon
  Boar's Head 30
  Heluva Good 6
  Kraft 50

Jams and Jellies, 1 tablespoon
  Smucker's, all varieties 0
  Kraft, strawberry, grape, and orange
      marmalade 0

Ketchup, 1 tablespoon
  DelMonte 190
  Heinz 190
  Hunt's 200
  Hunt's No Salt 10

Macaroni, any kind of pasta, 1 cup (cooked
with no salt in the water; you wouldn't
cook in sea water, would you?) 1

Mayonnaise, 1 tablespoon (that's pretty tiny
if you really measure it)
  Hellmann's Real 80
  Hellmann's Light 115
  Kraft Real 75
  Kraft Light 110
  Miracle Whip 85
  Miracle Whip Light 120

Mustard, prepared, 1 teaspoon
  French's yellow 55
  Grey Poupon dijon 120
  Goulden's spicy 50

Noodles, egg, 1 cup cooked without salt
in the water 11

Oils, all varieties, 1 tablespoon 0

Olives, 1 medium green olive (can you
eat just one?) 70

Pancake syrup, 1 tablespoon (makes you
think, doesn't it?)
  Aunt Jemima 120
  Golden Griddle 55
  Log Cabin 60
  Maple syrup, the real stuff, most brands,
      4 tablespoons 15

Pasta sauce
  Alfredo, 1/2 cup 1,080
  Pesto, basil, 1/4 cup 730

Pasta sauces, commercially prepared, 1/2 cup
  Healthy Choice (not so healthy on
      a low-sodium diet) 390
  Prego, plain (this is just a half cup,
      remember) 610
  Progresso Marinara 480

Peanut butter, 2 tablespoons (watch out for
low-fat varieties, the salt content seems
to go up as the fat goes down. There
are some good ones with nothing but
peanuts—no added anything,
including salt.)
  Peter Pan 120
  Skippy 140
  Smucker's 160

Pepper sauce, hot, 1 teaspoon (if you like
it hot, it pays to read labels)
  Durkee, Redhot 210
  Tabasco 30

Pickle relish, dill, 1 tablespoon 240

Pickle relish, sweet, 1 tablespoon 125

Pickles, 1 ounce (about 4 thin slices)
  Claussen bread and butter 170
  DelMonte sweet 210
  Hebrew National kosher dills 290
  Vlasic dills 260

Potato flakes, Hungry Jack instant,
1/3 cup flakes 45

Rice, dry, 1/4 cup
  Carolina, brown 0
  Minute, white, instant 3
  Uncle Ben's, white, instant 10
  Wild, 1 cup cooked 6

Salad dressing, 2 tablespoons (but what
about the big salad?)
  Bleu cheese
      Kraft 470
      Marie's 170
  Caesar, Kraft 370
  Coleslaw
      Kraft 420
      Marie's 210
  French
      Kraft Catalina 390
      Wishbone 170
  Italian
      Good Seasons, prepared from mix 320
      Seven Seas 580
      Viva 580
  Ranch
      Kraft 270

Seven Seas 250
Thousand Island
   Kraft 310
   Wishbone 340
Salt, 1 teaspoon (this is what the fuss
   is all about) **2360**
Shake and Bake mix, 1/8 package 230
Soy sauce, regular, 1 tablespoon (this is
   enough to make you very thirsty)
   Kikkoman 920
   Kikkoman "Light" 605
   LaChoy 1225
Steak sauce, 1 tablespoon
   A1 250
   A1 Bold 190
   Heinz 57 220
Taco mix, 2 teaspoons ("less" is still
too much)
   Old El Paso 550
   Old El Paso, Less Salt 330
Tartar sauce, 2 tablespoons (a rare time when
   cutting the fat is actually bad for you)
   Hellmann's 260
   Hellmann's Low Fat 360
Teriyaki sauce, 1 tablespoon
   LaChoy 920
   LaChoy Light 440
Vinegar, 1 tablespoon 0
Wheat germ, Kretschmer, 2 tablespoons 0
Worcestershire sauce, 1 teaspoon
   Lea & Perrins 65
   French's 55

Vegetables

Even the frozen stuff can get you here.
Fresh is still the best.

Asparagus, 4 spears 1
Asparagus, canned, 1/2 cup 346
Beets, 1/2 cup
   Raw 53
   Canned 260-325
Black beans, 1/4 cup
   Dried 20
   Canned 350-630
Broccoli, 1/2 cup chopped fresh 12
   Green Giant Harvest Fresh frozen,
      2/3 cup 150
   Spears, plain, 10-ounce package 49
Brussels Sprouts, 1/2 cup raw 11
   Green Giant frozen in butter sauce,
      1/2 cup 270
Butternut squash, 1/2 cup baked 4
Cabbage, 1/2 cup shredded 6

Carrot, raw, 7 1/2-inch 25
   Green Giant canned, 1/2 cup sliced 380
   Green Giant frozen, 1/2 cup sliced 40
Cauliflower, fresh raw, 3 flowerets 17
   Green Giant frozen, 1 cup 25
   Green Giant frozen in cheese sauce,
      1/2 cup 510
Celery, raw, 1 stalk 70
Chick peas, 1/2 cup
   Dried, boiled 6
   Canned
      Progresso 280
      Goya 360
Corn, 1/2 cup
   Most brands, frozen, loose pack 8
   Canned
      DelMonte.................... 360
      Green Giant 360
Cucumber, sliced, 1/2 cup 1
Eggplant, raw, 1/2 cup 2
Green Beans, fresh, 1/2 cup 3
   Canned
      DelMonte.................... 360
      Green Giant 400
Leeks, raw, 1/2 cup 11
Lettuce, Iceberg variety, 1 head 48
   Loose-leaf variety, 1/2 cup shredded 3
Lima Beans, 1/2 cup
   Fresh, boiled 14
   Green Giant, canned 450
   Green Giant, frozen 130
Mushrooms, 1/2 cup
   Fresh 1
   Green Giant canned 440
Onion, 1/2 cup
   Chopped raw 2
   Canned whole 410
Parsnip, boiled, 1/2 cup 8
Peas, 1/2 cup
   Fresh, cooked 2
   Canned
      DelMonte.................... 360
      Green Giant 380
      Frozen, Green Giant, plain, sweet 135
Peppers, sweet, any color, 1/2 cup 1
Potato
   Baked, 4 ounces, with skin 8
      Without skin 6
   Canned whole, 2 1/2 pieces 330
   Frozen
      Ore-Ida Crinkle Cuts, 3 ounces
         (about 8 fries, before the salt) 25
      Ore-Ida hash brown toaster patties,
         2 pieces 470

Food Item and Serving Size	Mg. of Sodium
Tator Tots, 3 ounces	300
Pumpkin, fresh, 1/2 cup boiled	2
Libby's canned, 1/2 cup	5
Spinach, 1/2 cup chopped	
Fresh, boiled	63
Frozen, Green Giant	65
Canned, DelMonte	360
Sweet potato, 5x2 inch raw	17
Canned, drained, 1/2 cup (surprise!)	38
Tomato, 2 1/2 inch fresh, whole	11
Canned, 1/2 cup	
Crushed, Hunt's	285
Progresso	95
Diced, DelMonte	25
Whole, Contadina	220
Hunt's "No Salt"	5
Paste, canned, 2 tablespoons	
Contadina	20
DelMonte	25
Hunt's	90
Progresso	20
Puree, canned, 1/4 cup	
Contadina	15

Food Item and Serving Size	Mg. of Sodium
Hunt's	100
Progresso	15
Sauce, canned, plain, 1/4 cup (you don't have to make your own sauce)	
Contadina	280
DelMonte	340
DelMonte No Salt	20
Hunt's	360
Hunt's No Salt	10
Progresso	260
Sun-dried, Flora, no oil, 5 pieces	15
Turnip, 1/2 cup, raw	44
Turnip greens, 1/2 cup, raw	11
Canned	325
Frozen	20
Water chestnuts, canned 1/2 cup sliced, (a rare exception to the canned rule)	6
Winter squash, 1/2 cup, raw	4
Yams, 1/2 cup, boiled	0
Yellow squash, 1/2 cup, boiled	1
Zucchini 1/2 cup, fresh	2
Canned, DelMonte	490
Progresso	400

Keep in mind, the fast food list is according to each company's own published "nutrient facts," a copy of which you can get at any one of these places if you ask. This is just meant to give you a rough idea of why you shouldn't expect to fit these into your healthy eating plan.

By now you've seen the point. There are plenty of foods that are good and not so good for you. Using these tables you can calculate the sodium content in the foods you normally eat and find ways to adjust your meals and snacks, allowing you to reduce your sodium intake dramatically. There are plenty of items I didn't include, but that doesn't matter because you can find the sodium content right on the label.

What It Boils Down To Is This:

1. Salt is poison. Put a skull and cross bones on the shaker and hide it up in a cupboard someplace and forget it. It's all up to you. There are no Salt Police.

2. Fresh is best. Mom was right when she said you should eat more fresh fruits and vegetables.

3. Always read the label on absolutely everything. Every time. Everywhere. No exception. And add up your daily salt intake as you go.

4. Think of canned foods as bombs. Don't take them off the shelf, let alone open one; they'll blow you up, resulting in an explosion of salt and fluid retention, weight gain, swelling, shortness of breath . . . you know the drill.

5. Don't add salt to cooking water, such as for pasta or vegetables (of course you couldn't anyway, because it's up in a cupboard out of reach, right?)

6. Keep your meals well balanced. Don't give up otherwise healthy foods; change the way you prepare or buy them instead.

7. Processed food is just that—processed. That means that almost all of the goodness has been replaced by salt.

8. Fast food restaurants want you to put them in your will. And regular restaurants should be approached with caution.

9. Your ancestors survived without salt, so can you.

10. The health of your heart is in your hands. Handle with care!

Remember!
SALT IS POISON

Recipes to Demonstrate a Point

Chicken and Rice Soup

How many times have you followed a recipe and not questioned its sodium content? Here's an example of how easy it is to tweek a recipe you may have used for decades and make it low sodium and still delicious.

Homemade the Standard Way
4 servings at 677 mg. sodium each

1 (32-ounce) carton chicken broth
$1/2$ onion, chopped
1 stalk celery, sliced thin
1 carrot, diced
1 garlic clove, minced
$1/2$ cup uncooked rice
$3/4$ teaspoon dried thyme
1 cup cooked chicken, diced
$1/4$ teaspoon salt
$1/4$ teaspoon ground pepper

Combine broth, onion, celery, carrots, and garlic in stock pot. Bring to a boil. Add rice and thyme. Reduce heat to low and simmer, uncovered, 30 minutes, stirring occasionally. Add chicken and heat through. Stir in salt and pepper.

Homemade My Way
4 servings at 85 mg. sodium each

4 cups salt-free chicken broth (make your own stock or look for it in the soup section, you can even find salt-free bouillon cubes or powder if you look carefully)
$1/2$ pound cooked diced chicken—salt free of course ($1^1/2$ cups)
2 cups chopped fresh or frozen salt-free vegetables (let your creativity flow, try zucchini, green onion, mushrooms, snow pea pods, bean sprouts, okra, broccoli, cabbage, or any of the old standards like onions, peas, and carrots, fresh or salt free, naturally.)
1 to 2 teaspoons fresh herbs, minced (any favorites work well; try tarragon, sage, thyme, parsley; whatever you have on hand—you are growing an herb garden now, right?)
$1/2$ cup uncooked rice—any kind you like

Bring broth to a boil and add remaining ingredients. Cover and simmer 20-30 minutes depending on the vegetables and rice you chose.

Easy Pork Mole

Makes 4 servings

The Old Way

1 lb. pork tenderloin, cut into bite-size pieces (340)
1 yellow onion, chopped (5)
1/4 cup bottled Italian dressing (1160)
1 square semi-sweet chocolate, chopped (0)
2 tsp. instant coffee (0)
1/2 teaspoon chili powder (13)
1/2 teaspoon ground cumin (0)
1 can (14 1/2 oz.) diced tomatoes, undrained (770)
2 green onions, chopped (4)
2 cups hot cooked long-grain white rice (0 cooked without added salt)

Cook meat and yellow onions in dressing in large saucepan on medium-high heat 10 min. or until meat is browned and onions are crisp-tender, stirring occasionally.

Add next 4 ingredients; stir until meat is evenly coated.

Sir in tomatoes; simmer on low heat 15 min. or until meat is done; top with green onions. Serve over rice. One serving has 570 mg. sodium.

The New Way

1 lb. pork tenderloin, cut into bite-size pieces (340)
1 yellow onion, chopped (5)
2 tablespoons olive oil (0)
1 square semi-sweet chocolate, chopped (0)
1/2 teaspoon cinnamon (0)
1/8 teaspoon cloves (0)
1 teaspoon chili powder (26)
1 teaspoon ground cumin (0)
2 tablespoons raisins (15) (optional)
1 can (14 1/2 oz.) no-salt-added diced tomatoes (5) OR 1 1/2 cups diced fresh tomatoes (11)
2 green onions, chopped (4)
2 cups hot cooked long-grain white rice (0 cooked without added salt)

Cook meat and yellow onions in dressing in large saucepan on medium-high heat 10 min. or until meat is browned and onions are crisp-tender, stirring occasionally.

Add next 5 ingredients (and raisins for a more authentic mole that's still quick and easy); stir until meat is evenly coated.

Sir in tomatoes; simmer on low heat 15 min. or until meat is done; top with green onions. Serve over rice. One serving (with the raisins) has 101 mg. sodium.

Make Your Recipes New Again, the Low-Salt Way

So you've been a cook for years, decades, maybe. You have all your tried-and-true recipes and change is not coming easy. I get it. Learn to use your old recipes but in new ways. Take those family favorites and scrub out the salt. Add new seasonings or change the method of cooking. Here's a good example of how you can adapt your old familiar recipes or any new one you find compelling. Change it up! Make it your own by varying the meat, seasonings, cooking method, sauces, and so on. Be a chef in your own kitchen. That's exactly what I did with this recipe. It originally called for chicken, and that worked, but it works well with other meats and dense fish, too. It called for rosemary, a good choice, but not the only herb in the garden. Plus you can up or down the heat and use any preserves or vinegar you like. Lets take a look (oh, by the way, the original recipe called for 2, yes TWO teaspoons of salt. Why, I ask, why? You will not miss it, I promise!)

1 1/2 tablespoons herb of your choice, minced, let's say, thyme

1/2 tablespoon brown sugar (or you could go with honey, let's say lavender honey)

1 teaspoon heat, hot paprika, minced jalapeño, oh, let's use dried red pepper flakes

1 teaspoon pepper, black that you grind yourself, white (that's just the inside of black peppercorns) or, let's say, pink peppercorns, a neat little prize I found in the regular grocery.

2 tablespoons canola or olive oil plus extra for the grill or sauté pan

2 pounds boneless meat, chicken (skip the breast meat here, it'll dry out too quickly, use whole boneless thighs), turkey, pork tenderloin, halibut, swordfish, cod, lamb, even tender beef. Cut the meat into large chunks you can handle with tongs or on a grill easily, say 3x4 inch pieces. I used turkey thighs cut into 4-5 pieces each.

1 cup preserves, pick one that works well with the meat. Maybe raspberry for chicken, apricot for pork, mint for lamb, blueberry for cod (yes, it works well). I like a nice little Irish whiskey-infused orange marmalade with everything.

1/4 cup vinegar—STOP. Don't drag out that old bottle of distilled white vinegar. It's flavor we're after, remember? Use champagne vinegar, or in heartier meats, try Balsamic or red wine vinegar. I used rice vinegar so as not to overrun all the other flavors, but still give it all a boost while balancing the sweetness of my special marmalade.

Mix 1 tablespoon of the herb you've chosen with the sweetener, heat, and pepper of your desire; set aside. Drizzle the 2 tablespoons of oil over the meat of the day and toss to coat. Sprinkle, or spoon the herb mixture on and toss to cover meat well.

Put the remaining herb together with the marmalade or preserves, and the vinegar. Warm in a saucepan or microwave gently just to melt and blend.

Heat the grill (thread meat on skewers for fun) or a sauté pan to medium-hot. Cook the meat, browning well on each side. If using a grill go for those grill marks. If using a sauté, don't crowd the meat; better to do in 2 or 3 batches so it browns well instead of stewing in a crowd! Serve with warm sauce.

This recipe serves 4 generously. Using my ingredient choices from the options we discussed above, each serving goes like this:

Ingredient	Sodium content for one serving
Thyme	Zip
Lavender honey	Nada
Pink peppercorns	Nothin'
Olive oil	Zilch
Turkey (say 6 ounces, mmm!)	120 mg.
Orange Marmalade	22 mg.
Rice vinegar	You guessed it—ZERO
My total	142 mg. sodium

My total if I used the prescribed salt:

Well, 2 teaspoons of salt is 4800 mg. of sodium and the recipe was for 4 servings so that's 4800 mg. divided by 4 servings, or 1200 mg. extra sodium totaling 1342 mg. per serving. Why? WHY? It didn't need any salt at all. Even my husband liked it!! The message here is simple: play with your food! There are so many flavors to experiment with. You'll see how much better food tastes.

The Spice of Your Life

Ways to flavor your food without salt

I know. You're probably thinking, "There has to be a better way. Food without salt has no flavor." Fear not, hungry reader, we have ways to add zest to your plate and zing to your palate. There are bazillions of flavor enhancers that range from jalapeño to citrus, and chili powder to thyme leaves. Step into the herb garden with me.

First, let me be perfectly clear: garlic salt, onion salt, or any other flavor enhancer that includes salt in its name or ingredient list has no place in your food or in your cupboard! Dispense with them all immediately before the salt police catch up with you! This includes MSG. Ah, yes, another source of the poison we seek to avoid. We discussed it briefly a few pages ago. Its name hints of the evil within it: monoSODIUM glutamate! It has little taste of its own, but while it is added to food to bring out the natural flavors of the food, it loads on sodium. If you have it on your shelf, lose it now! Hurry!

Whew! Safe again. Now let's explore alternative flavors, and then we'll spend some time on other flavor enhancement elements.

Let's start with a chat about **GARLIC**. Everybody knows what garlic tastes like, but there are ways you can vary that a bit. One way is to roast it. That really mellows out the flavor.

Roasted Garlic

From a whole head of garlic remove only the loosest papery layer. Now cut a thin slice off the root end in one good slice across to expose the meat of the cloves. Don't separate them, just brush or drizzle a little olive oil over the cut surface, wrap it in foil and bake. You could do several at once by putting cut side down in a baking pan first greased with a layer of olive oil. Do this when you have the oven going for something else so you don't heat it up just for a head of garlic. It can bake at any temp. To give you a timing idea, I find it softens and roasts through in about 30–40 minutes at 350°. Once done, let the garlic cool till you can handle it, grasp it at the uncut end and gently squeeze out the soft, aromatic cloves like toothpaste. Store airtight in the fridge. Try that on breads or veggies instead of salty butter!

Tuck whole cloves or thick slices of garlic into tiny pockets cut into meat roasts with the tip of a knife. Let them roast right along with the meat for a flavorful roast.

Add sliced or minced garlic to food you'll cook in a sauté or fry pan. To get the skin off the clove of garlic you want to use, lay the clove on a cutting board. Rest a wide chef-type knife with a flat side resting on the garlic. Holding it steady by the handle, hit the top flat side of the knife; go on, hit it like you mean it using the heel of your hand. That will flatten it and separate the papery cover from it. Wet your hands so the garlic doesn't stick to you. Now, just pull off the skin and mince up what you need. If you'll be adding other ingredients, have whatever else you are cooking all ready to go in before you begin cooking the garlic. First heat some oil, and then add in the prepared garlic. Cook on medium to medium high just a minute—no more or it will start to burn and turn bitter and ugly. Add the veggie or whatever you want to cook with the garlic and continue as usual. Who says you need salt?

And if you like shallots, do the same thing with them. If you don't know if you like shallots, why not? Try 'em! They are generally mild and some people see them as a melding of onion and garlic flavors. They look a lot like a small onion, so slice off the ends, peel, and chop or slice like an onion.

Of course ONIONS come in a wide range of flavors from sweet to biting. Try red onions, leaks (be sure to rinse these very well as sand tends to collect in the layers), or green onions. Also delicious are pearl and cipolline onions for cooking whole in recipes. These are small but easy to peel if you just toss them into a pot of boiling water for 2 minutes, and drain quickly. Then throw them into a bowl of ice and water to stop the cooking process. As you cut the root end off, put some pressure on the top where you're holding it. It will pop out of the skin from the bottom as you squeeze from the top. Now use them in a stew or sauté in a vegetable dish, as just a couple ideas.

Other members of the onion family (technically the Allium family) include Mayan or Vidalia sweet onions, scallions, aka green onions, and chives. Chives don't just come in onion flavor. Look for garlic flavored, too. Either way, snipped into short pieces they add color, flavor, and texture to more than just your baked potato! Sprinkle over scrambled eggs and omelets, all manner of salads, vegetable sides, and casseroles. And don't ignore those beautiful chive flowers; they work beautifully in a salad or just as garnish.

How about some Onions on the Side:

With NO SODIUM here, onions make a great flavor booster and go so well with meats on the side or rolled up in them: Slice a nice big sweet onion thickly, separate into rings, and cook in a little olive oil slowly over not-too-high heat until it's almost soft enough to spread like butter. Toss in a drop or two of your favorite vinegar—maybe balsamic, red wine, champagne? If there is any leftover, it will keep well, covered in the fridge.

Try them in **Chicken-Onion Roll-Ups**: pound a chicken breast to 1/4-inch thick, spread some of these onions over and roll up. Cover and bake 30 minutes at 350° until 165° shows on your meat thermometer. Sprinkle a little cheese (remember to account for the sodium in the amount and type of cheese you pick) over the chicken roll and let it set 5 minutes to melt. Mmm, juicy and flavorful.

PEPPERS offer a broad selection of tastes and choices. We are all familiar with green bell peppers. Did you know they are just unripe bell peppers? As they bask in the sun on the plant, green bells ripen into sweet, vitamin C-rich, red, yellow, orange, purple, and other colored, ripe bell peppers. Of course there is also a whole range of spicy and hot peppers to try either fresh or dehydrated.

Bells come in so many colors that they just brighten up any plate besides adding sweetness and nutrition, and they do this cooked or raw. In terms of nutrition, get this: there is more vitamin C in one cup chopped ripe bell pepper than in one cup fresh orange juice! A recessive gene is what gives these peppers their lack of heat, even though they are members of the chile pepper family. Most often when people talk of "peppers," and especially "sweet peppers," bells are what they mean. They are eaten raw, cooked, pickled, turned into salsa, and more. Grab a few extra in peak season; dice and freeze them for the long dark season. Be sure to wash them well before using.

Roasting peppers, as with any vegetable, brings out the intense, sweet flavor of bell peppers and makes them excellent when added to salads, sandwiches, and recipes. Preheat the oven to 500°, and line a baking pan with foil. Cut the pepper into quarters, place on the foil inside down so skin side is up to the heat, and roast until the skin turns black. Once out of the oven, cover the pieces with a tea towel or put them in a container with a lid or a paper bag and close it up. When the pepper has cooled, you can peel the skin off. Feel free to try the method that has you holding them over the gas flame; I'd take out extra fire insurance first.

Of course there are lots of **HOT PEPPERS**, too, and they vary from mild to blow-your-lid-off hot. Although bell peppers are also "chile peppers," only the hot varieties are called by that name. These are the capsicum fruits with moderate to extreme levels of capsaicins. What makes a "hot" pepper hot is that it contains capsicanoids, more commonly called capsicum, and this chemical is what gives the fruit the hot sensation when it is eaten. Most commonly seen in North American are "red chilies" a small bright-red to dark-red variety. Renowned are the round, yellow-orange "habañeros," the hottest of the chile peppers. Interestingly, birds don't taste this chemical, but mammals do.

Spicy peppers are used in many cuisines. Of course we know the flavor and heat they add to Mexican and southwestern cooking, but did you know Thai food is often enhanced by spicy chilies? Many types are used in Thai cooking, fresh and dried, whole and ground; the smallest and hottest is the Thai birds eye. Other cuisines that commonly include spicy peppers include those of China, India, North Africa, Spain, and South America. Hot peppers often have unique and excellent taste once the heat is tamed. Do this by being sure to remove the ribs and all seeds before using the peppers in cooking. Always wash your hands thoroughly or wear gloves so you don't risk getting the heat in your eyes.

It is usually best, at least as you begin this journey, to mince up the hot chile you plan to use so you don't get a big bite until you're used to the taste and want bigger bites. If you get into more heat than you can handle and your mouth is just on fire, do not drink water—it makes the heat hotter. Use milk. For some reason, milk efficiently neutralizes the burn of the capsicum in the hot pepper. If you are in a place, such as a restaurant, where you don't have ready access to milk, try plain bread, rice or yogurt. Don't pass up the opportunity to flavor up your food with some hot (or mildly spicy) peppers in your quest for a salt replacement.

A chile's heat is rated in Scoville heat units, ranging from 1 to 300,000 (mild to extremely hot). The common jalapeño, which most people believe is very hot, rates only 5000 units, whereas a habañero can get right up there at 300,000 units! There are many types

of chile peppers of varying "hotness" that you could look for. Some fairly mild chile peppers are the Anaheim chile, poblano chile, Hungarian wax chile, and the ancho chile (which is just a dried poblano, something that confused me for ages until I finally figured it out). Moderately hot chile peppers include the Cascabel chile, chilaca chile, pasilla chile, chipotle chile, and the jalapeño chile. Some really hot chile peppers are the cayenne chile, Serrano chile, Thai chile, and Pequín chile. Peppers to call the fire department for include the habañero and Scotch Bonnet, offering the strongest heat of all chile pepper varieties! I'd bet Peter Piper wouldn't touch these! Be sure to check out my absolute best-ever homemade chili powder, page 53.

In my own experience, fresh jalapeños work very well in fresh foods especially salsas. And I love it in a homemade béchamel sauce (fancy name, don't be intimidated, its basically a cream sauce and easy to make) for vegetables or a twist on lasagna. Here's my recipe:

Jalapeño Béchamel Sauce

2 tablespoons unsalted butter
2 tablespoons all-purpose flour
2 cups milk
1 jalapeño, halved, seeds and ribs removed, and finely minced

Melt the butter in a small pot over medium heat. Add the flour, stir with a wooden spoon working the flour into the butter until a paste consistency is achieved. Whisk in the milk slowly, whisking well to remove lumps and make the sauce very smooth. Continue to whisk over medium heat until thickened. Once the mixture thickens, add the minced jalapeño. Use to sauce a vegetable dish or as the sauce in a pasta dish. I used this in a seafood lasagna recipe for a cooking competition and took first prize. Who needs salt? There are 244 mg. of sodium in the whole 2 cups, so an average quarter cup per serving will have about 31 mg.

How about **CITRUS** for a little zing? Citrus fruits can add a bright flavor, or lift a recipe by drizzling in a little liquid sunshine. Remember what we said back on page 7 about fooling our salt taste buds by stimulating our sour receptors instead? Lemons and limes will work perfectly. When buying citrus fruits, choose them if they seem heavy for their size and have bright peels that don't have spots and blemishes or seem to be withering. Store them in plastic in the veggie drawer. They'll keep several days, but if you hit a good sale and can't use them up soon enough, zest them with a micro-plane (my personal favorite kitchen tool) and freeze the zest spread out on a cookie sheet, then once frozen, store in a plastic bag, or put zest in ice cube trays, add a little water and freeze that way. Then juice your citrus and freeze the juice in ice cube trays. Once frozen, transfer to a plastic bag and stash in the deep freeze. Be sure to label everything; you'll be surprised how much citrus juice from different fruits will look alike in ice cube form!

Now you have a tablespoon of citrus juice or a tea-spoon of citrus zest ready to go anytime you want to freshen the taste of a vegetable or fish, or add them to a sauce or salsa. Be creative—beat that salt craving! Use lemon juice (fresh is best, of course) in your vinai-grette. Melt unsalted butter, stir in lime zest and cayenne powder, and use it on your fresh hot vegeta-bles. Now that was an easy way to get flavor instead of salt on your food!

How about one of my favorites: remove the sections of a ruby red grapefruit, drizzle on a little honey (any kind), then sprinkle just a little ground cardamom over it all. What a yummy, sodium-free breakfast treat!

How about another flavor-enhancer and taste bud-fooler, **VINEGAR**? Whether you buy fla-vored vinegar or make your own, this is a big flavor booster. Vinegar is one of those ingredients that people don't think of as often as they should. Mostly it's just seen in salad dressings and pickles, which is a shame, because there is a whole world of flavor just waiting to be tapped into. Vine-gar results from a process of fermentation that changes it from a carbohydrate, to an alcohol, and to an acetic acid. Acetobacter aceti is the bacteria used to create vinegar from alcohol. It is widely found in nature and requires oxygen to func-tion. That's why a bottle of wine with an alcohol con-centration of 10 or 12% left uncorked and undisturbed in a cozy warm condition for a couple weeks becomes snappy vinegar. But, really good vinegar needs to start with a more dilute alcohol content base. Actually, it's not really hard, but I question whether it's really worth the time and work when you can buy vinegar cheaply enough. It is fun to enhance it!

Buy a red wine vinegar, white wine vinegar, rice wine vinegar, or true cider vinegar. Sterilize bottles you will make and store the vinegar in and let dry inside com-pletely. Water left behind may contaminate the vine-gar or at minimum cause cloudiness. There are two

schools of thought about heating the vinegar or using it room temperature. If you heat it, the herbs will defi-nitely fade. But that's not a problem because once you get to the flavor intensity you want, you can simply remove the used herbs and replace with a stem or two of fresh herb; now it's beautiful. I tend to the heat-your-vinegar club, but try it both ways and make your own decision. If you choose heat, don't boil it; just get it nice and hot. And use nothing metal at all.

My flavored vinegar:

You need a bottle of vinegar (type depends on your purpose and the herbs you want to use), lots of fresh herbs, either all of one type, or a mixture. Include cloves of garlic, strips of fresh citrus, chili peppers, whatever floats your boat: just be sure they are thor-oughly washed AND DRIED. Herbs can be prepared using the bleach-rinse described below but it isn't nec-essary (page 40). Jars and bottles should be sanitized, but a dishwasher is all you need. It isn't necessary to outright sterilize them like baby bottles.

Warm the vinegar but stop short of a simmer or boil. You could aim for 190° but never more than 200° on a reliable thermometer. Use a non-metallic (enamel) pot, or heat in the microwave. Lightly bruise and stuff as many herbs as you can, at least several stems or other ingredients, into the bottle. Using a non-metal funnel, pour in the vinegar to nearly the top. Use a cork or other non-metal top. Give it a little shake to seat the herbs and leave it in a dark place that's not hot or cold for 2 weeks. Then strain your brew through cheesecloth. I put some into a plastic funnel so I can pour directly through it into the decorative bottle (again sanitized and dry). Tuck in a stem of the (safely prepared) herb or a twist of the citrus peel for eye appeal, and enjoy! It will keep in the fridge for 6 months. It's high acidity also helps discourage bacteria growth.

One of my favorite executive chef-friends encouraged me to make chili vinegar. The process is the same, but use strips of seeded fresh jalapeños. Keep it in the fridge and tap into it when you need a little zing! Comes in very handy.

And yes, aged balsamic vinegar is a world above any-thing you can imagine. When a friend of mine brought me some from her trip to Italy, I totally fell in love with it! She also brought back a very small bottle that had been aged for 30 years—and we ate it over ice cream! Oh, baby was that heaven. I know, you think I'm nuts, but if you have the opportunity, try it. In the mean-time, give good balsamic a chance, wherever it comes from, however old it is. You won't be sorry.

Good news, you can make **HERBAL OILS** almost the same way! I love having homemade garlic oil at my fingertips. Choose a light oil with little or no flavor of its own (sunflower, safflower, extra-virgin olive oil) and place the amount you want to make in a large saucepan. Throw in 1 or 2 whole heads of garlic that have been sliced in half horizontally so every clove is exposed. Don't bother with removing the papery stuff. Bring the heat up so the oil is hot, but just below a simmer/sizzle point. The purpose here is not to cook the garlic, but to extract as much flavor as possible while creating a germ-discouraging (especially *Clostridium botulinum* bacteria) hot environment. Let it sit on the heat for 20 minutes. Once the garlic is all softened, press it up against the side or bottom of the pot with a wooden spoon to further extract flavor. Remove from the heat and let cool. Once you can handle it without fear of burns, pour through cheesecloth and store in plastic squirt bottles (I use the kind you see ketchup or mustard in on diner tables). Keep them cool until you need them. I go through this fast enough that I can keep a bottle next to the stove with my pour-bottle of plain olive oil. I've never had it go bad on me. In general it is best to use the oils in a couple months, so don't make more than you can use!

If you want herb oils, warm your choice of oil and pour into sterilized glass bottles or jars containing herbs you have thoroughly sanitized in a bleach solution (see page 40), washed, dried, and lightly bruised. Use as much herb as you can to infuse the most flavor. Cover and stash your oil in a dark place. Check for intensity of flavor now and then. Once you get the flavor concentration where you want it, filter it through cheesecloth and discard the old herbs. You can add a single stem of the herb you used as a "label" but be aware it will continue to add a little more flavor to the oil. Tasty and a whole lot cheaper than store bought!

We can't forget about **PEPPER**! You know: salt's alter ego. It's time pepper came out from the shadows I'd say. Pepper comes in so many colors and flavors that it can enhance many dishes. There is evidence that it was being used in food over 4000 years ago. In medieval times, pepper was actually used as money; and, yes, it was one of the spices on Christopher Columbus's shopping list.

If you don't have a peppermill, it's an investment you should seriously consider. Fresh grated pepper is all about the flavor, not the bite, something you are certainly missing if you are using powdered pepper in a shaker. That old powdered stuff lost its flavor before it even found its way into the container at the powdered pepper factory, long before shipping to your local store, never mind how long it sat on the shelf at in the spice section of your local megamart. Yuck. Grate, grind, or crack it as you need it! Fresh grated pepper can really zip up a recipe. You don't need a fancy or expensive one, just look for a mill that holds a couple tablespoons of peppercorns securely and twists smoothly. A simple, hand turned peppermill will be just perfect. It will be frequently used as well. Once you taste fresh grated pepper, you'll never look back. And do look in that spice section of your megamart for those dandy new devices that contain whole peppercorns and a grinder top on the bottle.

When cooking with black pepper, keep in mind that flavor deteriorates as food cooks, so be aware that long-cooking recipes may be better served (no pun intended) if the pepper gets grated into the delicious simmering potion later rather than sooner. However food that has been "peppered" then frozen may have a stronger pepper flavor. Who knew? When buying your peppercorns, don't be confused if they are labeled with such names as Bangkok, Belém or Malabar; these are just the locations of their growth, production, or shipping.

However, you may want to keep a couple other pepper varieties around, as well. Happily, spice companies are also marketing many kinds or combinations of kinds of peppercorns in their own little disposable peppermills that are very handy if you want to try out a variety of pepper flavors. Just be wary, if you start trying pepper combos with garlic or other additives in the little mill, that they haven't added salt, too. I've found them housing many kinds of peppercorns just waiting to be released into my rations, thanks to a twist or two of the fancy grater do-dad on the top. Experience the variety of flavors this devise can supply!

Consider white pepper for a milder taste and a color that works best in light colored foods such as fish, potatoes, and creamy foods, sauces, and dressings. These are actually black peppercorns with the black coat removed. White pepper can be used interchangeably with black, as well, but little black flecks may not look as appealing in light colored foods.

I recently discovered pink peppercorns; this has an almost fruity flavor with a mild spicy-peppery taste that's hard to describe but delicious to eat on vegetables, eggs, fish, poultry, and almost anything that isn't a hardy flavor in its own right. They are actually berries of the Bais Rose plant from Madagascar and are cousins of the mango. This, like white pepper, is best added at the end of cooking so as not to dull its flavor. This is totally worth looking for and totally worth a slightly higher price. Do be aware that another form of "pink pepper" exists that is from an entirely different source, the *Schinus terebinthifolius*, also called the Brazilian Peppertree. The flavor is more like menthol, and it can cause allergic reactions if eaten in much quantity—read labels—oh yeah, you already do that anyway.

Green peppercorns impart a pungent, "green" flavor and are actually just immature black peppercorns. Also great in foods that call for a lighter pepper flavor such as salads, vegetables and sauces. Don't be confused by names such as "French Peppercorns", or "Rainbow Peppercorns" as they are all just mixtures in different proportions and of different intensities of peppery bite, usually combining black, green, and white peppercorns, nothing scary or haute. Really.

Now let's look at **CULINARY HERBS**. Humans have been using seasonings for almost as long as we've been eating. And various blends of herbs and spices have evolved over the centuries just as various cuisines and recipes. Many areas of the world have geographically specific blends that lend emphasis to the cuisine of the local region. For example, there are many variations on curry powder, some with as few ingredients as two or three, some with a dozen or more according to the local taste. We have no need to settle for the single, homogenous offerings of grocery store sources. Once you have a grasp of the various individual scents, tastes, and palatable applications, you can be the architect of your next meal's seriously good, salt-free flavor! So let's take a look at some of the options from the hundreds of herbs and spices at your disposal. And many come with nutritional extras, like lysine, vitamins, and antioxidants. Of course, history suggests herbs have myriad medicinal uses, and whole books have been written for you on that alone. As seekers of flavor, we'll look at some of the easier to find or grow herbs no one should live without!

If you want to consider an herb garden, keep in mind a few herbs that attract butterflies when in bloom: basil, chives, dill, lavender, mint, oregano, and thyme. Let's assume you got the herb "bug" and just came

home (or better yet, in from the garden) with an armload of the enticing aromas and, oh my, now what? Of course you want to preserve your harvest; how do you prevent its deterioration into a slimy green, primordial soup before you can use it all? Well, you could make flavored oils and vinegars as described above beginning on page 38. Or try some of these ideas . . .

Quick herb preparation

Roll out several sheets of paper towels—keep them attached to each other in one long train. Lightly moisten them, easily done with a spray bottle for the express purpose of atomizing water only. Now lay out your emerald beauties across the papers in single layers. Starting at one end, roll up the whole length snuggly, but not too tightly. These aren't sardines! Now take your roll and wrap it around with a length of plastic wrap. They will keep nicely on the top shelf (not the veggie drawer) for many days. Some herbs like to keep their toes in water. Thyme, rosemary, parsley and the like can be placed stem down in a container of water (not so deep the leaves are in the water) with a loose plastic bag over the top. Stash this in the door of the fridge. Now go look for recipes to use them before you lose them!

Other ways to extend the life of your herbs

Prepare herbs with sanitizing bleach solution

I prepare all my herbs for drying, freezing, and oil-making the same way: with a bleach sanitizing solution. There will be NO residual bleach on the herb, and the risk of botulism is essentially eliminated this way. (Because vinegar is high in acid, it does not support the growth of *Clostridium botulinum* bacteria, making this step unnecessary. But if you feel inclined, it's ok.)

1. Pick herb stems from your garden or porch pots after the dew is off the leaves when the essence is fully redistributed from the roots and back into the leaves, but not too late in the day so as to avoid burning of the leaves by the sun.

2. Be sure the leaves are picked through and sorted to exclude any leaves that aren't beautiful, any with signs of insects, and any other debris.

3. Fill a large pot (I actually use my smaller side sink) with 1½ quarts cool water and stir in 1 teaspoon liquid bleach, no more. Briefly dip and swirl the fresh herbs in the sanitizing bleach solution, rinse thoroughly under cold running water, and pat gently so as not to bruise, but thoroughly to dry all absorbable liquid off the leaves

Dehydrating herbs

Gather several stems of the herb, but not so many as to impede air movement around the leaves and stems so that mold might be encouraged. I like to wrap a rubber band around the stems down toward the cut ends. This way it will shrink down to hold tightly to the stems as they dry and shrink. Nothing worse than doing all that work, then finding half-dried stems on the floor because they shrank and slipped out of a string tied around them! Once you have snuggly fit your rubber band girdle on the stems, work a piece of string through a loop of the band; tie it off and use to hang the stems to dry. Choose a dark place where there will be air changes (not in a closet that never gets opened, for example) and check them now and then. Don't leave them hanging so long they get dusty, but don't take them down before they are completely dry. Store in jars or plastic bags tightly closed and away from light and heat. Or buy an electric food dehydrator—I couldn't live without mine! (Makes great jerky and fruit leathers, too.)

Freezing herbs

Start with finely chopped fresh, young herb leaves (see chiffonade, below) and divide the herbs into the compartments of an ice cube tray. Gently pour filtered water over the herbs and freeze. Once solid, remove herb cubes and keep frozen in labeled plastic bags. These herb-pops will stay well until the next growing season when fresh herbs are available again and make a handy way to toss flavor into your cool-season cooking.

How to chiffonade herb leaves

(Use this method with any leaf large enough that you need to cut it up). See photos below.

1. Stack a few rinsed and dried leaves one on top of the next.

2. Roll the stack into a fairly tight bundle.

3. Using a very sharp knife (sharp is key here), cut using a gentle, slide-through slicing motion to prevent bruising and brown edges; making very thin slices.

4. Fluff out the resulting tiny ribbons and distribute over the food and plate.

Hints on using herbs

Delicate herbs in quick recipes or ones that require high temp cooking are best added toward or at the end of cooking to keep the flavors fresh.

In stews and braising, however, tie that bunch of thyme stems tightly together with butcher string and toss in for the long haul. This is also the best method for cinnamon sticks, bay leaves, and Bouquet Garni—see page 53. (For easy retrieval these are best tied up in a little cheesecloth bundle or in a tea ball or similar contraption for infusing herbs in these types of brews—something for your wish list, perhaps?)

Toasting seeds

This process can accentuate the taste and aroma of most any spice seeds such as cumin, coriander, fennel, sesame, and mustard seeds. To toast, heat a heavy skillet over medium heat until hot. Add seeds; toast 2–5 minutes or until spices are fragrant and lightly browned, stirring frequently, or shaking the pan back and forth to prevent burning. Stay right there with them; it's a quick trip from toasty and tasty to charcoal. Remove from heat, cool, and store airtight. You might want to use a splatter screen over the skillet because seeds can pop high as they toast. By the way, fennel, caraway, and cumin seeds aren't really seeds at all. They are little, bitty, teeny, tiny fruits. Thought you'd want to know.

Ground seeds from your herbs

Frequently, recipes will call for ground spices, often seeds that you can grow and grind yourself. If you are collecting seeds from your herb garden, be sure to dry well and toast for storing safely and flavor enhancement (except of course the ones you air dry and store for planting next year). Then, unless you're off the grid and have to grind in a mortar and pestle to crush them (old reliable method, but more work than I'm willing to do) assign a small electric grinder, such as a coffee bean grinder, to spices only. Don't get a fancy expensive one, stay with the plain and low cost. It'll whirl your aromatic toasted seeds into delicious freshly ground seeds for recipes very quickly. It's also handy for grinding any small amount of spice, as well. Do wipe it out well and don't use for coffee beans unless

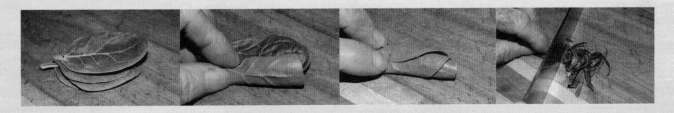

you want to have spicy coffee! Keep in mind seeds, when whole, can keep well for 2 years, but storage in the ground state will cut them back to 6 months. It's just a taste thing.

And now, the herb parade:

BASIL

Don't blow this off as just a pesto herb, it is so much more than that. And it boasts highbrow cousins: mint and thyme. What fresh herb fills a kitchen with the scent of summer more than basil, even on a cold February day? If you do much Italian-style cooking, you are familiar with the sweet, clove-fragranced, typical Italian basil. But do you know it comes in lemon, lime, cinnamon, and even camphor scents as well? In fact, more than 60 varieties exist, most heralding from the Mediterranean area. Some have large leaves, some purple and ruffled (opal basil). Thai basil is one especially associated with Southeast Asian cooking and has a slight sweet-licorice flavor. In any variety, the smaller leaves will have more robust flavor.

If you want to grow basil (and do consider this because of its valuable culinary addition or just because of its heady aroma), but live in a setting where you can't grow it in a yard or garden, it does very well in patio pots, giving you the advantage of being able to bring it indoors if a cold snap threatens, or in window gardens inside the home with its inherent advantages.

If you want to grow it in your garden it will ask you for a warm, sunny spot and well-drained soil. It's not going to winter over, so be sure you dry all you'll want before a cold snap. The leaves will turn brown and curl up if it gets very chilled so don't expect to wait till a frost warning to harvest, it'll already be too late. The seeds are very tiny, and I find it hard to start the plants, so it's worth it just to buy a couple already healthy growing plants in the spring. For a steady supply of beautiful leaves, consider sequential planting so old plants are replaced by new seedlings routinely. Pop 'em in the ground, keep the dirt moist but not soggy, and stand back. Pinch off developing flower spikes to keep the plant growing and encourage bushing out. If you let it put much energy into flowering, that's what it will do and the leaves will not develop as before the floral display.

This is an herb whose leaves you may want to dehydrate and store for yearlong use, but be aware that the dried herb is not nearly as flavorful as its fresh version.

I use a gadget specifically designed for food and herb dehydrating, but typically the volume used in most kitchens would not warrant the investment just for this. For most purposes it's easier to hang dry in bunches (see dehydrating herbs above). Consider looking for hydroponically grown basil in the supermarket produce section during the winter.

Basil also makes nicely flavored oil. It's a little too mild to survive in a vinegar bath, however. Freezing, done carefully to avoid the classic brown leaf of chill damage just as seen in the late fall garden, is an excellent way to keep basil and maintain its original fresh flavor.

When cooking with basil, as with most herbs, add the herb toward the end of the cooking time called for in a recipe to get the best flavor and avoid the bitterness of overcooking. Basil has a natural affinity for tomato dishes, but it adds a lovely note to vegetables, fish, and chicken dishes and pairs well with garlic and onion. I like to sprinkle it as a chiffonade (see How to chiffonade herb leaves above) over finished dishes and salads. Remember that dried herbs are more intense so 1 teaspoon dried basil interchanges with 1 tablespoon (aka 3 teaspoons) fresh. Unsure how much chopped basil really fits in a cup measure? Me too; it varies every time. Try this: 1 cup chopped fresh herb equals about half an ounce on a food scale.

Common, or Italian basil is what you see in Caprese Salad which layers whole basil leaves between slices of ripe tomato and fresh mozzarella cheese. Sprinkle on some good olive oil and a few more pieces of torn or chiffonade-cut basil leaves for a classic salad.

In making pesto, avoid including any stems or the veins of larger leaves since these will contribute to unappetizing browning of the final product.

Classic Pesto

Younger leaves are important in this recipe to provide the best flavor. You can freeze the finished pesto as long as you leave out the cheese; just add it when you defrost it for use. Pesto can be made with other soft-leafed herbs, such as parsley, or try lemon basil. You can also substitute other nuts such as almonds, walnuts, or peanuts for the pine nuts.

2 large cloves garlic, chunked up
3–4 tablespoons pine nuts (pignolia)
¼ cup freshly grated Parmesan cheese
¼ cup, heaped up, chopped basil
3 tablespoons good olive oil

Blast the garlic, pine nuts, cheese, and basil in a food processor. With machine running, stream in the olive oil until grainy textured and well incorporated. If you need another tablespoon to make it look and taste right, go for it. Keeps 2 weeks covered in the fridge. Each tablespoonful carries 32 mg. of sodium.

Great, now what are you going to do with it? I have a couple ideas:

Basil-Pesto Chicken

Makes 2 generous servings for 235 mg. sodium each.

1 pound boneless, skinless chicken cut into cubes
1 bell pepper, chopped, red, orange, or yellow are all
    pretty
1/2 pound mushrooms, sliced, any kind you like
2 cups sliced young zucchini
1 recipe Classic Pesto, above
2–3 tablespoons olive oil

Heat the olive oil in large skillet on medium-high until shimmering. Add chicken pieces and brown and stir for 2 minutes. Toss in vegetables and continue to cook and stir another 4–5 minutes or until vegetables are tender and chicken is cooked through. Stir in pesto and cook and stir another minute to heat through and finish cooking. Serve with pasta, rice, or noodles for a tasty meal.

Pesto Bread

Begin with the White Bread recipe on page 78, except after the first rise is complete, instead of shaping into a loaf, do this:

Roll out to a 9 x 14 rectangle. Spread half a recipe of pesto (above) and 1/4 cup grated or finely shredded Parmesan cheese on top, then roll the dough like a jelly roll. Pinch the seam closed and place into greased 4½ x 8-inch loaf pan. Sprinkle another 1/4 cup Parmesan over the top. Cover with plastic wrap and let rise in a warm place until not quite doubled, another 35–45 minutes. Remove wrap and bake in preheated 375° oven 40–45 minutes until golden and hollow sounding when tapped gently. If it browns too quickly, cover with a tent of aluminum foil for last 10 minutes or so of baking. Cool 5 minutes in pan then remove to rack to finish cooling. Remember that the sodium cost per slice goes up about 77 mg. to 182 mg. per slice, with 12 slices per loaf.

CILANTRO

Also known as coriander, this is really a better reference to the seeds of the cilantro plant (which, by the way, taste nothing like the leaves, thank goodness!) this old herb is said to have been found buried with pharaohs in the pyramids. Tender and fern-like, its flat leaves (usually referred to as cilantro) can be mistaken for parsley at a glance. However, once the aroma is inhaled, you would never think of it as a parsley wanna-be, and it isn't interchangeable. Cilantro is commonly used in Mexican, South American, Middle Eastern, Southeast Asian, and Indian cooking. Seeds from this plant, commonly known as coriander, are often roasted or toasted to bring out the flavor, which is very different from its parent plant's leaves. Dried cilantro is pretty much flavorless, so if you like cilantro's flavor, go for the good stuff—the fresh. And what is it we want? FLAVOR!! It's common in grocery stores year 'round.

Growing cilantro is easy; it's really a bit of a weed. It needs a sunny spot that's not too crowded so it will fill out well. It thrives in sunny, damp locations. If you want to start from seed, soak them first, at least 24 hours, then keep the soil moist till the seedlings emerge. You will need to keep soil from drying out, especially in hot summer months. Take clippings from the leaves as you need them. Once the seeds form and turn brown, they are ripe for harvest and the plant has about had it. Seeds that fall onto the dirt may become volunteers next season. You can put paper bags (plastic will cook them in the sun) over seed heads to catch them. You can leave the bag on a day or even two if no rain is expected. This seems to allow stragglers to ripen up. Shake them gently and only keep the seeds that fall willingly. Bend the stem down so gravity will keep the seeds in the bag, remove the bag and let seeds finish drying on a tray in a single layer. Toast them for extra flavor and longer shelf life (see Toasting Seeds above).

Middle Eastern Vegetables

5–6 tablespoons extra virgin olive oil
2 cloves garlic, minced
1 large potato, cubed small (leave peel on if you like)
1 cup fresh or frozen green beans in 2-inch pieces
1 small zucchini, sliced 1/4 inch thick
1 small onion or 2 medium shallots, sliced
1 packed tablespoon coarsely chopped cilantro
    (coriander) leaves
Juice of one lime and one lemon

Heat oil in large skillet and sauté all the vegetables about 5 minutes until toasty brown. Add coriander and citrus juices. Cover and cook over medium heat, stirring occasionally, until vegetables are crisp tender, 20–30 minutes adding a tablespoon of water from time to time if too dry. Garnish with more coriander leaves or parsley. Makes 4 servings at 8 mg. sodium each. Go on, have a second helping.

Mediterranean Rub for Lamb

1 teaspoon cumin seeds, toasted (or $^1/_2$ teaspoon ground)

1 teaspoon coriander seeds, toasted (or $^1/_2$ teaspoon ground)

2 garlic cloves, chunked up coarsely

1 tablespoon chopped fresh cilantro

1 teaspoon minced fresh mint

1 teaspoon grated lemon zest

3 tablespoons olive oil

2 teaspoons finely minced fresh rosemary

Freshly grated black pepper

$1^1/_2$ pounds lamb shoulder roast

Place whole toasted cumin and coriander seeds, if using, in your spice grinder and give 'em a good whirl. Add with garlic, cilantro, mint, and lemon zest to small container of food processor and blend using several pulses. With processor running continuously, slowly add olive oil. Stop and stir in rosemary and several grinds of pepper. Use to coat all sides of the roast, cover and chill half an hour to 2 hours before roasting. Makes 6 servings costing less than 80 mg. of sodium each. Leftovers make killer sandwiches. Yummy.

DILL

Used in the Middle Ages to ward off witches, dill is commonly the flavor of pickles. Much more than just for pickling, fresh dill compliments seafood nicely. It also works well with vegetables, lamb, poultry, soup, dips, eggs, and potato salad. Dill seeds can be used in many ways, also, such as in cabbage and root vegetable dishes, bread, stew, bean soup, salmon dishes, and with fresh tomatoes and cucumbers.

Another easy-to-grow herb, that if allowed, will readily drop seeds that become volunteers next season. Give it a well-drained, sunny spot and it will do you proud. It has a quick season so you may want to drop a few seeds intentionally about 6 weeks after the start of the season, especially if you want to time fresh dill with your cucumber crop. Get those feathery leaves while they are still young and tender and dry or freeze them. Seeds need to be very dry, preferably toasted, before storing to prevent mold. Nothing says summer more than a crisp cucumber sliced thinly and sprinkled with minced up fresh dill. Mmmm.

Homemade, Low-Sodium Refrigerator Pickles

First, the disclaimer: Pickles have salt for the same reason other foods do—or, er, well, used to—to preserve them and prevent spoilage. That is why there is really no such thing as a low-sodium processed pickle! The amount of salt can be decreased significantly in refrigerator pickles, but they must always be stored in the refrigerator, not the pantry shelf. A big plus here is that you avoid the hot water processing—no small deal in the hot summer when the cukes are ripe. That said, remember that this is also not a salt-free product. But if you crave a pickle badly enough, and you are willing to be careful and attentive to how much you eat of these, then this will work. Be alert to the sodium here as it is hard to give exact sodium content per pickle! Of course, you removed all salt from your house when you started reading this book, so now you will borrow—not buy—salt from your neighbor, sister, son, cousin, boss, whomever. But they won't let you have it because they have your best interests in mind and don't want to see you fall off the salt wagon. So show them this book, turn to this page, and let them see this recipe. Then promise them a pint of pickles when you're done. And remember to only borrow one teaspoon for this recipe only. Good luck! I know you can do it!

6–8 pounds pickling cucumbers—ok, hold up a minute. A few hints: Be sure you get pickling cucumbers; others will not be as crisp. Be sure they are about 4, no more than 5 inches long (it will take about 4 of these per pint jar) and be sure they are just ripe, but not overripe. Nicely ripe cukes still have their warts. Unlike us, as they get older they smooth out, and more like us, they plump out. Older cukes are not crispy inside anymore.

Brine (oh, just the sound of this word sends shivers up my spine—be careful!)

$^1/_2$ to $^3/_4$ cup fresh dill and 1 full dill head per pint

1–2 cups thinly sliced sweet onions such as Mayan or Vidalia

$1^1/_2$ cups sugar (you can use part honey)

$1^1/_2$ cups white vinegar (5% acidity is important here)

1 teaspoon table salt (not bad for 6 pints of pickles!)

I also throw in $^1/_2$ teaspoon whole mustard seeds and $^1/_2$ teaspoon celery seeds

Rinse and trim off both ends, especially the blossom end because it contains some kind of chemical that reduces the crispness of the final product. Cut the cukes into spears that are just a ¼ inch shorter than the jars.

Wash and rinse your jars (should take 6, but I prepare a seventh, too, just in case) and the tops and rings in the dishwasher on the hottest cycles and set it to dry them as well. Try to time it so they finish the drying cycle about when you are prepped to fill them. If a dishwasher is not an option, submerge them completely in boiling water for 10 minutes (your old canner will work well for this). Use a non-aluminum pot and bring the brine ingredients just to a boil, reduce and simmer gently for 5 minutes.

Meantime, load your prepared jars, still hot from sanitizing, with the cucumber spears. Carefully pour the hot brine mix over the cukes leaving just a ¼-inch headspace, being sure to include one head dill per jar. Let them come to room temperature, about 2 hours, then store in refrigerator for at least 24 hours to several days to let the flavors blend. They will hold easily for 2 months.

So what's 1 teaspoon of salt divided over all those pickles? Hmmm. If you made 6 pints, it's 400 mg. per pint. If it took 4 cucumbers per pint, that's 100 mg. per cucumber. If you cut those cucumbers into 4 spears, it's 25 mg. per spear. And that assumes you consume some of the liquid, so it probably comes out to less than 25 mg. per spear. Compare that to those store-bought salty things! Crunch! Take that, Mr. Stork (or was he a pelican?).

Salmon with Yogurt and Dill

Each serving has 259 mg. of sodium

4 ounces plain yogurt

1 tablespoon plain yellow mustard

¼ teaspoon fresh ground pepper (here's a great place for a special pepper like pink, see pepper discussion above)

1 handful fresh dill leaves, minced (about 2 tablespoons)

1 handful fresh parsley leaves, minced (about 2 tablespoons)

4 4-ounce portions salmon fillet, patted dry with paper towels

Combine yogurt, mustard (if you are thinking of substituting Dijon, remember that it has more than twice the sodium of plain and spicy mustard), pepper, and herbs. Spread over fish and bake 20–25 minutes in preheated 400° oven.

FENNEL

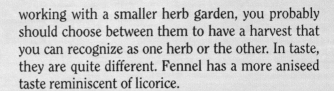

Fennel and dill do not play well together, or perhaps it is that they play too well. Given the opportunity and proximity, they will cross breed. If your garden is a big one, do separate them as much as possible. If you are working with a smaller herb garden, you probably should choose between them to have a harvest that you can recognize as one herb or the other. In taste, they are quite different. Fennel has a more aniseed taste reminiscent of licorice.

Fennel has a big history. Valued by Roman soldiers, ladies, and gladiators for its healing properties, Charlemagne used it for its power against evil. In the modern garden, it attracts hoverflies that eat those garden pests—aphids—and is said to be a flea repellent that some rub on their dogs and place in their bedding. It has been touted as a digestive aid, as well.

A rather robust perennial, there are several varieties of fennel, including Florence fennel from which the edible bulbs come. These can be sliced and used in salads and vegetable trays, or halved and roasted like other root vegetables. Both the feathery leaves and seeds are used for culinary purposes, and can be dried or frozen for future use. If you are drying seeds, be sure they are thoroughly dry before stashing away to prevent mold.

Chopped fresh fennel leaves are delicious in salads or stuffed in fish before steaming or baking. The leaves can be a tasty surprise in a sandwich along with the lettuce and tomato. The fronds work well in good, mild vinegar or even in a mild-flavored oil. An herb often used in Italian cooking, fennel seed is a staple in sausages (see Faux Sausage, page 112).

Italian Meatballs

Assuming 10 meatballs, each is worth 35 mg. of sodium

1 pound lean ground pork or beef, or a mix of both

2 cloves garlic, minced

2 teaspoons toasted fennel seeds

½ teaspoon red pepper flakes

2 tablespoons finely chopped onion

2 tablespoons olive oil

Combine meat, garlic, fennel seeds, red pepper, and onion. Form into 10–12 balls. Heat oil over medium-high in large skillet. Add meatballs and turn to brown evenly. If desired, at this point move meatballs into an inch or two of prepared tomato sauce and simmer or bake until done. Alternatively, reduce heat in skillet and continue to cook meatballs until cooked through.

Tunisian Chick Pea and Fennel Stew

Here's a tasty stew for 4 that lets you use dried chick-peas instead of worrying about all the sodium in canned ones. Comes to 155 mg. sodium per serving.

Scant 1¹/₄ cups dried chickpeas soaked in 4 cups water
  at least 6 hours, preferably overnight
1 small bunch Swiss chard (I like the red in this),
  stemmed, washed, chopped
2 tablespoons olive oil
1 medium sweet onion, coarsely chopped
1 leek, thoroughly rinsed, white part sliced, discard
  green part
1 large fennel, remove, chop, and set aside fronds;
  halve, core and chop bulb
2 large garlic cloves, minced
1 teaspoon coriander seed
1 teaspoon cumin seed
1 teaspoon fennel seed
dash cayenne pepper
1 tablespoon tomato paste
1¹/₂ cups plain dry couscous
2 cups salt-free chicken or vegetable broth, boiling hot

Drain chick peas and transfer to a large pot. Add 6 cups
water. Bring to a boil, then reduce to a simmer. Simmer for an hour.

In a Dutch oven, heat olive oil, stir in onion, leek and
fennel bulb. Cook until tender 8–10 minutes, stirring
often. Combine seeds (best if toasted, first) in a spice
grinder and grind fine. Add to onion mixture with garlic, stirring in well. Add cayenne. Dissolve tomato
paste in a little water to loosen and stir into onion mixture. Stir in chick peas and the water in which they
were simmering. Cover and simmer 30 minutes until
chick peas are almost tender, adding more water if
needed. Uncover and stir in chopped chard and fennel
fronds. Simmer, uncovered another 10 minutes until
chard and chick peas are tender.

Reconstitute couscous in boiling broth. To serve, place
some couscous in bowl and ladle stew over top.

LAVENDER

One of my (apparently many)
favorites, lavender was used
in Greek and Roman baths,
it often finds its way into
sachets for drawers as a moth
repellent and into linen closets.
It is only half-hardy, so it won't winter over well in the
colder, snowy, or heavy frost areas of the country, although my northern-area sister-in-law can't kill hers!

The main focus is the flower, but leaves can be used,
too. They like poor soils, especially drier, sandy ones.
They need full sun to produce aromatic oils. Aside

from teas, and scented bathwater, I love it for culinary
uses. Surprise!

Lavender Cookies

¹/₂ cup shortening
¹/₂ cup unsalted butter, softened
1¹/₄ cups sugar
2 eggs
1 teaspoon vanilla extract
¹/₂ teaspoon almond extract
2¹/₄ cups all-purpose flour
4 teaspoons dried lavender flowers, chopped
1 teaspoon baking powder

Preheat oven to 375°. In a large bowl, cream the shortening, butter and sugar until light and fluffy. Add eggs,
one at a time, beating well after each addition. Beat in
extracts. Combine remaining ingredients. Gently stir
dry ingredients into creamed mixture thoroughly.
Drop by rounded teaspoonfuls 2 inches apart on
cookie sheet lightly coated with cooking spray. Bake
in preheated oven 8–10 minutes until golden. Cool 2
minutes before removing to wire racks. Store airtight.
Makes 7 dozen delicate, pretty little cookies. Each little
morsel counts for 12 mg. of sodium. As you know by
now, the sodium count comes primarily from the baking powder and salt. If you make the cookies bigger,
be sure to recalculate.

Lavender Pound Cake

Makes 2 loaves. Each loaf cut into 10 slices will give
you 20 servings at 75 mg. sodium each.

2 sticks unsalted butter
2 cups sugar
5 eggs
2¹/₂ cups all purpose flour
1 teaspoon baking powder
¹/₄ teaspoon salt
1 tablespoon dried lavender blossoms, chopped
1 cup buttermilk
2 teaspoons vanilla

Preheat oven to 350°. Grease and flour two 8¹/₂ x 4¹/₂
x 2⁵/₈ loaf pans. Cream butter and sugar. Beat in eggs
one at a time, beating thoroughly after each. Combine
dry ingredients in another bowl. Stir vanilla into buttermilk. Add wet and dry ingredients alternately to egg
mixture. Divide batter between prepared pans. Bake
one hour until toothpick tester comes out clean. Cool
on rack 10 minutes, then remove from pans and cool
completely. Eat as is or drizzle something on it. Works
well under fruit, too.

LEMON-SCENTED HERBS

There are many lemon-scented herbs. Some to look for include lemon verbena (often used in desserts), lemon basil, and lemon thyme (great with fish). Lemon balm grows like, well, a weed. But if you have a nice spot to let it go a little wild, it will give you more than enough sweet lemon fragrance for home-scenting in potpourri, as well as eating. Reports from earlier centuries credit lemon balm tea with lengthening life to as old as 116! Unlike most herbs, lemon balm flavor is best after blossoms begin to appear.

Here are some goodies enhanced by more common lemon-flavored herbs . . .

Lemon Thyme Bars

Unsalted butter, for greasing baking dish
Flour, for dusting baking dish

Bars:
1 cup all-purpose flour
2 tablespoons chopped fresh lemon-thyme leaves
1 stick (4 ounces) unsalted butter, at room temperature
1/2 cup powdered sugar
2 tablespoons fresh lemon juice
1/2 teaspoon pure vanilla extract

Glaze:
2 tablespoons fresh lemon juice
1/2 cup powdered sugar

Place an oven rack in the center of the oven. Preheat the oven to 325°. Butter and flour an 8 x 8-inch baking dish. Set dish aside.

For the bars:

In a small bowl combine flour and lemon-thyme. Set aside. Using a stand mixer fitted with the paddle attachment, beat together 1 stick of butter and powdered sugar on high speed until light and fluffy, about 30 seconds. (You can do this with a hand mixer, but it takes longer.) Beat in the lemon juice and vanilla. Gradually add the flour mixture on low. Moisten fingers and press the dough into the prepared pan. Bake for 30 minutes until golden. Cool for 30 minutes.

For the glaze:

In a medium bowl, whisk the lemon juice and powdered sugar together until smooth. Spoon the glaze over the cooled crust. Allow the glaze to harden, at

room temperature, for at least 1 hour. Cut into 1½-inch square bars and arrange on a serving platter or store airtight in a plastic container at room temperature. There is less than 5 mg. of sodium in each one! (Yes, I'm licking my fingers.)

Lemon-Basil Butter Cookies

You'll love these delicately sweet butter cookies. Lemon brightens the flavor of the basil.

1 cup fresh lemon basil leaves, packed
1 3/4 cup sugar, divided
1 pound (2 sticks) unsalted butter, softened
1/4 cup lemon juice (fresh if you have it)
1 large egg
6 cups all-purpose flour

Process basil and 1/4 cup of the sugar in a food processor until well blended. Beat butter at medium speed with electric mixer until creamy. Gradually add remaining 1½ cups sugar. Beat until fluffy. Beat in lemon juice and egg. Gradually beat in flour and basil sugar mixture on medium speed until well blended.

Shape dough into 1-inch balls. Place on cookie sheets and flatten slightly with the bottom of a glass dipped in sugar. Bake at 350° in preheated oven for 8–10 minutes until lightly browned. Cool on racks. Makes 6½ dozen. Again, less than 5 mg. sodium per cookie!

MINT

Now the first thing that comes to mind might be a mint julep, but wait, there's more! Yes, there's mint tea, chocolate mint candy, mint chewing gum, minted balms and salves, mint-flavored mouthwash and toothpaste . . . Why so many mint-flavored and scented concoctions? It's popular! People love it! And it's another herb that grows like the weed that it really is. Mint comes in many flavors. I have grown pineapple mint, apple mint, orange mint, chocolate mint (sprinkle this minced up over raspberries, mmmm), and of course, spearmint and peppermint. Seems like a lot, but it demonstrates the versatility of this weed, eh hem, herb. Of course, its scent when you brush by it is refreshing, too. Historically, in many cultures, mint symbolized hospitality and was offered as a sign of welcome and friendship to guests as they arrived. The two most popular cooking mints are peppermint and spearmint, with peppermint a bit more pungent. High in vitamins A and C, mint is extremely popular in Middle Eastern cooking, and used in many sweet and savory dishes. Mince up some chocolate mint and stir it into your hot chocolate. Delicious. OK, just for fun:

Mint Julep

5–6 large mint leaves (peppermint variety)

1¼ teaspoons superfine sugar

2 tablespoons cold water

Finely crushed ice

2 ounces Kentucky Bourbon (Kentucky to do it right, but use what bourbon you have, and for anyone who isn't drinking alcohol, replace the water and bourbon with lemonade.)

In a highball glass, muddle the mint and sugar forcefully; get that mint flavor out of the leaves. Add the water and stir until the sugar dissolves. Fill the glass with crushed ice, packing it in. Pour the bourbon over the ice and stir gently to blend all the ingredients. Garnish with a fresh sprig of mint and enjoy.

Cucumber Raita

2 cucumbers, peeled, halved and seeded, thinly sliced

2 cups plain yogurt

3 tablespoons fresh lemon juice

2 tablespoons, packed, chopped fresh mint

¾ teaspoon sugar

Stir together and chill at least 2 hours to blend the flavors. Serves 4 at 82 mg. sodium each. Goes beautifully with Middle Eastern dishes such as Moroccan Lamb Tagine with Raisins, Almonds, and Honey, page 121.

OREGANO

Varieties of oregano and its cousin, marjoram, add flavor ranging from sweet to pungent and are easy to grow and preserve by drying. At it's best in tomato-based foods, oregano originated in Greece where it is known as wild marjoram and grows freely. You can work with oregano or marjoram interchangeably; just use a little less if subbing oregano for marjoram.

Broiled Tomatoes

Four servings at 180 mg. sodium each

4 large tomatoes

4 tablespoons unsalted butter

1 tablespoon chopped fresh oregano (or 1½ teaspoons dried)

1 small clove garlic, minced

a couple grinds of black pepper

4 tablespoons freshly grated Parmesan cheese

Halve the tomatoes and place in shallow pan or flame-proof dish. Thoroughly combine remaining ingredients, beating till fluffy. Spread mixture over cut surfaces of tomatoes. Run under broiler for five minutes or so, until tomatoes soften and are hot through, and topping takes on a yummy golden color.

Lemon Chicken with Oregano

A mere 59 mg. of sodium each

2 large tomatoes

4 sprigs fresh oregano

fresh ground black pepper to taste

4 chicken thigh fillets, skinned and boned

1 tablespoon lemon juice

1 tablespoon extra virgin olive oil

Chop the tomatoes. Remove the oregano leaves from their stems and add them and the pepper to the tomato.

Pound the chicken gently to encourage uniform thickness. Pat them dry and pour the lemon juice over the chicken pieces, turning them till thoroughly coated. Heat the oil in a medium skillet and brown the chicken pieces on all sides. Add the tomato mixture, stir, and cover. Simmer gently till the chicken is cooked through (10–12 minutes depending on their thickness).

If serving with pasta, you can use a can of chopped, no-salt-added tomatoes instead of the fresh ones to give more sauce for the pasta.

PARSLEY

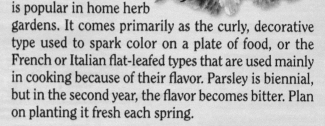

Parsley's ubiquitous use makes it easy not to notice, but it is popular in home herb gardens. It comes primarily as the curly, decorative type used to spark color on a plate of food, or the French or Italian flat-leafed types that are used mainly in cooking because of their flavor. Parsley is biennial, but in the second year, the flavor becomes bitter. Plan on planting it fresh each spring.

Lemon-Garlic-Parsley Tilapia

Two amazing servings of deliciousness for 100 mg. sodium each

2 tilapia fillets, about 6 ounces each

1 tablespoon fresh lemon juice

1 tablespoon unsalted butter, melted

1 clove garlic, finely chopped

1 tablespoon fresh parsley, minced

Pepper to taste

Preheat oven to 375°. Spray a baking dish with non-stick cooking spray. Rinse tilapia fillets under cool water, and pat dry with paper towels. Place fillets in baking dish. Pour lemon juice over fillets, then drizzle butter on top. Sprinkle with garlic, parsley, and pepper. Bake in preheated oven until the fish is white through, 20–30 minutes depending on thickness. This will work with many varieties of fish fillets including snapper, and cod for about the same sodium cost.

Parsley Potato Chips

A little labor intense, but very beautiful. Large potatoes only run about 25 mg. of sodium each, so sticking with the unsalted butter and adding no salt makes the sodium count here negligible.

2 sticks unsalted butter, melted
6–8 large, similarly sized Idaho potatoes, peeled
1 cup (at least) flat-leaf parsley (curly won't flatten enough) handled gently during the rinse and dry process to keep the leaves beautiful

Heat oven to 400°. Line a baking sheet with parchment paper. Using a pastry brush, paint a thin coat of butter on the parchment. Using a mandolin, slice the potatoes very thinly into lengthwise, even, translucent slices. Place the slices on the buttered parchment and brush them with a thin, even layer of melted butter; completely cover the slice, but don't use too much. Place 1 or 2 dry, perfect parsley leaves on top, and smooth with your fingers dabbing it lightly with some of the butter. Place another similar sized and shaped slice on top, smooth with your fingers and brush lightly but completely with butter. Cover potatoes with a piece of parchment paper, and place another sheet pan on top. Weight the top baking pan with something heavy and heat proof: a baking dish filled with water, a couple bricks, or a large amount of raw beans. It is essential to use two perfectly level baking pans so the potatoes cook evenly. Bake, rotating the baking pans until potatoes are crisp and golden brown all over, about 12 minutes (check after 6 minutes). Remove from oven, and serve.

ROSEMARY

Rosemary, one of my favorites, is grown as a hedge or shrub in milder climates than mine, but luckily, lends itself easily to cuttings and window gardens for yearlong availability. I understand it can be grown as a deer barrier around plants deer tend to find tasty. Seems they just don't appreciate rosemary!

When stripping the evergreen-like leaves for a recipe, don't toss the woody stems. They are perfect for barbecue or indoor grill skewers. Or toss them on the hearth for a wonderful house-filled scent. Dry the intact stems for future use, but then remove the needle-leaves, crushing only when you are ready to use them. Commonly used in chicken and lamb, don't forget about some other good pairings.

Rosemary-Garlic New Potatoes

2 pounds new potatoes, scrubbed and halved
6–8 cloves garlic, peeled and chopped
2 tablespoons chopped fresh rosemary
2 tablespoons olive oil

Preheat oven to 400°. Toss all ingredients in a large bowl. Spread potatoes on baking sheet, cut side down, in a single layer. Bake 30–45 minutes until tender and golden. Serve hot. Makes 4 servings at 18 tiny, tasty mg. of sodium each.

Grilled Carrots with Rosemary

1 cup carrots, sliced thick, or if mini ones, leave whole
1 sprig rosemary
1/2 teaspoon olive oil
2 tablespoons orange juice, fresh if you have it

Cut a large piece of aluminum foil and place carrots and rosemary sprig on half; pour on orange juice and olive oil. Fold foil over carrots, sealing edges well all around to make a tight pouch. Place on grill over medium heat for 15 or 20 minutes, flipping once, until carrots are perfectly softened and caramelized. Makes 2 people very happy for about 20 mg. of sodium each!

SAGE

Another easy to grow herb, sage has a few variations you may like. Aside from common sage (the sage for sausage, stuffing, and turkey), it also comes with tri-colored leaves, purple leaves, and pineapple scent. When used in culinary applications, it is best used as the only herb in the recipe—it doesn't play well with others because it is so strong. In general 10 medium fresh leaves will equal 3/4 teaspoon of dried.

In my garden, I find sage gets woody with age. I tend to cut it way back when that begins to happen, and I never feel badly about pulling a plant after a few years and starting fresh. It also does well in a kitchen garden, provided it gets enough light. Ever try loosening the skin of the turkey over the breast and sliding whole leaves in so they rest on the meat? A beautiful presentation because the leaves show through the cooked skin as they flavor the breast meat. Do it in chicken, too.

Pork Tenderloin with Sage and Balsamic Sauce

1½ pounds pork tenderloin trimmed
2 tablespoons all purpose flour
⅛ teaspoon pepper, freshly ground
1 tablespoon unsalted butter
1 tablespoon olive oil
⅔ cup balsamic vinegar
¼ cup salt-free chicken stock
1 tablespoon fresh sage, minced

Cut the tenderloin on a slight angle into eight 1¼-inch slices. Pound them lightly with the flat side of a large knife to flatten. On a plate, combine the flour with the pepper. Dredge the pork slices in the seasoned flour and shake off the excess. In a large skillet, melt the butter in the oil over moderately high heat. Add the pork in two batches and cook until nicely browned and medium-done, 2 to 3 minutes per side, don't over-cook. Transfer to a plate, cover with foil and keep warm. Drain the fat from the pan. Add the vinegar and boil, scraping the bottom of the pan with a wooden spoon to release any brown bits, until the mixture is thick and reduce by about half. Add the chicken stock and any juices that have accumulated on the plate from the pork and boil until reduced to a dark, shiny sauce, about 1 minute. Add the sage and season to taste with pepper. Arrange the pork on a platter or plates and spoon the sauce on top. No mistaking the flavors here and the sage is a strong enough herb to stand up to the balsamic vinegar. Makes 4 generous servings at 55 mg. sodium each.

Fettuccine in Creamy Mushroom and Sage Sauce

Two main course servings for 30 mg. each

8 ounces spinach fettuccine pasta
1 tablespoon extra virgin olive oil
1 shallot, chopped
1 clove garlic, chopped
4 ounces chopped fresh mushrooms
½ cup heavy cream
1 tablespoon chopped fresh sage
Pepper to taste

Bring a large pot of water to a boil. Add pasta and cook for 8 to 10 minutes, or until just tender. Drain.

Meantime, heat olive oil in a saucepan over medium. Sauté shallots and garlic two minutes until softened but not yet translucent. Stir in mushrooms, and cook until tender. Mix in heavy cream and sage. Cook and

stir until thickened. Toss sauce with cooked fettuccine, and season with pepper to taste.

TARRAGON

Once said to cure bites of serpents and small dragons, there are two varieties used for culinary purposes today. French tarragon is the primary type with more refined flavor, but the plant is less cold tolerant, and tends to lose flavor over years. This is the type often used in vegetable, fish and foul dishes for its more delicate taste. The Russian variety is hardier and improves its flavor as the plant ages, but its flavor is more unsophisticated. Either way, tarragon can overwhelm your food; go gently.

Indispensable in cream sauces, including béarnaise and hollandaise, and white wine vinegars, tarragon is said to have a flavor reminiscent of licorice. It can be a fairly strong herb, so use gently until you know how well you like it. See also Chicken in Creamy Herb Sauce, page 90.

Tarragon Chicken

Four servings for 81 mg. sodium each

¼ cup (half a stick) unsalted butter
1 tablespoon olive oil
4 8-ounce skinless chicken breasts
2 scallions (green onions) finely chopped
1 clove garlic, finely chopped
¼ cup dry white wine or sherry
½ cup light cream
1 tablespoon roughly chopped fresh tarragon

Melt butter with oil over medium heat in a large skillet. Add chicken and cook through until lightly browned, 4–5 minutes each side. Remove and keep warm. Add onion and garlic, stirring over medium high just until garlic is softened. Add wine, cream, and tarragon, simmering about 2 minutes. Return chicken to pan and warm through, turning to coat with sauce.

Béarnaise Sauce

3 tablespoons white vinegar
3 tablespoons white wine
10 peppercorns crushed
2 tablespoons finely chopped shallot
1 tablespoon chopped tarragon
1 tablespoon water
3 egg yolks

1 cup unsalted butter, melted

freshly ground black pepper or, if you don't like black spots in your white sauce, use white pepper

1 tablespoon finely chopped fresh parsley

In a medium saucepan, combine the vinegar, wine, peppercorns, shallots, and tarragon. Bring to a boil and continue boiling until reduced to 1 tablespoon. Add 1 tablespoon of water and set aside to cool.

Once cool enough not to make scrambled eggs, add the egg yolks and whisk, over low heat, or use a double-boiler, until frothy, about 3–4 minutes.

In a steady stream, add the butter and keep whisking until the sauce thickens. Season with pepper. Strain the sauce through a fine sieve. Garnish with the parsley. You'll have about one cup sauce, all of which only counts for 58 mg. of sodium, making a tablespoon less than 4 mg.

THYME

Ok, I have to say it: I never have enough thyme. I know, it's lame, but I mean it. It is without doubt my favorite, and I believe the most adaptable herb on earth. It comes back reliably, year after year, even after central New York winters, and comes in a number of delicious varieties. Even bees love it; try thyme honey if you have the opportunity! It is said that fairies dance where thyme grows, and a centuries-old recipe exists for a thyme-oil said to make it possible to see them. No, I'm not sharing that one.

There is a creeping variety that looks pretty on stone walls and between stones or bricks in a walk (go ahead, enjoy the aroma; it will tolerate being stepped on without a whimper). The most used culinary variety is the common, or garden thyme, but look for lemon thyme, too. It works so well with seafood!

Thyme-Roasted Pork Tenderloin and Potatoes

Serves 4 at 145 mg. sodium each

1/3 cup extra virgin olive oil

4 cloves garlic, minced

2 tablespoons fresh thyme or 1 tablespoon dried, crushed (of course you can switch out this herb for your own favorite—try rosemary)

1/2 teaspoon freshly ground black pepper

1 1/2 pounds pork tenderloin

2 pounds potatoes, thinly sliced, peel on or off as you like

Preheat oven to 375°. In a small mixing bowl combine olive oil, garlic, thyme, and pepper. Coat pork tenderloin with 3 tablespoons of the garlic mixture and place in a roasting pan. Toss potatoes with remaining garlic mixture and arrange around roast in the pan. Roast for 35–40 minutes, stirring potatoes once.

Thyme for Tilapia

Four tasty servings at only 177 mg. sodium each

4 tilapia fillets (or sole, catfish, even cod, really any mild white fish you like) about 6 ounces each

4 tablespoons unsalted butter, softened

1 large clove garlic, minced

1 teaspoon fresh thyme (use lemon thyme if you can), or 1/2 teaspoon dried, crushed

4 tablespoons grated Parmesan cheese

Rinse fish, pat dry and arrange on a baking dish or rimmed pan that will be safe under the broiler, sprayed with cooking spray or lightly greased. Bake at 400° about 10 minutes, a couple minutes longer for thicker fish, but not all the way to done. Meantime, thoroughly combine remaining ingredients. After the fish is nearly done, give it a flip and divide the herb-cheese mixture, spreading it evenly on each portion of fish. Run it under the broiler to finish cooking and to make the cheese all brown and bubbly.

There are many other herbs and spices you may choose to try, so give them consideration as well. They may not be easy to grow in your own herb garden, but you can find them in most well-stocked grocery stores, fresh and dried, and online. Examples to think about: allspice, bay leaves, caraway, cardamom, celery seeds, cinnamon, cloves, coriander, cumin, ginger, (crystallized, dried and fresh), grains of paradise, lemon grass, lime leaves (kaffir), lovage, mace, mustard (seeds and powder), nutmeg (get the whole nutmeg and a nutmeg grater for the freshest flavor: what do we want? FLAVOR!), paprika, (plain, smoky, and hot), poppy seeds, saffron, sesame seeds, star anise, sumac (another one I really love), turmeric, and vanilla beans, just to name a few.

A few words on **SPICES**. Don't ignore spices, they add a whole different dimension to eating and have been valued for this for centuries. In fact, Columbus and Magellan spent their lives discovering things about our world all for the sake of finding easier access to the spices craved by the populations of their times. Even though they don't grow in a culinary herb garden, you will still want spices for FLAVOR! One thing is certain; spices fade over time just as herbs do. So toss old stuff and figure on doing that every six months or so, depending on the spice and how well it has been stored. A few worth mentioning:

Allspice berries resemble large brown peppercorns. It takes its name from its aroma, which smells like a combination of spices, especially cinnamon, cloves, ginger, and nutmeg. Whole dried allspice will keep indefinitely when kept out of light in airtight jars. It can be ground in a spice mill or an electric coffee grinder. The ground spice loses flavor quickly. Allspice can be used as a substitute in equal amounts for cinnamon, cloves, or nutmeg. And to make a substitution for allspice, combine one part nutmeg with two parts each of cinnamon and cloves.

Cardamom is an expensive spice, so beware of substitutions of lower quality, only *Elettaria cardamomum* is the true cardamom. The small, brown-black sticky seeds are contained in a pod, the texture of which is that of tough paper. The flavor inside is totally worth the effort of opening the pods.

Cassia is an aromatic bark, similar to cinnamon, but differing in strength and quality. It is less costly than cinnamon and is often sold, ground, as cinnamon. Where cinnamon and cassia are distinguished, cinnamon is used for sweet dishes, or those requiring a subtle flavor, and cassia for strong, spicy, main dishes. In many countries the two spices are used interchangeably and in the US the more intense cassia is usually used.

Cinnamon is the inner bark of a tropical evergreen tree. A native of Sri Lanka (formerly Ceylon) the best cinnamon grows along the coastal strip near Colombo. True cinnamon quills or sticks will be curled in a telescopic form, while cassia quills curl inward from both sides, like a scroll.

The nutmeg tree is a large evergreen cultivated in the West Indies. It produces two spices—mace and nutmeg. **Nutmeg** is the seed kernel inside the fruit and mace is the lacy covering. Whole nuts are preferable to ground nutmeg, as flavor deteriorates quickly and will keep indefinitely. It can be grated as required with a nutmeg grater. One whole nutmeg grated equals 2 to 3 teaspoons of ground nutmeg. **Mace** is the bright red, lacy covering of the nutmeg seed shell. The mace is removed from the shell and its broken parts are known as blades. Mace and nutmeg are very similar, though mace is somewhat more powerful.

Sumac comes from the berries of a bush that grows wild in all Mediterranean areas. The berries are dried and crushed to form a coarse purple-red powder. It is used in Mediterranean and Arabian cooking as we might use lemon, tamarind, or vinegar in the US.

HERB and SPICE BLENDS

There are literally hundreds of spice mix combinations on the market. There is no set amount or ingredient list for most spice mixtures. They have evolved based on personal tastes and should always be adjusted to suit your own preferences. Some basic international and regional spice combos and their common ingredients include several you may find delicious. **Chinese five spice powder** includes star anise, fagara, (somewhat bitter tasting leaves and bark with a lime scent), cassia, fennel seeds, and cloves. If you bought **picking spice** that left out the salt, you would have black peppercorns, yellow mustard seeds, hot red pepper flakes, allspice berries, dill seed, mace, cinnamon, bay leaves, whole cloves, and ground ginger. The Middle Eastern herbal blend called **zahtar** (also spelled za'atar) is made of sumac, (no, this isn't poisonous), roasted sesame seeds, and ground thyme. However, the blend varies from home to home and region to region. **Ras-el-hanout** is a North African blend of peppercorns, cardamom, mace, galangal, (a peppery rhizome), nutmeg, allspice, cinnamon, ash berries, (also called Szechuan peppercorns and are actually berries from the prickly ash tree with a lemon-pepper flavor), cloves, ginger, turmeric, nigella, (a peppery, onion flavored seed), lavender, rosebuds, orrisroot, cassia, and fennel seeds. **Jamaican jerk** seasoning includes chiles, thyme, cinnamon, ginger, allspice, cloves, garlic, and onion. The Indian **garam masala** can vary quite a bit, but commonly includes most of these: cumin, coriander seed, cardamom, black peppercorns, cloves, mace, bay leaves, and cinnamon. **Curry powder** is especially variable but usually has dried red chiles, coriander and mustard seeds, black peppercorns, ground ginger and turmeric, and fenugreek seeds (pungent, a little bitter, reminiscent of celery, often used in pickling in India, as well). **Chili powder** is another blend that varies from region to region, but often includes garlic, onion, cumin, oregano, allspice, and other spices. You are going to love the one below!

Of course commercial preparation of these combination spices almost always includes salt; why, I just don't know. But as a result, we usually need to create our own. Besides, that keeps our supply fresh and flavorful. And when we cut sodium out of our lives, what do we want in its place? Yes, FLAVOR!! OK, I'll put away my pompoms now. I'm giving you my very best chili powder below, and I'll share a few more of my tasty combos here, as well. When you make them, don't double the recipes. The amount given here will last a good while, and since seasonings lose their flavor power after six months or so, you don't want to invest a ton of cash in large volumes you'll end up tossing out instead of into the food.

The instructions for all the combo recipes below are the same: combine and place in an airtight container; store away from heat and light; toss and make new after six months. If you decide to buy combos, always read the label and be sure to avoid any with salt or sodium anywhere in the ingredients.

Blackening Seasoning

A spicy blend for making blackened fish and chicken.

1 heaping tablespoon paprika
1 heaping teaspoon garlic powder
1 heaping teaspoon onion powder
$1/4$ to $1/2$ teaspoon ground cayenne pepper
2 teaspoons fresh ground black pepper
$1/2$ teaspoon dried thyme
$1/2$ teaspoon dried oregano

Bouquet Garni

This is a classic herb mixture used in cooking meats and vegetables. Traditionally, this combo gets tied up in a little cheesecloth with butcher twine to make it easy to grab out when the cooking is finished. This makes about half a cup.

$1/4$ cup dried parsley
2 tablespoons dried thyme
2 tablespoons dried, broken bay leaf
2 tablespoons dried rosemary

The Best Chili Powder You Will Ever Use

3 dried ancho chilies stemmed, seeded, and sliced or torn to lay flat
2 dried cascabel chilies stemmed, seeded, and sliced or torn to lay flat
2 dried arbol chilies stemmed, seeded, and sliced or torn to lay flat
2 dried jalapeño peppers, seeded, and sliced or torn to lay flat
2 tablespoons whole cumin seeds
2 tablespoons garlic powder
1 tablespoon dried oregano
1 teaspoon smoked paprika

Place all of the chilies and the cumin into a medium nonstick sauté pan or dry cast iron skillet over medium-high heat. Keep the pan moving constantly while heating and gently toasting the peppers and cumin seeds, approximately 4–5 minutes. Set aside and cool completely.

Once cool, place the chilies and cumin into the carafe of a blender (works better than a food processor for this) along with the garlic powder, oregano, and paprika. Process until a fine powder is formed. Allow the powder to settle for at least a minute before removing the lid of the carafe; the alternative is a lung full of spicy pepper powder—ouch. Store in an airtight container for up to six months; it'll give you about a half cup of excellent chili powder. This is tremendous and has no sodium in it. Compare that to the store-bought, sodium-laden stuff! I won a chili cook-off using this chili powder. I always keep a jar around.

Creole Seasoning I

1 tablespoons garlic powder
1 tablespoon black pepper
1 tablespoon onion powder
1 tablespoon cayenne pepper
1 tablespoon dried leaf oregano
1 tablespoon dried thyme

Creole Seasoning II

A more robust combination and the one I keep in my cupboard. Makes 18 tablespoons, or just over a cup.

2 tablespoons onion powder
2 tablespoons garlic powder
2 tablespoons dried oregano leaves
2 tablespoons dried sweet basil
1 tablespoon dried thyme leaves
1 tablespoon black pepper
1 tablespoon white pepper
1 tablespoon cayenne pepper

1 tablespoon celery seed
5 tablespoons sweet paprika

Combine thoroughly (might be easiest in a food processor to be sure it is well blended) and stash out of the way of heat and light. If you think this is more than you are likely to use in the next six months or so, make less by substituting "teaspoon" for every time the ingredients say "tablespoon" and you'll have one-third as much or about 18 teaspoons instead (or 6 tablespoons).

Curry Powder

As we mentioned earlier, there are many variations on curry ingredients. Here are two. The first one is fairly mild:

4 tablespoons cumin seeds
4 tablespoons coriander seeds
$1/2$ teaspoon mustard seed
2 teaspoons turmeric
$1/2$ teaspoon crushed red pepper
$1/2$ teaspoon ground ginger

Toast the seeds over medium heat in a heavy skillet being watchful to keep stirring so to avoid burning the seeds. When they have a toasty look and aroma, remove from heat and let cool. Once the seeds are at room temperature, whirl them with remaining ingredients until a fine powder. Store airtight away from heat and light.

And this one has more bite:

3 tablespoons Hungarian paprika
2 teaspoons ground cumin seed
2 teaspoons ground fennel seed
2 teaspoons ground mustard seed
2 teaspoons ground cayenne pepper
1 tablespoon ground coriander
1 teaspoon ground turmeric
1 teaspoon ground cardamom
$1/2$ teaspoon ground black pepper
$1/2$ teaspoon ground cinnamon
$1/2$ teaspoon ground cloves
$1/2$ teaspoon ground ginger

Still not hot enough? Simply increase the cayenne and/or black pepper and the ginger.

Fines Herbes

This is a classic French herb mix. Often made up fresh in a little piece of cheesecloth to be tossed in near the end of cooking to preserve the flavor, it can also be dried ahead and a teaspoon or so tied up in the cheesecloth. This makes about a quarter of a cup:

1 tablespoon tarragon
1 tablespoon chervil
1 tablespoon chives
1 tablespoon parsley

Garam Masala

The best cooks in India make their own Garam Masala fresh right before they need it, but this will keep in an airtight container away from heat and light for several months and always be ready when you want it.

4 tablespoons coriander seeds
1 tablespoon cumin seeds
1 tablespoon black peppercorns
1 teaspoon black cumin seeds (also called shahjeera)
4 cardamom seedpods
$3/4$ teaspoon whole cloves
2 inches good cinnamon stick
2 large bay leaves, broken up
$1 1/2$ teaspoons powdered ginger

Toast all spices except the powdered ginger in heavy skillet over medium heat, stirring and watching carefully to avoid burning them, something that will happen more quickly than you can imagine if you walk away for just a minute! Once they have darkened some, and the aroma is heady, remove skillet from heat and let the spices cool. When toasted spices are room temperature, remove seeds from cardamom pods and place all ingredients in a spice or specially designated coffee grinder. Grind to a fine powder. Store airtight away from heat and light.

General Purpose Blend

Change it and make it yours!

$1 1/2$ teaspoons garlic powder
$3/4$ teaspoon dried thyme leaves
$1/2$ teaspoon dried oregano
$1 1/2$ teaspoons onion powder
$1 1/4$ teaspoons paprika
1 teaspoon celery seed
$1 1/2$ teaspoons white pepper
$1 1/2$ teaspoons dry mustard
1 teaspoon dried lemon peel
1 teaspoon ground black pepper

Jerk Seasoning

2 tablespoons dehydrated minced onion
2 teaspoons dried, crushed thyme

2 teaspoons ground allspice

2 teaspoons ground pepper

1 teaspoon ground cinnamon

1/2 teaspoon cayenne pepper

Combine spices and store airtight away from heat and light. When ready to use, rinse meat, pat dry with paper towels, rub on a little olive oil, and rub in the jerk.

Mediterranean Herbs

4 tablespoons crushed, dried basil

4 tablespoons crushed, dried thyme

2 teaspoons crushed, dried lavender

2 teaspoons crushed, dried rosemary

2 teaspoons minced garlic

1 teaspoon crushed, dried tarragon

1 teaspoon freshly ground black pepper

Ras-el-Hanout—The Simple Version

1 teaspoon ground cumin

1 teaspoon ground ginger

1 teaspoon ground black pepper

1/2 teaspoon cinnamon

1/2 teaspoon ground coriander

1/2 teaspoon cayenne pepper

1/2 teaspoon allspice

1/4 teaspoon ground cloves

Ras-el-Hanout—The Very Serious, Herb-Loving, Low-Sodium Cook's Version

The name ras-el-hanout, by the way, translates as "top of the shop," which some have taken to mean "best of the best."

4 whole nutmegs

10 rosebuds (dried)

12 cinnamon sticks

12 blades of mace

1 teaspoon aniseed

8 pieces of turmeric

2 small pieces orrisroot

2 dried cayenne peppers

1/2 teaspoon lavender

1 tablespoon white peppercorns

2 tablespoons whole gingerroot

6 cloves

24 allspice berries

20 white or green cardamom pods

4 wild (black) cardamom pods

Grind all the ingredients until you obtain a fine mix. Store airtight away from heat and light.

Zahtar (Za'atar)

1 tablespoon sesame seeds

1/4 cup sumac (if you can't find it in a local source, it is available for order from spice houses and not too expensively)

2 tablespoons dried thyme

2 tablespoons dried marjoram

2 tablespoons dried oregano

Toast the sesame seeds in a heavy skillet over medium heat, watching carefully to avoid burning, to develop a darkened color and lovely toasty aroma. Cool completely to room temperature and whirl it all in the spice grinder or processor. You know the drill—keep airtight away from heat and light.

Fish with Mediterranean Herbs

Works best on solid, fleshy fish such as red snapper, sea bass, or swordfish. Works well in a skillet or on the grill. If you're worried about losing the fish through the grill grates, use a well-oiled grilling basket. Using swordfish, each of 4 servings will be about 200 mg. sodium.

2 pounds fish such as described

6 tablespoons Mediterranean Herbs (page 55)

3 tablespoons extra-virgin olive oil

When you are ready to cook your fish, combine the herb mixture with the oil. Make the paste in a small bowl by working all ingredients together. Spread the paste evenly on both sides of 2–4 fish fillets (depending on size of fish you've chosen). Sauté in a small amount of olive oil or grill over hot coals until the flesh is opaque throughout and just starting to flake (flaking fish is overcooked fish!), 5–7 minutes, turning once halfway through grilling time. Of course you can do this with fresh herbs, too, just remember the proportions: you'll need two to three times as much fresh herb to equal the more concentrated flavor of dried.

Jazzed Sirloin Steak

This is so easy and so good.

1 sirloin steak, fatty edges trimmed

2 teaspoons The Best Chili Powder (page 53)

2 teaspoons ground coriander

Fresh ground pepper to taste

Combine the seasonings. Pat the steak dry (wet steak doesn't crust up nicely), then rub the seasoning all over both sides of the steak. Rub it in like you mean it. Grill over medium hot coals, or in an oiled grill pan on the stove. Pass the Honey Sweet Potato Biscuits (page 74) and some Grilled Corn on the Cob (page 131) and you will have the happiest, low-sodium-fed tummy in town! If your steak weighs in at 1½ pounds, and you serve four with it, it will cost 115 mg. sodium each. See how you don't pay for the flavor in spices? Cool, huh?

EDIBLE FLOWERS

While edible flowers aren't exactly herbs or spices, they warrant a brief mention here. Any blossom on an edible herb plant will also be edible, best taken as soon after opening as possible before they grow old or set seeds. An ideal example is the chive flower: oniony and beautiful on a salad. Blossoms from our flower gardens can also be tasty and beautiful in culinary uses, as long as they have not been subjected to poisonous bug killers and other lawn and garden chemicals.

Here's a partial list of safe-to-eat flowers:

Blossoms of any edible herb, fruit, or vegetable

Squash blossom

Peach blossom

Chive blossom

Calendula

Carnation

Chrysanthemum

Daylily

Dianthus

Hibiscus (remove stamen and pistil)

Impatiens

Hollyhock

Johnny Jump-Up

Lilac

Lavender

Marigold

Nasturtium

Orange or other citrus blossom

Pansy

Rose petals

Scented geranium

Violets

I once made a two-tiered birthday cake for my mother-in-law that I covered with candied pansies and Johnny jump-ups. I was good for years on that one!

Candied Edible Flower Blossoms

Start a couple days before you'll need them to allow time for all the drying to take place.

A handful of edible blossoms, or as many as you are willing to give up from the garden and take the time to candy

1 egg white at room temperature

$1/4$ teaspoon water (yup, just a few drops)

Superfine sugar (if you don't have any, make it by processing regular granulated sugar until it's superfine; you'll need a cup or so) on a plate or shallow dish

A small paintbrush like you would use to paint models or paint by numbers

Racks to dry the blossoms on

Pick perfect blossoms and gently but thoroughly rinse and dry them all completely. Best to let them air dry an hour before you do this. Whisk the egg white and

The Handbook of Practical Low-Salt Living

tiny bit of water together just until it starts to get bub-bly, don't go all the way to foamy. Hold the stem of the blossom you want to candy in your non-dominant hand. With your dominant hand dip the bristles of your brush into the egg white and paint a thin layer on all surfaces of each petal, separating petals to get to areas that overlap. Don't put so much on that the overlapping petals glue together.

Now set the brush down, hold the flower over the plate of sugar, and sprinkle it on all the painted surfaces until covered. Don't try to dip the flower into the sugar, it just makes a mess and ruins the your hard work. Very gently set the blossom on a rack to air dry. You'll get faster and more proficient as you practice. Let them air dry in a safe place away from any breeze or draft. Once dry, decorate your cake or cupcakes or anything else you will serve and want to look like a work of art. No sodium is added, only ooo's and ahh's. Who says you don't eat with your eyes? You don't have to eat them, but it's good to know your decorations won't put anyone in the hospital.

Be Safe! Know Your Flower

Here are a few poisonous blossoms to be sure to avoid:

Azalea

Buttercup

Clematis

Foxglove

Hyacinth   Iris   Larkspur

Lily of the valley

Lobelia

Daffodil

Four o'clock

Morning glory   Sweet pea

There are many others. When in doubt, throw it out! Be certain about what you are putting in your mouth. And be certain it has been grown without pesticides!

Unsalted sippers? Really? You don't mean that there's salt in what I drink? Naw, nobody shakes salt into a drink—except maybe a Margarita—certainly not my soda or my milkshake!

Yes, I know. It seems like an oxymoron, but it's a real problem. Sodium hides everywhere. Often it's a naturally occurring dose of sodium like that in milk, but it has human help sneaking into many things we drink. Salt has even been found in some bottled water! So read those labels and enjoy sipping on some of the following suggestions instead.

Old Fashioned Hot Cocoa

Way better than the stuff in the can and just the thought of it sends swirling memories of sledding as a kid through my head. We always came back shivering but hot cocoa warmed us up.

Serves 4 at 110 milligrams sodium each

1/4 cup unsweetened baking cocoa
1/4 cup brown sugar, packed
1/4 teaspoon cinnamon
1/4 cup hot water
3 1/2 cups milk
1/2 teaspoon vanilla

Using a medium saucepan, thoroughly combine cocoa, brown sugar and cinnamon. Beat in hot water with a whisk. Stirring constantly, bring to a boil over medium high heat. Now whisk in milk and continue to cook but not boil for 12 minutes or so. Stir often while cooking, then stir in vanilla. If you garnish with whipped cream or marshmallows, account for the sodium content of what you use.

Creamy Strawberry Sipper

Dressed up with champagne or made without, strawberries, OJ, and yogurt make this a healthy treat.

Serves 4 at 28 milligrams sodium each

2 cups sliced strawberries
1 cup orange juice
8 ounce carton plain yogurt
1 tablespoon sugar
1/2 teaspoon vanilla
3/4 cup champagne (see note)
strawberries for garnish
orange slices for garnish

Place all but champagne in blender. Blend until smooth. Chill. Just before serving, gently stir in champagne. Pour into glasses and garnish with an orange slice and a strawberry. NOTE: Instead of champagne, substitute dry white wine or sparkling grape juice, or plain white grape juice.

Springtime Punch

Family get-together, bridal or baby shower? What a tasty and easy way to quench everyone's thirst.

Serves 32 at 5 milligrams sodium each

2 cups sugar
2 1/2 cups water

1 cup fresh lemon juice
1 cup fresh orange juice
6 ounces pineapple juice, frozen concentrate, thawed
2 quarts ginger ale, chilled

Bring sugar and water to boil. Boil 10 minutes and remove from heat. Stir in juices and chill. Just before serving combine with cold ginger ale in a large punch bowl.

Hot Buttered Rum

Never mind the hot cocoa, give that to the kids and warm your toes and nose with this tasty little number.

Serves 20 at 15 milligrams sodium each

1/2 cup unsalted butter
3 cinnamon sticks
6 whole cloves
1/2 teaspoon grated nutmeg
2 cups rum
Whipped cream

Combine all but rum and whipped cream in crockpot. Add 2 quarts hot water. Stir well. Simmer low 5 hours or high 2 1/2 hours. Add rum, stir, turn to low if not already. Serve in warm mugs with a scoop of whipped cream and a dusting of nutmeg. The crockpot is a great help here, you can set it and go about other party preparations or entertaining and then serve when ready.

Hot Spiced Wassail

Sounds like Christmas, but if you call it Witch's Brew, it can work all through the fall, too. This is another recipe that stays warm nicely in the crockpot. Make it with or without the rum, of course.

Serves 10 at 17 milligrams sodium each

6 inches stick cinnamon broken into pieces
16 whole cloves
1 teaspoon whole allspice
2 medium oranges
6 cups apple cider
2 cups cranberry juice
1/4 cup sugar
1 cup rum (are you beginning to see a pattern here?)

Tie all the spices together in a cheesecloth bag. Slice and stud the oranges with a few more cloves. Combine juices and sugar in large saucepan. Add spice bag and oranges (reserve a few slices for garnish). Simmer, covered 10 minutes.

Stir in rum and heat just until warmed through. Remove spices and oranges. Serve in warmed punch bowl or crockpot with fresh orange slice garnish. Warms you through and through. One of my favorites for fall and winter get-togethers. I keep it hot in the crockpot.

Gramma Balch's Fruit Punch

Or The Dressed-Up Hawaiian

Serves 20 at 15 milligrams sodium each

1 46-ounce can red real-juice punch
1 1/2 cups orange juice
1/4 cup lemon juice
1 10-ounce package frozen red raspberries
2 12-ounce cans lemon-lime soda

Combine all but soda in punch bowl and stir well. Gently pour soda down side of bowl to avoid foaming and carefully stir just to blend. Very tasty, in fact we all look forward to it when we gather at Gramma's on special occasions.

Raspberry Peach Coolers

When it's peach season, these are heavenly.

Serves 4 at 50 milligrams sodium each

2 large, pitted and peeled ripe peaches
1 pint raspberry sherbet
1 1/2 cups chilled ginger ale

If you are lucky enough to have a juice extractor, use it to extract about one cup juice from the peaches. I'm not that lucky so I beat the death out of them in a food processor. The final consistency is different but all the flavor is there. I only use very ripe fruit. Of course you could use canned peach nectar, but it's not the same and you'll have to check labels. Pour 1/4 cup juice into each of 4 glasses. Add 1/4 of the sherbet (about 1/2 cup) and top with the ginger ale. Ahh, the taste of summer.

Breakfast Smoothie

Switch out flavors and make it your own. Put this in the kids' breakfast glasses or in your travel mug for the trip to work in the morning.

Serves 2 at 85 milligrams sodium each

1 cup orange juice
1 cup plain low fat yogurt
    (or strawberry-banana)
1 medium ripe banana
3/4 cup strawberries, fresh
    or frozen without sugar

3–4 ice cubes (less if using frozen berries)
1 teaspoon honey (skip if using flavored yogurt)

Whir it all together in the blender until it's smooth and enjoy. Sodium content changes slightly depending on yogurt brand chosen, but flavor or no flavor doesn't effect it much.

Grown-Up Hawaiian Punch

The sodium here comes from ginger ale at 35 mg per 8 ounce serving, so a "punch-cupful" (1/3 cup or so) will cost you about 12 mg. of sodium.

1/3-cup serving contains 12 milligrams sodium

1/2 cup agave nectar
3 cups pineapple chunks (1 pineapple)
Juice of 2 limes (1/4 cup)
1 cup rum
1 quart (half a 2-liter bottle) ginger ale

Puree all but ginger ale in blender till smooth. Pour into pitcher; gently stir in ginger ale.

Spiced Apple Cider

Ahhh, the taste of autumn, and just 22 mg. sodium in the whole batch! Not that I'm recommending drinking the whole batch in one sitting, you understand . . .

1 quart contains 22 milligrams sodium

1 quart cider
4 whole cloves
3 whole allspice berries
1 teaspoon candied ginger, chopped
8 inches cinnamon sticks
1/4 cup brown sugar, packed

Combine cider and all spices in large pot; bring to a boil. Reduce heat, stir in brown sugar, and simmer gently. Strain and serve. Holds well in a thermos if you're planning an autumn leaf-peeping trip.

Blueberry Peach Float

8 servings at 20 mg. sodium each.

1 cup sugar
2 cups water
1 vanilla bean; split
2 cups frozen peaches
1 tablespoon fresh lemon juice
2 cups fresh blueberries
16 ounces tonic water or other carbonated beverage to
    taste

In a saucepan, bring to a boil the sugar, water, and vanilla bean. Once it boils add the frozen peaches and lemon juice and let them sit in the hot syrup 5 minutes. Remove the vanilla bean and puree the liquid. Strain into a shallow pan and freeze overnight. Scrape out the frozen puree with a spoon, moving it all to a freezer container. Keep frozen until ready to use.

To serve the floats, place a spoonful of the scraped peach puree into a small juice glass. Top with a few fresh blueberries. Pour carbonated beverage over to cover and serve with a straw.

Irish Coffee

(Come on, you didn't think I'd leave this out did you?)

Serves one at 5 milligrams sodium

½ cup hot strong coffee
1 tablespoon Irish whiskey
2 teaspoons sugar
Whipped cream
Ground cinnamon or nutmeg

In a coffee cup or Irish coffee mug, stir together hot coffee and Irish whiskey. Stir in sugar. Top with a dollop of whipped cream (it's so much easier than floating heavy cream on top, but you can try it: hold a spoon right down at the surface of the coffee mixture tilted toward the surface but not under it even a little. Very gently pour heavy cream into the spoon and let it slide off the spoon and float on the surface); sprinkle with cinnamon or nutmeg. Makes 1 (6-ounce) serving.

Lemon Basil Tea

An unusual but enjoyable way to savor the herb garden. Tastes as good as it smells.

Serves 2 at zero milligrams sodium each

2 cups water
3 tablespoons thinly sliced fresh green basil or lemon basil leaves
1 teaspoon grated lemon peel
2 teaspoons English breakfast or other black tea leaves

In a small saucepan, bring water to a boil. Remove from the heat. Add the basil, lemon peel, and tea leaves; cover and steep for 4 minutes. Strain, discarding lemon peel and tea leaves. Serve immediately with a sprinkle of sugar, if desired.

Pink Lemonade Champagne Punch

Make a pretty ice block or ring by freezing fruit slices, herb leaves and edible flowers (see page 56) in water.

Serves 8 at about 25 milligrams sodium each

2 cans frozen pink lemonade concentrate
1 bottle champagne
Sliced fruit

In a large punch bowl, combine pink lemonade concentrate and champagne. Stir to combine and dissolve frozen lemonade. Add sliced fruit or ice ring, as you like.

Desalted snacks: isn't that an oxymoron?

These are areas of great sodium potential. Most foods in this category use chips, crackers, pretzels, cheese, bacon, prepared dressings and sauces, olives, pickles and shellfish, which are all scary in the sodium content column. Microwave popcorn is another source of sodium you might not realize. It not only comes pre-buttered but manufacturers often shake on salt and chemicals, too. Care should be taken to stay within the measurements or servings as described, but avoiding what is uncalculated or unprepared by you is usually safest. Boring, but safest. Try some of these instead . . .

Onion Salsa

A tasty balance to a rich pork roast, flavor develops with a good chill before serving.

Makes 2 cups at 12 milligrams sodium per tablespoon

2 medium sweet red or purple onions, finely chopped (about 1 1/2 cups)
1 large tomato, seeded and finely chopped
1/4 cup chopped green onions or chives (chives grow like weeds in a garden!)
2 large cloves garlic, finely minced
1/4 cup lemon juice
2 tablespoons chopped fresh cilantro or flat parsley (the herb garden sure is handy)
2 tablespoons balsamic vinegar
1 tablespoon olive oil
1 teaspoon low-sodium soy sauce (measure very carefully)
Dash cayenne pepper

Combine in glass container with cover and chill at least a couple hours to blend flavors.

"Corn" Chips

Don't reach for those salty crackers! This lets you dip without danger.

Each "chip" contains about 5 milligrams sodium!

1 6-ounce package stone-ground corn tortillas
Nonstick cooking spray

Spray a couple cookie sheets with the nonstick spray. Cut each tortilla into 8 wedges and arrange in single layer on baking sheets. Bake 6 minutes in oven preheated to 450° until crisp, not brown. Serve cooled chips with onion salsa. (No reason you can't do just one or two tortillas at a time to keep them crisp and fresh.)

Garden Mousse

Makes a very attractive molded dish for parties. Here's another chance to use an herb from your garden.

Makes 4 cups at 15 milligrams sodium per tablespoon

1 envelope unflavored gelatin
1/4 cup white wine, white grape or apple juice
2 1/2 medium cucumbers, peeled, seeded and finely chopped (about 2 1/2 cups)
1/2 cup buttermilk (you can get it in a powdered form and make it as you need it)
1/2 cup sodium-free chicken broth (see recipe in soup section)
1/4 cup lime juice (fresh if you can)
1/3 cup chopped green onions (usually 3)
1/4 cup light mayonnaise

1 tablespoon chopped fresh dill (can use 1 teaspoon dried)
1/4 teaspoon white pepper

Prepare a 4-cup mold by lightly coating with nonstick spray. Sprinkle gelatin over wine in a medium saucepan and let sit a few minutes to soften. Place over medium heat and stir constantly for 2 minutes until dissolved. Remove from heat and cool slightly at room temperature. Meanwhile, combine 2 cups of the chopped cukes and the remaining ingredients in food processor or blender. Process or blend till smooth. Whir in gelatin for just a few seconds. Stir in remaining cucumber and pour it all into prepared mold. It takes about 4 hours to chill firm. Unmold and serve with fresh veggies and "corn" chips.

Stuffed Mushrooms

Don't be afraid to rinse mushrooms well in running water. I never understood the big deal about washing mushrooms—no, don't soak them. Then they will absorb water. But a good running water rinse makes sure you have all the muck off and does not saturate the cap. Promise.

Makes a dozen at 35 milligrams sodium each

12 medium-large mushrooms, rinsed and wiped clean
1 tablespoon unsalted butter or margarine
3 tablespoons finely minced onion
2 slices plain white bread in little pieces
2 tablespoons white wine or sherry
2 tablespoons grated Parmesan cheese, divided
1/4 teaspoon dried thyme
1/8 teaspoon freshly ground black pepper
1/8 teaspoon dried oregano
1 tablespoon melted unsalted butter or margarine

Remove mushroom stems and finely chop them. Heat 1 tablespoon butter in saucepan and add mushroom stems and onion. Sauté until softened and tender but not browned. Stir in all remaining ingredients reserving 1 tablespoon Parmesan cheese, mushroom caps and last tablespoon melted butter. Place caps round side up on cookie sheet and brush with half the remaining melted butter. Run under preheated broiler for 2 to 2½ minutes. Remove, invert and fill with stuffing mix. Brush with remaining melted butter and sprinkle with remaining Parmesan cheese. Broil about 3 minutes until lightly browned and tender.

Garlic Dip

Be careful, makes about 1 cup, but 1 tablespoon is 90 milligrams of sodium. Dip lightly. Kinda gives you a new respect for the sodium in "regular" dips.

Makes 1 cup at 90 milligrams sodium per tablespoon

1 8-ounce package cream cheese
1 tablespoons dill

1/4 teaspoon fresh ground pepper

1–2 tablespoons finely chopped onion

2 cloves garlic, minced

1/2 cup finely diced raw vegetables such as carrot, celery and red bell pepper

Combine everything the day before you want to serve it to give it enough time to take whatever shape you want it in and blend flavors. Sprinkle with paprika or chopped parsley. Pretty at holiday get-togethers.

Chicken Fingers with Honey Mustard Sauce

When dipped lightly, each finger contains a poultry—I mean paltry—95 milligrams sodium each. The leftover chicken (ya, right) can be reheated the next day wrapped in foil.

16 appetizers at 95 milligrams sodium each

1/2 cup honey

2 tablespoons spicy brown mustard (not Dijon, it's too high in sodium)

4 4-ounce chicken breasts, (one pound), skinned, boned and cut into 4 even pieces each

1 cup all-purpose or unbleached flour

1/4 teaspoon freshly ground pepper

3/4 cup milk

1 cup vegetable oil

Combine honey and mustard in a small bowl and set aside. Combine flour and pepper on wax paper. Dip chicken in milk, and then roll in flour coating well. Pour oil to 1/4-inch depth in large frying pan and heat over medium high. Place chicken in hot oil in single layer and fry 5–6 minutes until done, turning once or twice. They should be golden brown and crispy. Place on paper towels to drain. Serve hot with sauce.

Homemade Potato Chips

Okay, first let me say, I'm not condoning fried snack foods. But if you don't overdo, these can help you with your craving. What you sprinkle on these is where the sodium, if any, will come from.

One peeled, 2 1/2-inch round potato contains 7 milligrams sodium; unpeeled it's about 10

1 large all-purpose potato, peeled or not, your choice

Garlic powder, onion powder, dried herbs, chili powder, or nothing at all

Oil

Slice the potato thinly, easier done with a slicer than a paring knife. Heat an inch or so of oil in a heavy saucepan to 365°. Fry a few slices at a time for about a minute

and a half or until desired golden color is achieved. Remove with slotted spoon and drain well on paper towels. Sprinkle with seasoning if desired. Don't go looking for the salt shaker; that would be poison, remember? Experiment with flavors; broaden your horizons.

Black Bean Dip

Yes, beans are good for you. You don't have to eat them in large amounts if it worries you, but if you like them, make up a batch of dip and some "Corn Chips" (above) and have a snack. Just don't use canned beans—dried aren't so hard to work with and you cannot get the salt out of the canned version no matter how long you rinse them.

Makes 1 cup at 15 milligrams sodium per tablespoon

1 cup prepared black beans from dried (see my discussion about beans and easy instructions for working with dried beans on page 70)

Half an 8-ounce package cream cheese, softened (Add more if it seems too intense for your palate, but wait till you taste the end product as presented here, and be sure to add in the additional sodium.)

2 canned green chilies, drained and minced

1 tablespoon chili powder (see recipe page 53)

1/2 teaspoon garlic powder

Mash beans with fork; stir in the remaining ingredients. Serve with homemade chips (page 64) or salt-free purchased chips.

Shrimp for the Buffet

What a treat. Use the fresh parsley. It makes a difference in taste and appearance.

Serves 4 at about 28 milligrams sodium per shrimp

2 tablespoons olive oil

2 medium cloves garlic, peeled and sliced thickly

1 bay leaf

Pinch of red pepper flakes

1 pound raw shrimp (about 25 of the 21–25 count size) peeled and deveined

2 tablespoons dry sherry

Juice of half a lemon

1–2 tablespoons chopped fresh parsley

Heat oil over medium in a large sauté pan. Add garlic, bay leaf, and red pepper flakes and cook, stirring, about 3 minutes. Retrieve the bay leaf and garlic (garlic gets bitter when it spends too long frying in hot oil). Toss in the shrimp and stay with the pan as shrimp cook quickly and it's a short run to rubbery and tough. As soon as all the shrimp are pink on both sides (about 4 minutes) add sherry, lemon juice, and parsley. Stir and cook another minute and pile 'em high on a platter and pass the toothpicks. (Don't lose count!)

Zucchini Chips

Panko crumbs are the trick here. There are very dry and help keep the chips crispy.

Serves 4 at 120 milligrams sodium each

2 small zucchini, about 1 1/2 inches in diameter
1/4 cup Panko crumbs
1/4 cup Parmesan cheese
1/2 teaspoon garlic powder
2 teaspoons dried thyme, crushed hard before adding
1/4 teaspoon dry mustard
1/2 cup milk

Preheat oven to 450°. Spray a baking sheet with cooking spray. Combine crumbs, cheese, and seasonings in flat dish or pie pan. Slice zucchini and soak in bowl with milk. Dredge zucchini in crumb mixture a few slices at a time. Tap to shake off extra and place slices on prepared baking sheet. Bake 15 minutes,; flip them over and bake another 15 minutes.

Spiced Pecans

As long as you start with salt-free nuts, this is a tasty snack you can keep around during holidays for guests or to grab a handful yourself now and then.

Makes 2 cups and the whole thing has 10 mg. sodium

2 cups pecan halves
1/4 cup unsalted butter, cubed
1/4 cup sugar
1 teaspoon ground cinnamon
1/4 teaspoon ground nutmeg
1/4 teaspoon ground cloves

In a large skillet over low heat, toast pecans in butter for 15 minutes or until lightly browned, stirring often. Drain on paper towels. In a large bowl, combine the sugar and spices. Add pecans and toss to coat. Spread on a foil-lined baking sheet. Bake at 325° for 10 minutes. Cool. Store in an airtight container.

Sweet Potato Fries

Serves 4 at 21 milligrams sodium each

2 medium sweet potatoes cut into 8 wedges each
2 tablespoons olive oil
1/4 teaspoon black pepper
1 teaspoon chili powder (see page 53)
1 tablespoon sugar

Toss potato wedges with olive oil. Combine remaining ingredients and sprinkle over wedges, toss to distribute evenly. Spread onto parchment paper on baking tray. Bake 425° 20 minutes or until fork tender. Dip these

babies into Black Bean dip (page 65) or Blueberry Chutney below. Excuse me while I lick my fingers.

Blueberry Chutney

This so good I could eat it with a spoon or ladle over vanilla bean ice cream!

The whole batch costs 39 milligrams sodium

3 cups fresh blueberries
1/4 cup chopped onion
1 tablespoon grated fresh gingerroot
1/2 cup brown sugar
1/3 cup cider vinegar
1 tablespoon cornstarch
3-inch cinnamon stick

In large saucepan, combine all ingredients. Bring mixture to boil over medium heat, stirring frequently. Boil 1 minute. Remove cinnamon stick. Cool. Cover and refrigerate. Serve as a condiment with meats or as a dip with Sweet Potato Fries, above.

Avocado Stuffed Tomatoes

Pretty easy and very pretty!

Only 16 milligrams sodium each

30 cherry tomatoes
1/2 ripe avocado peeled, pitted and roughly chopped
2 ounces cream cheese at room temperature
2 tablespoons pesto (see page 145)
1 teaspoon fresh lemon or lime juice
30 tiny basil leaves or several larger leaves cut chiffonade-
    style (see page 41)

Cut a thin slice from the top of each tomato. You can also cut a thin slice from bottoms of tomatoes so they stand upright. With a small spoon or small lemon baller (I have had success with a grapefruit spoon but be gentle) carefully hollow out the tomatoes. Line a baking sheet with paper towels. Invert tomatoes on the towels. Let stand 30 minutes to drain.

Meanwhile, for filling, in a food processor bowl combine avocado, cream cheese, pesto, and lemon juice. Cover; process until smooth. Spoon filling into a pastry bag fitted with a large plain round or open star tip or a plastic bag with a very small cut-off corner to feed the mixture through.

Pipe filling into the tomato cups and arrange on platter. Serve immediately or cover loosely and refrigerate up to 4 hours before serving. Add a tiny basil leaf to each or sprinkle with chiffonade-cut basil before serving. Makes 30 appetizers.

As you have seen, store-bought canned, dehydrated, and even frozen soups are sky high in sodium content. You may be able to find some that claim to be reduced in sodium, but even then, you probably don't want to give up your allowance of sodium to a bowl of soup or to a can of broth to use in cooking. Homemade stock may take a little time, but it's worth the investment. You can keep it in the refrigerator for use over the following several days or freeze it in small amounts to use over several months.

A good way to get started with homemade chicken stock is to save the carcass from your next roast chicken and simmer the bones in a large kettle on the stove to extract the flavor. Or use a whole bird or parts on sale, simmer until the meat is tender and remove the meat for that night's dinner and continue to cook the bones for stock. Another way to attack this is to buy whole chickens, cut them up yourself to use the breasts and legs for meals, and save the extras, like the wings, backs, and so on, for the stock. You can store the stock parts in the freezer, along with the leftover chicken skeleton from a meal, until you have enough. That saves some on the cost of the chicken parts you would have bought, too. The broth will make great soup just by adding some herbs, vegetables, and rice or noodles.

Seasoned Croutons

The sodium content of this recipe depends on the sodium content of the bread you use. Using the low-sodium bread available in my area, this runs 21 milligrams of sodium for each half-cupful. Nice addition to soups and salads.

1 teaspoon garlic powder
1 teaspoon dried oregano
1 teaspoon dried basil
1 tablespoon grated Parmesan cheese
3 cups cubed fresh, low-sodium bread
Olive-oil-flavored cooking spray

Preheat oven to 350°. Mix garlic, oregano, basil and cheese in a large zipper plastic bag until well blended. Dust bread cubes lightly with a shot of olive-oil-flavored spray. Add bread cubes to bag and shake until coated with spices. Not all spices will stick to bread, but that's O.K. Place bread cubes in a single layer on baking sheet. Bake until croutons are crisp and golden brown, about 10 minutes (keep your eye on them). Stir once or twice during toasting. Let cool. Store in an airtight container or plastic bag for up to one week.

Beef Stock

This is a little different because of the fat content, but the idea is the same as for chicken stock.

8 one-cup servings at 55 milligrams sodium each

4 pounds beef shank bones (they're fattier but worth it for the better flavor)
3 quarts water
1 medium onion, peeled and quartered
1 bay leaf
1 sprig thyme
Several sprigs parsley
5–6 whole black peppercorns

Preheat oven and place bones in roasting pan in oven at 400° for half an hour to collect fat. Turn the bones once or twice while de-fatting. Transfer bones to waiting stock pot and cover with water. Add remaining ingredients and bring to simmer. Partly cover and simmer at least 4 hours, longer for better flavor. Add a little water if needed. Skim as much fat as possible. Strain, chill and remove any fat layer that forms. Use in soup, gravy and for other cooking needs. Freezes well. Makes about 2 quarts.

Chicken Stock

Can't babysit the stockpot all day? I've used the slow cooker with good results.

16 one-cup servings at 40 milligrams sodium each

1 chicken carcass, 6 or 8 chicken pieces or 1 whole chicken, about 5 pounds (see page 67)
Cold water to cover
1 large sprig each: rosemary, parsley, thyme
1 bay leaf
1 medium onion, peeled and quartered
1 medium carrot, peeled and quartered
5–6 whole black peppercorns
3 celery tops, the leafy stuff

Rinse the chicken and place in large stockpot. Add enough water to cover, usually about 4 quarts. Toss in remaining goodies (these are where all the great flavor will come from). Bring to a boil then turn down until it just simmers partly covered. If using bones with meat on them, remove meat after 20 minutes or so then continue to simmer bones. One neat trick I learned a long time ago is to tie all the bones up in a big piece of cheesecloth. This makes it easier to remove and makes you feel more certain that you didn't miss any tiny bones. Simmer for at least 3 hours; add a little water if you need to. Cool until you can handle it safely then strain the broth. Chill and remove any fat that forms on top. Use in soup, gravy, cooking sauces. Freezes well. Makes about 4 quarts. You can do exactly the same thing with a turkey carcass, too.

Vegetable Soup

This is so delicious. If you use store bought stock pay close attention to the sodium content. It's not easy to find truly low-sodium stock. If you don't like barley, think about alphabet pasta.

4 one-cup servings at 80 milligrams sodium each

1 tablespoon olive oil
$1/2$ cup chopped onions
$1/2$ cup diced celery
$1/2$ cup chopped carrot
$1/2$ teaspoon dried oregano or $1 1/2$ teaspoons fresh
2 cloves garlic, minced
4 cups (1 quart) very low sodium beef stock
$1/2$ cup chopped green beans
$1/2$ cup chopped ripe tomatoes
Freshly ground pepper to taste
$1/2$ cup barley

Sauté onion, celery, and carrots in large saucepan over medium until soft, 5–6 minutes. Add garlic and cook another minute or two. Add remaining ingredients and simmer 45 minutes or until vegetables are done and flavors are well blended.

Old Fashioned Cream of Tomato Soup

Quick and so much better than canned stuff.

Serves 4 at 151 milligrams sodium each

2 16-ounce cans no-salt-added diced tomatoes
1¼ cups salt-free chicken broth (you can use sodium-free bouillon in a pinch)
2 tablespoons unsalted butter
1 tablespoon sugar
1 tablespoon chopped onion
2 cups cream

Mix tomatoes, chicken broth, butter, sugar, and onions. Simmer 1 hour. Heat cream in double boiler or microwave until just hot, not simmering or boiling. Slowly add cream to hot tomato mixture. Blend until smooth using a stick blender or cooling a bit and adding to blender or food processor. Float a chiffonade (see page 41) of basil on top and serve.

Best Cream of Broccoli Soup

Don't waste your money on broccoli florets; cut your own and use the stems for flavor!

Serves 6 at 103 milligrams sodium each

2 tablespoons unsalted butter
1 onion, chopped
1 stalk celery, chopped
3 cups low-sodium homemade chicken broth (see page 68)
8 cups broccoli florets
3 tablespoons unsalted butter
3 tablespoons all-purpose flour
2 cups milk
Ground black pepper to taste

Melt 2 tablespoons butter in medium-sized stock pot, and saute onion and celery until tender. Add broccoli and broth, cover and simmer for 10 minutes. Puree soup and return to heat. I like to hold back some of the broccoli rather than puree it all so I can have actual pieces of it in my soup. In small saucepan over medium heat, melt 3 tablespoons butter, stir in flour, and add milk. Stir until thick and bubbly, and add to soup. Season with pepper and serve.

Asparagus Soup

I stole this recipe from an old friend. Then I loved it so much I actually went out and bought a stick blender just for this soup! That makes it so much easier compared with pouring hot soup in and out of a blender. If you don't have one, no big deal, just be careful not to get splashed with hot liquid.

Makes 4 cups at 65 milligrams sodium each

1 pound fresh thin asparagus spears (these are more tender than the thicker ones)
3 cups very low sodium chicken stock, divided
1 tablespoon unsalted butter or margarine
2 tablespoons all-purpose flour
½ teaspoon curry powder
Several grinds fresh black pepper, to taste
1 cup milk
1 teaspoon grated lemon peel

Cut off tips of asparagus and set aside. Cut remaining spears into 2-inch pieces. Heat these pieces and 2 cups of the chicken stock to boiling. Reduce heat to simmer and cook 10 minutes until tender. Pour stock and all into blender and process until smooth. Heat unsalted butter in large saucepan until melted. Add flour and whisk in well. Cook, stirring constantly until smooth and bubbly. Remove and stir in remaining 1 cup stock. Whisk till smooth. Heat to boiling, stirring constantly; boil and stir one minute. Stir in asparagus mixture, reserved tips and seasonings. Simmer uncovered 10 minutes. Stir in milk and heat just till hot. Sprinkle each serving with lemon peel.

Colorful Corn Chowder

Makes 10 tummy-warming servings at only 82 milligrams of sodium each. You could skip the cheese topping to drop each serving without it to 56 milligrams, but why?

Serves 10 at 82 milligrams sodium each

2 tablespoons unsalted butter
1 onion, chopped
1 green bell pepper, chopped
1 red bell pepper, chopped
2 carrots, chopped
2 (10-ounce) packages frozen corn kernels, thawed
1½ cups dry potato flakes
¼ teaspoon ground black pepper
¼ teaspoon ground cayenne pepper
3 cups water
2 cups milk
1 cup half-and-half
¼ cup grated jack or cheddar cheese

In a large saucepan, melt butter over medium-high heat. Cook onion, red and green bell peppers, and carrots until tender. Stir in thawed corn, potato flakes, ground peppers, and 3 cups water. Bring to boil. Reduce heat. Cover, and simmer for 10 minutes. Stir in milk and half and half. Warm only. Do not boil. Serve sprinkled with grated cheese.

Winter Warmer Soup

Here's a soup that's warming just to look at on a cold evening.

Serves 4 at 106 milligrams sodium each

2 tablespoons unsalted butter
2 onions, chopped
2 carrots, shredded
2 potatoes, peeled and cubed
3 cups low-sodium homemade chicken broth (but you could just use water)
1 tablespoon dried parsley
1/2 teaspoon dried thyme
1 bay leaf
2 cups milk
Pepper to taste

In a large pot over medium heat, melt the butter and saute the onions for 5 to 10 minutes, or until tender. Add the carrots, potatoes, broth, parsley, thyme, and bay leaf. Reduce heat to low and simmer for 30 minutes, stirring occasionally. Remove the bay leaf. Puree the soup in a blender or food processor in small batches and return to the pot. Stir in the soup, mixing well, and season with pepper to taste. You can invent your own soup recipes if you use your homemade stock. Leave out added salt and check the sodium content of all the ingredients you want to add. There's nothing like a steamy hot bowl of homemade soup on a wintry day. Now, what to serve with it?

Favorite Hash

This makes a great easy supper; just add a salad and maybe some crusty bread. Leftovers are tremendous once all the flavors have blended. Make it hotter or milder as you like.

Serves 6 at 92 milligrams sodium each

1 pound ground beef
2 cups chopped bell peppers (mix up the colors!)
1/2 cup chopped onion
1 cup sliced mushrooms
2 garlic cloves, minced
2 small potatoes, peeled and cut into 3/4-inch pieces
1 16-ounce can no-salt-added tomatoes, diced (You can buy whole if it's hard to find no-salt diced; dice them yourself by dragging a sharp knife through them a bunch of times right in the can. Use with all the juice.)

1 8-ounce can no-salt-added tomato sauce
1/2 cup red wine or beef broth
1/2 teaspoon Tabasco sauce (more or less to taste, but remember, we're going for flavor in place of salt)
1 tablespoon Worcestershire sauce
1 teaspoon dried oregano
1/2 teaspoon freshly ground pepper
1/2 teaspoon dried thyme
1/2 teaspoon chili powder (see my recipe page 53)
1/4 teaspoon cayenne powder

Cook ground beef, peppers, onions, mushrooms, and garlic till meat is no longer pink. Add remaining ingredients and bring to a boil. Reduce heat and simmer, uncovered until potatoes are tender and flavors have mellowed, about half an hour.

Black Bean Cowboy Chili

I must digress here and talk about beans. Mainly about canned vs. dried. By now you know canned vegetables are generally loaded with that poison we know as salt and anything from a can no matter how much it is rinsed and drained is still sodium laden. There are some brands that offer some varieties of beans labeled "no salt added"—a good deal for convenience. But the costs tend to go up when components are removed from processed and prepared foods (go figure). And canned anything tends to be more mushy so they don't hold up as well to cooking. Dried beans have no sodium to poison you with, but they are less convenient because you have to plan ahead, unless you did plan ahead and now you have a stash in the freezer, tah-dah. If buying dried beans—don't be sucked in by expensive pretty colored and speckled beans. Those more costly colors disappear when cooked.

That said, consider this: beans cook up and freeze beautifully. Don't ask me why the frozen vegetable companies haven't jumped on that one yet. Anyway, here's how to do it yourself easily. Buy a one-pound bag of dried black beans. Sort them for little stones or debris and rinse them. Simmer them in water or any salt-free liquid you like. Toss in onion or other flavor enhancers; as long as there is no sodium going into the pot you're good. Watch them for the next two hours or so, depending on your bean, temperature under the pot, and so on. Of course, soaking them in liquid in the fridge overnight before you cook them considerably speeds the cooking time. Stir to keep from sticking and burning. When soft enough for your taste, but not too soft— they have to withstand more cooking—drain and cool. Measure out 1-cup portions and freeze. Now you have the same convenience of canned beans but for less cost and more nutrition.

And so here is a tasty recipe to start you off on a bean experience! (PS, my mom always added a pinch of cloves to any bean recipe—claimed it cut the gas issue down. You try it and let me know!)

Serves 8 for only 115 milligrams sodium each made just this way

2 pounds lean ground beef

1 tablespoon olive oil

1$^1/_2$ cups chopped onion

2 medium bell peppers, chopped (mix it up: try different colored peppers)

1 jalapeño pepper, seeded and chopped

2 tablespoons chopped garlic

$^1/_4$ cup salt-free chili powder (see my recipe page 53)

1 tablespoon cumin

1 teaspoon dried oregano, crushed

1 teaspoon dried thyme, crushed

1 can (28 ounces) no-salt crushed tomatoes, undrained

1 can (14$^1/_2$ ounces or so) no-salt diced tomatoes, undrained (yep, you can buy the tomatoes in any form in the can, whole will work if that's all the no-salt-added canned tomatoes your grocer carries, and crush, chop or otherwise change to meet your needs)

1$^1/_2$ cups salt-free beef broth

12 ounces dark beer

$^1/_2$ cup tomato paste (this one is harder to find without sodium, I calculated the recipe's sodium content based on Contadina, DelMonte, and Progresso brands which are pretty reasonable in terms of sodium contribution)

1 tablespoon honey

4 cups black beans prepared from dry state as above (would take about $^2/_3$ of a pound bag of dry beans before you prepare them as above)

Fresh chopped cilantro

Brown the ground beef in a stockpot over medium heat 8–10 minutes until loose and no longer pink. Remove with slotted spoon and pour off drippings. Heat olive oil in pot over medium. When shimmering, add onions and bell peppers, cook and stir 3–4 minutes until crisp-tender. Stir in jalapeño and garlic, continuing to cook another 3–4 minutes until all vegetables are tender. Return beef to pot along with seasonings; cook and stir 2–3 minutes until you just love all those aromas. Stir in all tomatoes, beef, beer, paste, and honey. Bring to a boil; reduce heat. Cover and simmer about 45 minutes, then uncover. Stir in beans and continue to simmer, uncovered now until liquid reduces and chili is thickened to desired consistency, stirring occasionally. Serve garnished with cilantro. What cowboy wouldn't love that?

Italian Wedding Soup

Tastes traditional and it's filling!

Serves 4 at 216 milligrams sodium each

Meatballs

$^1/_2$ pound ground beef or turkey

$^1/_4$ cup chopped flat parsley

2 tablespoons chopped fresh oregano

1 small clove garlic, finely minced

1 slice hearty Italian white bread whirled in a processor to small crumbs

Olive oil

Soup

$^1/_2$ mild cooking onion, diced small

1 stalk celery, diced small

2 medium carrots, diced small

1 quart salt-free chicken or vegetable stock

$^1/_4$ cup white wine if you have some handy

$^1/_2$ cup small pasta such as orzo or Acini di Pepe

1 cup chopped escarole or whole baby spinach leaves

2 tablespoons grated Parmesan cheese

Combine all meatball ingredients but oil. Form into small, rounded teaspoon-sized balls. Brown in hot oil and cook through over medium heat, about 5–6 minutes. Remove and set aside to drain. Remove all but 2 tablespoons pan drippings.

Cook onion, celery, and carrots in remaining hot oil over medium-low heat, stirring frequently for 6–8 minutes until softened but not browned. Add stock, bring to a boil and reduce to medium. Add wine, pasta, and escarole (not spinach) and simmer about 5 minutes. Stir in meatballs and spinach if using, and simmer another 2–3 minutes until pasta and escarole (if using) are tender and meatballs are done. Serve sprinkled with half a tablespoon of grated cheese.

Fish Chowder

If you can think to save shells from shrimp, or other shellfish, freeze them and when you have enough, use them to make stock and replace the chicken broth with it in this soup.

Serves 4 at 191 milligrams sodium each

About $^1/_2$ pound firm-fleshed fish such as flounder or cod, thawed if frozen

$^1/_2$ pound peeled and deveined raw shrimp, thawed if frozen

1/2 cup chopped onion
1 clove garlic, minced
1 tablespoon olive oil
1 tablespoon unsalted butter
1 15-ounce can no salt added diced tomatoes with the juice
1 cup salt-free chicken broth
2–3 medium red or gold boiling potatoes, washed and cubed
1 teaspoon Creole Seasoning (see page 53)
1 cup frozen, salt-free corn
1/2 cup canned evaporated milk
2 tablespoons heavy cream
2 tablespoons chopped fresh parsley or chives

Cut fish into bite-sized pieces; set aside. Heat oil and butter over medium in 3- to 4-quart pot. Add onion, stir cooking until almost soft, about 8–10 minutes. Add garlic, continue to stir occasionally until onion and garlic are translucent, not browned. Stir in tomatoes, broth, and potatoes. Bring to a boil and reduce to simmer. Cover and simmer until potatoes are almost tender. Add Creole seasoning, corn, and seafood. Cover and simmer about 4–5 minutes until shrimp are pink and pieces of fish are opaque. Gently stir in evaporated milk and cream. Do not boil. Serve each bowlful sprinkled with a half-tablespoon of parsley or chives.

Chicken and Bean Stew

Be sure to read through the discussion about preparing dried beans on page 70. Remember that canned beans are like any canned vegetable: you have to find them canned salt-free or cook them from scratch. But that's how Grandma did it, and darn, it just tastes better, anyway.

Serves 4 at 375 milligrams sodium each

2 pounds mixed bone-in skinless chicken parts
2 teaspoons olive oil
10 ounces pearl onions; peeled and halved
3 carrots; diced
5 cloves garlic; chopped
2 tablespoons balsamic vinegar
1 teaspoon liquid smoke
1 cup dry white wine

4 cups cooked cannelloni or Great Northern beans
2 teaspoons fresh rosemary; chopped, (or 1 tablespoon dried)
2 cups sodium-free chicken broth
Freshly ground black pepper; to taste

Heat the olive oil in a large, nonstick soup pot over medium-high heat. Add chicken and brown on all sides. Add pearl onions, carrots, and garlic; sauté until onions are lightly browned. Stir in balsamic vinegar, liquid smoke, and white wine; bring to a boil and then simmer over medium-low heat until the liquid is reduced by about one third. Stir in beans, rosemary and chicken broth. Bring back to a simmer, reduce heat to low, cover and let cook for 20 minutes.

Dilled Potato-Leek Soup

The dill adds a great flavor.

Makes 2 hearty servings at 119 mg. sodium each.

1 cup sliced leeks (white portion only)
1 celery rib, chopped
1 1/2 teaspoons unsalted butter
2 cups salt-free chicken broth
1 1/2 cups cubed, peeled Yukon Gold potatoes (2 medium)
1 large carrot, finely chopped
1/2 teaspoon dried thyme
1/4 teaspoon white pepper
1/2 cup buttermilk
1 1/2 teaspoons snipped fresh dill or 1/2 teaspoon dried
Shredded leeks for garnish

In a large saucepan, sauté leeks and celery in butter until tender. Stir in the broth, potatoes, carrot, thyme, salt and pepper. Bring to a boil. Reduce heat; cover and simmer for 10–15 minutes or until vegetables are tender. Cool slightly.

Transfer to a blender, cover, and process until smooth. Return to the pan. Or, if you have an immersion hand blender, here's a good time to pull it out. Whisk a small amount of soup into buttermilk; return all to the pan, stirring constantly. Add dill; heat through (do not boil).

Garnish with shredded leeks or more fresh dill if desired. Yield: 3¾ cups.

Quick breads get their rise from baking powder or baking soda, as compared to yeast breads that require long rising times before baking. Yeast-free quick breads like banana bread, scones, and all kinds of muffins are a snap to prepare, if you remember a few caveats:

• Stick with the pan size in the recipe.

• Don't grease the sides of the bread pan. The batter will rise better if it can grip the sides and climb up without slipping.

• Measure carefully to keep the texture right. Too much or little of anything can make your bread too wet or dry.

• That especially includes fruit and vegetables—if it says 1 cup of berries, don't use 1½, because it may make your batter too wet. Be sure to prep your fruits, veggies, and nuts so the batter doesn't have to sit and wait. It may do too much rising while you are chopping and shredding the add-ins!

• Don't beat bread batters; it incorporates too much air and toughens the gluten.

• Don't try to cut the fresh bread until it cools a good bit to avoid crumbling and mashing.

• Store wrapped, cooled quick breads in the fridge a week or the freezer a month.

Sour Cream Blueberry Muffins

Very tasty!

Makes one dozen at 74 milligrams sodium each

$1/3$ cup unsalted butter
1 cup sugar
1 egg
1 teaspoon vanilla
2 cups flour
2 teaspoons baking powder
$3/4$ cup milk
$1/2$ cup sour cream
1 cup blueberries, fresh or frozen

Preheat oven to 375°. Cream first 4 ingredients. In a separate bowl, sift flour and baking powder together. Add to creamed mixture alternately with milk and sour cream. Fold in blueberries. Spoon into greased muffin tins (something that works well for me is to use paper cupcake liners but spray lightly inside the paper liner with nonstick cooking spray). Sprinkle with crumb topping made by mixing together $1/3$ cup unsalted butter + $1/3$ cup flour + $1/3$ cup brown sugar + $1/2$ teaspoon cinnamon. Bake 20–25 minutes.

Honey Sweet Potato Biscuits

A great way to get your vitamin A, sweet potatoes give these a lovely orange, as well as a texture that is light and still holds up to a drizzle of honey.

Makes one dozen at 92 milligrams sodium each

2 cups flour
1 tablespoon baking powder
$1/4$ cup shortening
2 tablespoons grated orange peel (2 teaspoons dried)
$3/4$ cup sweet potatoes, mashed (One large sweet should do it. Cooks in about 5 minutes in the microwave.)
$1/3$ cup honey
$1/2$ cup milk

Combine flour and baking powder; cut in shortening until mixture resembles size of small peas. Add peel, sweet potato and honey; mix well. Add enough milk to make soft but not sticky dough. Knead lightly on a flour-dusted surface. Divide dough into 12 equal parts. Form into flatten balls. Place on ungreased baking sheets. Bake in preheated 400 degree oven 14–16 minutes or until lightly browned. Don't overbake! Serve warm.

Fresh Peach Muffins

These will cost you 125 milligrams sodium each but they sure taste like summer!

Makes one dozen at 125 milligrams sodium each

2 cups flour
1 cup milk
$1/2$ cup sugar
1 egg
6 tablespoons unsalted butter, melted
4 teaspoons baking powder
1 cup fresh peaches, chopped

Sift dry ingredients into bowl. Combine liquid ingredients and stir into dry just until moistened. Fold in peaches, spoon into greased or cooking spray prepared tins. Sprinkle with sugar. Bake in preheated oven at 400° for 25 minutes.

My Favorite Blueberry Muffins

My favorite because it's easy, fairly low fat, and very delicious!

Makes one dozen at 100 milligrams sodium each

2 cup flour
$1/2$ cup sugar
1 tablespoon baking powder
1 teaspoon lemon peel (1/2 teaspoon if using dried)
$1/2$ teaspoon pumpkin pie spice
$3/4$ cup milk
1 egg
$1/3$ cup oil
1 cup blueberries, fresh or frozen

Preheat oven to 400°. Line muffin tins with paper cups and spray lightly with nonstick cooking spray. In a medium bowl, combine dry ingredients; mix well. In measuring cup, beat milk, egg and oil with a fork until frothy. Pour egg mixture into dry ingredients and quickly stir with fork just until moistened. Lumpy is good. Fold in berries. Spoon gently into tins to $2/3$ full. Bake 20–22 minutes or until wooden pick comes out clean. To cool, tilt each muffin up slightly on its side so the bottoms don't get soggy. Cool in pan 5 minutes then remove to rack. Dip tops of warm muffins in melted unsalted butter and sprinkle with cinnamon sugar if desired.

Lemon Loaves

Makes 2 scrumptious loaves, 10 slices each.

Each slice contains 105 milligrams sodium

1 cup unsalted butter, softened
2 cups sugar
4 eggs
3 cups all-purpose flour
1/2 teaspoon salt, measure very carefully
1/2 teaspoon baking soda
1 cup buttermilk
Grated zest of one lemon
1 cup unsalted nuts, chopped, if you like them, just as good with none
Juice of 3 lemons
1 cup powdered sugar

Cream butter and sugar. Beat in eggs, one at a time. Sift together flour, salt and soda. Add to egg mixture alternately with buttermilk. Stir in zest and nuts. Pour into 2 greased loaf pans and bake in oven preheated to 350° for one hour. Combine lemon juice and powdered sugar. As soon as loaves come out of oven, prick all over with a fork or long pick and cover with lemon syrup before removing from pans. Cool before slicing. Freezes very well. You'll get rave reviews on this one.

Peanut Butter and Jelly Muffins

These are soooo good and only 95 milligrams sodium each with unsalted peanut butter. The grocery store I use carries its own brand of peanut butter made with nothing added at all and it's excellent, so it can be done!

Makes 12 at 95 milligrams sodium each with unsalted peanut butter

2 cups flour
1/3 cup sugar
1 tablespoon baking powder
1/2 cup smooth unsalted peanut butter
1 cup milk
1 egg
1/4 cup oil
1/2 cup grape jelly

Combine dry ingredients and mix in peanut butter until crumbly. Add milk, egg and oil stirring just till blended. Spoon half the batter into muffin tin with greased paper liners. Spoon 1 tablespoon jelly into center of each and cover with remaining batter. Bake 400° for 18–20 minutes until lightly browned.

Rosemary-Corn Muffins with Marmalade

I've made these using the orange marmalade with Irish whiskey in it, oh, yeah!

6 tasty muffins at 143 mg. sodium each

1/2 cup flour
1/2 cup cornmeal
3 tablespoons sugar
1 1/4 teaspoons baking powder
1/4 teaspoon baking soda
2 teaspoons minced fresh rosemary (use 3/4 teaspoon crushed dried if you have no fresh)
1 egg
1/3 cup sour cream
2 tablespoons orange marmalade

In a medium bowl, combine dry ingredients. In another bowl, combine the rest and stir gently into dry ingredients just till moistened. Divide into 6 muffin cups that were lightly coated with cooking spray, or use paper muffin liners. Bake in preheated 375° oven 16–18 minutes. Cool slightly before removing from pan; serve warm or split and toasted.

Batter Beer Bread

The beer substitutes for yeast and makes it a quick rise so you can eat it sooner. Do measure the baking powder and slice carefully. It makes 12 slices at 125 mg. sodium each—now don't spoil it by using salted butter! Any beer will work; change the one you choose and change the flavor. You can up or down the sugar a bit if you like it more or less sweet, and you can add whatever else you like—seeds, garlic powder (not salt, of course), and any herbs. You can even make this as muffins.

Each slice contains 125 milligrams sodium

3 cups unbleached flour
1/4 cup sugar
3 scant teaspoons baking powder
12 ounces any beer you like (of course I tested this with Guinness . . .)

Preheat oven to 350°. Lightly grease or spray a loaf pan. Combine flour, sugar, baking powder, and any extras you may want to use (my tasters loved it with toasted caraway seeds added), in a large bowl. Stir in beer. Add a little more flour if it seems very sticky, but it will be a stickier dough than that of regular yeast bread. Let it rest 30–45 minutes and bake 50–55 minutes.

Banana Bread

Delicious. Change what you want as long as you respect the sodium content. Made as presented it will provide 10 slices at 175 mg. sodium each.

10 slices at 175 milligrams sodium each

$2^{1}/_{4}$ cups flour (you can up the fiber by switching the $^{1}/_{4}$ cup to whole wheat flour)

$1^{1}/_{2}$ teaspoons baking powder

$^{1}/_{2}$ teaspoon baking soda

1 8-ounce package cream cheese, softened

$^{1}/_{4}$ cup (half a stick) unsalted butter

1 cup sugar

1 cup fully ripe bananas, about 3 medium, well mashed with 1 teaspoon lemon juice

2 eggs, lightly beaten

1 teaspoon vanilla

$^{1}/_{2}$ teaspoon ground cinnamon (or try apple pie spice)

1 cup chopped nuts of your choice if you like them— unsalted of course

Preheat oven to 350°. Grease and flour a 9x5-inch loaf pan. Combine dry ingredients; set aside. In large bowl, beat cream cheese, butter, and sugar until fluffy and well combined, about 3 minutes. Beat in bananas, eggs, vanilla, and cinnamon. Stir in dry ingredients gently just until combined. Fold in nuts. Transfer to prepared pan, smooth surface of batter, and bake 60–70 minutes until toothpick comes out clean. Cool in pan a few minutes then turn out to finish cooling on a rack. Don't cut until it's cooled significantly or it won't slice nicely.

Pumpkin Bread

Makes 2 loaves, 10 slices each.

Each slice contains 180 milligrams sodium

$3^{1}/_{2}$ cups flour

2 teaspoons baking soda

$^{1}/_{2}$ teaspoon salt

1 teaspoon cinnamon

$^{1}/_{4}$ teaspoon nutmeg

3 cups sugar

1 cup olive oil

4 eggs, slightly beaten

2 cups pumpkin (This is a rare vegetable that tends not to be "sodium-ized" in the can, but read the label to be certain.)

1 cup water

Grease and flour 2 regular loaf pans. Preheat oven to 350°. Combine dry ingredients. Combine remaining ingredients and add to dry. Stir gently only until just moistened. Bake 75 minutes.

Apple Fritters

A tasty side dish or eye-opener

Serves 4 at 46 milligrams sodium each

2 eggs separated

$^{1}/_{2}$ cup milk

2 teaspoons vanilla

1 tablespoon unsalted butter, melted

1 cup all purpose or unbleached flour

1 tablespoon sugar

1 cup olive oil

4 apples, cored and sliced $^{1}/_{4}$-inch thick

Whisk egg yolks, milk and melted butter together. Stir in flour and sugar combining well. Chill one hour. Heat the oil in a heavy skillet, (I use a cast iron skillet), over medium heat. Beat the egg whites until stiff but not dry. Fold into batter. Dip apple slices into batter to coat completely. Remove with fork and gently place in heated oil. Cook in small batches until deep golden brown, about $1^{1}/_{2}$ minutes per side. Drain briefly on paper towels and serve dusted with confectioners sugar or real maple syrup.

Homemade Stuffing

Store bought low-sodium white bread isn't so good by itself, but in this stuffing the bread works well because of all the flavor added to it. Although I haven't had much luck finding nationally known brands of low-sodium bread, my grocery store has its own brand at 5 milligrams per slice. Don't be shy about asking your grocer to stock low-sodium bread or any other low-sodium ingredients you need.

Six 1-cup servings at only 48 milligrams sodium each

1 1-pound loaf, 20 slices, low-sodium bread

1 cup diced celery

$^{1}/_{2}$ cup chopped onion

4 tablespoons unsalted butter

$^{1}/_{2}$ cup milk

$^{1}/_{2}$–$^{3}/_{4}$ cup homemade no-salt Chicken Stock or Turkey Stock (see soup section)

2 teaspoons dried crumbled sage

2 teaspoons dried parsley

Tear bread into chunks. Combine all ingredients in large bowl adding enough stock to moisten thoroughly without saturating. Turn into 2-quart casserole which has been sprayed with non-stick cooking spray. Bake $^{3}/_{4}$ to $1^{1}/_{4}$ hours depending on the temperature the other food in the oven may require and on the moisture content of the stuffing. If baking alone it should take about $^{3}/_{4}$ of an hour at 375°. Vary the herbs to suit your taste.

Now a Word about Yeast Breads

Yes, you can make them with no salt. Those recipes tend to turn out tougher bread and flat-tasting loaves. They also rise funny. Store bought no- or low-salt bread isn't so bad because they have all those chemicals at their disposal that fool our taste buds into thinking it's more like ordinary bread. I don't like homemade bread without salt, so to be practical, I'm not going to try to convince you that you should try them. I will offer you a couple of low-salt versions that I think are worth a try, however. Do remember that each quarter teaspoon of salt provides 590 milligrams of sodium. And it's important to get the prescribed number of slices from a loaf of homemade bread to account correctly for the sodium content, no matter how tempting fresh-from-the-oven bread smells and tastes. These yeast bread recipes can easily become rolls. When you reach the point where you would shape them into loaves for the final rising, cut or pull them apart into roll shapes instead. You can bake them in muffin tins or put them an inch apart on a cookie sheet. Reduce the rising and baking time of course. I like to make cloverleaf rolls by taking the amount of dough for each roll and breaking it into three pieces. Then I put the three pieces together into a lightly greased muffin cup to bake back together again. If you want, you can very lightly brush the tops of the rolls after baking with melted, unsalted butter to keep the crust soft. That said, try these:

White Bread

This makes one loaf of 12 slices.

Each slice contains 105 milligrams sodium

$^3/_4$ cup water
$^2/_3$ cup milk
1 tablespoon shortening
4 to 4$^1/_4$ cups all-purpose or unbleached flour, divided
2 tablespoons sugar
$^1/_2$ teaspoon salt
1 package ($^1/_4$-ounce) active dry yeast

Combine water, milk and shortening in medium sauce - pan. Heat over medium high 2–3 minutes until liquid is about 120°. In large mixer bowl, combine 2 cups flour, sugar, salt and yeast on low speed. Add warm liquid and beat on medium about 2 minutes. Add another $^1/_2$ cup flour, scrape sides of bowl well and beat another 15–20 seconds on low then turn up to high for 2 minutes more. Scrape sides of bowl often. All this beating sure saves kneading time. Switch to a wooden spoon and stir in enough more flour to make moderately stiff dough. Turn out onto floured board and knead until smooth and elastic, 8–10 minutes. Place in greased bowl turning once to grease top and cover. Let rise in a warm place 1 to 1$^1/_4$ hours until doubled. Punch down, turn out on floured board, cover and let rest 10–15 minutes. Shape into loaf and place in greased loaf pan. Cover and let rise 35–45 minutes until not quite double. Bake in oven preheated to 375° 40–45 minutes until golden and hollow sounding when tapped gently. If it browns too quickly, cover with a tent of aluminum foil for last 10 minutes or so of baking. Cool 5 minutes in pan then remove to rack to finish cooling. Now that you've checked out the plain stuff, try the easy variations on the following page.

Herb Bread

Choose your favorite herb or herb combination (some that work well for me are thyme, lemon thyme, basil, flat-leaf Italian parsley and chives). Use about 2$^1/_2$ tablespoons chopped fresh, or put 4 teaspoons dried in a little water to soften first, then drain. Prepare the dough as above. When shaping, roll out into 15x9-inch rectangle. Spread thinly with a tablespoon of unsalted butter and sprinkle with herbs evenly to within $^1/_2$ inch of edges. Roll dough jellyroll fashion starting at a short edge. Pinch seam together and place in prepared pan tucking edges under. Continue to rise, bake and cool as above.

Spice Swirl

As above, prepare and roll out dough, spread thinly with 1 tablespoon unsalted butter. This time, sprinkle with a combination of $^1/_4$ cup brown sugar and 1 teaspoon of your favorite spice. Try cinnamon, nutmeg, (especially freshly grated), or cardamom. You could add raisins or chopped unsalted nuts here, too. Roll and finish as above.

Oat Bran Bread

Looking for a hearty sandwich bread? This not only tastes great, it offers the healthy benefit of oats and works well with salt-free peanut butter or try slices of leftover roast chicken, home made mayo, and thin apple slices.

Each slice contains 95 milligrams sodium

4$^1/_2$ to 5 cups all-purpose or unbleached flour
1 cup uncooked oat bran hot cereal
1 cup quick-cooking oats
$^1/_3$ cup molasses
3 tablespoons shortening
1 teaspoon salt
2 packages active dry yeast
2 cups very warm water (120°–130°)
1 egg white, slightly beaten
1 tablespoon cold water
Quick-cooking oats

Combine 2 cups of the flour, bran cereal, oats, molasses, shortening, salt and yeast in large bowl. Beat in warm water on low for a minute or so then increase to medium for another minute. Stir in another cup of flour and beat on medium-high 2–3 minutes, scraping sides of bowl often. By hand, stir in enough more flour to make a moderately firm dough that's easy to handle. Turn out onto floured board and knead 8–10 minutes adding more flour as needed. Dough should be firm and elastic. Grease a large bowl with shortening and put dough in bowl, turning to bring up greased top. Cover and let rise in warm place about an hour until double in bulk. Spray 2 loaf pans with nonstick cooking spray. Punch down dough and let it rest 10 minutes. Divide into 2 loaves and shape. Place in prepared pans and cover. Let rise another hour until almost doubled. Mix egg white and 1 tablespoon cold water; brush over loaves. Sprinkle with oats. Bake in lower third of oven preheated to 375° for 35–40 minutes or until deeply golden brown and hollow sounding to a light tap. Cool in pans 10 minutes then remove to wire racks to finish cooling.

Honey Whole Wheat Bread

This makes one loaf, 16 slices containing 94 milligrams sodium (depending on your cereal choice) and the extra benefit of 3 grams of fiber.

Each slice contains 94 milligrams sodium

2$\frac{1}{2}$ to 2$\frac{3}{4}$ cups all-purpose or unbleached flour

$\frac{1}{2}$ teaspoon salt

1 package active dry yeast

1$\frac{1}{2}$ cups very warm water (120°–130°)

$\frac{1}{4}$ cup honey

1 tablespoon olive oil

1 cup whole wheat flour

1 cup high-fiber bran cereal (Kellogg's All-Bran Extra Fiber seems to have the least sodium content of all the high fiber cereals I've checked)

Mix 1½ cups of the all-purpose or unbleached flour, the salt and yeast in a large bowl. Add the water, honey, and oil, and beat on low speed a minute or so. Scraping the bowl sides frequently, beat another minute on medium. Stir in the whole wheat flour and beat on medium another 2–3 minutes. By hand, stir in cereal and then enough remaining all-purpose or unbleached flour a little at a time until dough is easy to handle. Turn out onto floured board and knead 8–10 minutes until smooth and elastic. Grease a large bowl with shortening and place dough in bowl, turning to bring up greased top. Cover and rise an hour or a little longer until doubled. Punch down and shape into round loaf. Place on greased cookie sheet and cover. Let rise in warm place about 40 minutes or till almost doubled. Bake in oven preheated to 350° for 30–35 minutes. Cool on wire rack.

Potato Bread

This is a recipe for a bread machine. If you have one you know you can adapt regular bread recipes for the machine, but here's one you don't have to do the calculations for. It's a one-pound loaf that works best cut into 10 slices. Each will give you 115 milligrams of sodium. It's one of my favorites because it has a delicate texture, and it's a cinch to throw together.

Each slice contains 115 milligrams sodium

6 ounces warm water

1 tablespoon unsalted butter

1 egg

2 tablespoons buttermilk powder

2 tablespoons dry milk

2$\frac{1}{2}$ tablespoons mashed potato flakes

$\frac{1}{2}$ teaspoon salt

2 cups + 2 tablespoons bread flour

4 teaspoons sugar

$\frac{1}{2}$ teaspoon yeast

Put ingredients in pan in the order recommended by your machine's manufacturer. Set for one pound loaf, medium crust. Don't use the delay cycle because of the egg. Cool on rack.

Flavorful Breadsticks

Here's an easy to make way to enjoy low-sodium but very tasty bread. You'll get 24 bread sticks at 79 mg. sodium each. Experiment with any non-salt-containing flavorful substitutes for the herbs and seeds, maybe finely minced and sautéed garlic or onion?

24 breadsticks at 79 milligrams sodium each

$\frac{3}{4}$ cup milk

1 tablespoon sugar

$\frac{3}{4}$ teaspoon salt

1 tablespoon unsalted butter

1 packet ($\frac{1}{4}$ ounce) quick-rise yeast

$\frac{1}{4}$ cup warm water

3 to 3 $\frac{1}{4}$ cups all-purpose or bread flour

1 egg white, beaten

1 tablespoon warm water

Minced herbs or seeds

In a saucepan, heat milk, sugar, salt and butter. Cool to lukewarm. Dissolve yeast in warm water. Combine milk mixture, yeast, and 1½ cups flour; beat until smooth. Add enough remaining flour to form a stiff dough. Turn out onto a lightly floured surface and knead until smooth and elastic, about 4–5 minutes. Place in a greased bowl, turning once to grease top. Cover and let rise in a warm place until doubled, about 30 minutes.

Punch dough down. Pinch off golf ball-size pieces; roll into pencil-size strips. Place on greased baking sheets 1 inch apart. Cover and let rise 15 minutes. Combine egg white and water; brush over sticks. Sprinkle with herbs or seeds. Bake at 375° for 10 minutes or until golden.

No-Knead Bread

When you taste this with a little jam or pumpkin butter you will "need" more! Start this the day before you want to serve it and accept all the compliments. A wedge will cost you a chunk of your sodium allowance, so be sure the sodium content of the rest of your meal is on the very low side.

10 wedges at 177 milligrams sodium each

3 cups unbleached flour

$\frac{3}{4}$ teaspoon salt (measure carefully)

$\frac{1}{4}$ teaspoon active dry yeast

1$\frac{2}{3}$ cups warm water (should be 120° to 130°)

5–8 tablespoons additional flour

1 tablespoon corn meal

In a large bowl, whisk 3 cups flour, salt, and yeast. Stir in warm water till moistened, batter will be soft and sticky. At this point, cover and let stand at room temperature for at least 4 hours but you can leave it for as long as 24 hours.

Sprinkle 3–4 tablespoons flour onto a sheet of parchment or wax paper; you can use your counter or cutting board, but its very sticky and you will probably need a bench scraper or spatula to scrape it off. Turn batter out onto flour and sprinkle another 1–2 tablespoons flour over the top. Fold it over on itself and sprinkle another 1–2 tablespoons over the dough. Cover and rest at least 15 minutes up to 30 minutes.

Pull out an oven-safe 5- or 6-quart Dutch oven, and grease the bottom and sides. Sprinkle with cornmeal over bottom and about 2 inches up sides. Move dough into the pot. Cover and let rise another hour or two until it has risen another inch. Preheat oven to 450° and bake, covered with lid or foil, for 30 minutes. Uncover and bake 10–15 minutes until golden brown. Turn out onto rack to cool immediately. If you like, brush top with melted, unsalted butter. You can sprinkle with minced herbs or toasted seeds as you like.

Chuck Wagon Bread

Similar to pita breads, this is round fried bread that supposedly traces its origins back to the cowboy days. As you might suspect from its history, you can take your cast iron pan out to the grill or campfire and cook it there like trail cooks did!

Makes 8 "loaves" each for 94 mg. sodium

$1/2$ cup boiling water

$3/4$ cup cold milk

1 teaspoon white sugar

$1^1/2$ teaspoons active dry yeast

1 egg, beaten

2 tablespoons unsalted butter, melted and cooled

$1/4$ teaspoon salt

$1/4$ teaspoon ground nutmeg

4 cups all purpose flour

In a large bowl, stir together the water, milk, and sugar. Sprinkle the yeast over the top, and let stand for 5 minutes to dissolve.

Stir the egg and butter into the yeast mixture, then stir in the salt (measure carefully), nutmeg, and 2 cups of the flour. Mix until everything is well blended. Mix in remaining flour, ½ cup at a time until the dough pulls away from the side of the bowl. Turn out onto a floured surface, and knead for 10 minutes (no cheating!). Place dough into a greased bowl, and let rise until doubled in size, about an hour.

Divide dough into 8 balls, and let rest for another 15 minutes. Roll each ball out to 8 to 10 inches in diameter.

Heat a cast-iron skillet over medium-high heat. Fry (no need for oil in the cast iron pan) each of the pieces of bread for 30 to 60 seconds on each side, or until light to medium brown spots appear. Keep covered with a damp cloth, or store in a plastic bag until serving.

Herbed and Flavored Butters

Unsalted butter on your bread can be pretty flat and blah tasting, but before you slap on big pats of the regular salted stuff, consider making herb butter instead. It's very simple. Take softened unsalted butter and beat it a bit with a big spoon. Then stir in your favorite herb. Start with about ½ teaspoon chopped herb to 2 or 3 tablespoons butter and adjust to taste. Almost any herb will due. My favorite combination is 1 tablespoon fresh lemon thyme leaves to a stick (8 tablespoons) of unsalted butter. Fresh is best, but if that's not what's available, use dried; just remember to use about ⅓ of the fresh amount and let it stand awhile to freshen the herbs and blend the flavors. You can also make sweet butters by adding a touch of honey and some orange or lemon zest. Makes breakfast extra special. Let your creativity help you experiment with combinations of flavors you and your family will enjoy.

Another hint: Jams and jellies help, too. And if you're lucky enough to have the time and talent to make your own, you have ultimate control over the contents of the "fruits" of your labors. There are however, for the rest of us, some good choices in the grocery stores with little or no sodium. So check out the labels and offer yourself some variety.

For the most part, salads are not going to be a problem. After all they are usually fresh vegetables and we know that's low-sodium eating. When you want potato or macaroni salad, just use low sodium ingredients and cooking methods (e.g. no salt in the cooking water) and leave out the added salt. For tuna salad, use the canned tuna that is processed without salt (yes it does exist, I've bought it). Check your recipe ingredients against the sodium tables in this book and calculate a reasonable, serving-sized portion. You don't need to throw out all your old recipes, just be cautious. Dressing is another story. That's tough to get without salt. Give these a try:

Italian Dressing

This recipe makes about one cup and the whole cupful only has 48 milligrams of sodium. Adjust the herbs to taste.

Makes 1 cup at 3 milligrams sodium per tablespoon

$1/4$ cup red wine vinegar (splurge on the good stuff, it's worth the flavor)

$1/3$ cup olive oil (again, this is the time to use the good label)

$1/3$ cup + 1 tablespoon water

$1/4$ teaspoon freshly ground pepper

$1/4$ teaspoon garlic powder (or if feeling energetic, use $1/2$ teaspoon minced garlic)

$1/4$ teaspoon sugar

1 teaspoon fresh lemon juice

$1/2$ teaspoon dried crumbled oregano

$1/2$ teaspoon dried crumbled basil

Combine all ingredients in jar with a tight lid; shake well. Keep refrigerated.

French Dressing

This is a great way to dress up a lettuce wedge or a bowl of fresh veggies.

Makes $3/4$ cup at less than 2 mg. sodium per tablespoon

$1/2$ cup Coleen's Mayonnaise (recipe this section)

$1/4$ cup low-sodium Ketchup (recipe this section)

1 tablespoon minced sweet onion

1 tablespoon minced fresh parsley

Combine thoroughly. Stores for several days in the refrigerator.

Vinaigrette Dressing

Here's a chance to be inventive; try using different flavors of vinegar. There's no sodium in it the way it's presented here.

None. Nadda. Zero. Zip.

$1/3$ cup olive oil

2 tablespoons fresh lemon juice

2 tablespoons tarragon vinegar

1 teaspoon chopped fresh parsley (or $1/2$ teaspoon dried)

$1/4$ teaspoon freshly ground pepper

$1/4$ teaspoon dry mustard powder

1 tablespoon plain low-fat yogurt (optional, but don't skip it if you've never tried it)

Shake it all up in a jar with a tight lid. Keep refrigerated. Trade the parsley for some basil and you can't beat it on sliced tomatoes fresh from a garden.

Raspberry Vinaigrette Dressing

If you love raspberries, this is for you. Try making your own raspberry vinegar.

Makes $1 1/4$ cups at 3 milligrams sodium per tablespoon

$1/2$ cup olive oil

$1/2$ cup raspberry wine vinegar

$1/2$ cup white sugar

2 teaspoons (non-Dijon) prepared mustard

$1/4$ teaspoon dried oregano

$1/4$ teaspoon ground black pepper

In a jar with a tight fitting lid, combine the oil, vinegar, sugar, mustard, oregano and pepper. Shake well and refrigerate until chilled.

Fruit Dressing

This is healthy, but more important, it's full of flavor. Once you try it, consider dressing it up your way. For example, add a little cinnamon, or fresh grated nutmeg. Try switching out the orange juice for pineapple juice.

Makes about $1 1/4$ cups at 10 milligrams sodium per tablespoon

1 cup plain nonfat yogurt

$1/4$ cup orange juice

1–2 teaspoons honey

Blend well and keep in refrigerator, (why do recipes always tell you that— like you might put it on a shelf? Really, now.)

Farmstead Dressing

This is a variation on Ranch. Don't substitute Dijon unless you find a low-sodium brand. Dijon mustard increases the salt quite a bit.

Makes about $1 1/2$ cups or 24 tablespoons at 25 milligrams sodium per tablespoon

1 cup buttermilk (you can reconstitute it from powder, I do that all the time or I'd be throwing out old, unused buttermilk)

$1/4$ cup plain low-fat yogurt

1 tablespoon spicy brown mustard

2 teaspoons minced onion

1 tablespoon chopped fresh dill

1 tablespoon chopped fresh parsley

$1/4$ teaspoon garlic powder

$1/4$ teaspoon freshly grated pepper

Combine in bowl or jar and refrigerate (I can't seem to stop saying that).

Cole Slaw Dressing

Makes about 3/4 cup dressing, enough for 10 cups shredded vegetables. The best part is that there's no sodium in it, so you can use all you want.

None. Nadda. Zero. Zip.

1/2 cup sugar
1/2 cup white wine vinegar
2 tablespoons water
1 teaspoon celery seed
1 teaspoon mustard seed
1/4 teaspoon onion powder

Combine all ingredients in medium saucepan and bring to boil over high heat. Reduce heat and cook 1 minute. Cool to at least room temperature before pouring over vegetables.

Coleen's Mayonnaise

Want to make your own mayonnaise so you can make mayo-based dressings, tartar sauce and bread spread? Try this. If you use fresh lemon juice and the expensive olive oil, you should get enough flavor not to mind the missing salt. Don't use this recipe if you have any concern about your eggs since they don't get cooked in real mayonnaise. Doesn't keep as long as the processed store-bought stuff.

Makes 1 1/2 cups at almost no sodium

1 egg yolk
1 teaspoon dry mustard
1 teaspoon sugar
Dash cayenne red pepper
2 tablespoons fresh lemon juice
1 cup good olive oil

In small mixer bowl, beat egg yolk, dry mustard, sugar and 1 tablespoon of the lemon juice on medium speed until blended. Continue beating on medium adding the oil very slowly, literally one drop at a time. This is key. As the mixture thickens you can speed up this process a little. Slowly stir in remaining lemon juice. Beat well and keep it in the you-know-what.

Winter Fruit Salad

Substitute tangerines for the oranges (you'll need about 5). If you have access to pears or apples, chunk up one or two and toss them in, too. Red grapes make a pretty addition.

Serves 6 at 72 milligrams sodium each

2/3 cup orange juice
2 teaspoons cornstarch

2 tablespoons honey
1/3 cup sour cream
Lettuce leaves
3 oranges, peeled and sliced
2 kiwi fruit, peeled and sliced
2 bananas, peeled and sliced

Stir cornstarch into juice until dissolved. In small saucepan heat over medium-high just till boiling, stirring constantly. Cool one hour, then stir in sour cream. Chill thoroughly. At serving time, arrange lettuce leaves on plates. Then arrange fruit slices over lettuce. Top with dressing.

Cranberry Orange Mold

This makes a beautiful addition to the holiday table. It's also a great way to use some of those pretty molds you have stashed in the back of that high cupboard—yup, that one.

Serves 12 at 52 milligrams sodium each

1 12-ounce package fresh cranberries
1/2 cup sugar
1 1/2 cups boiling water
2 3-ounce packages or 1 6-ounce package cranberry-flavored gelatin mix (you can use any red flavor)
1/2 teaspoon cinnamon
1 1/2 cups cold water
1 11-ounce can mandarin oranges, drained
1/2 cup unsalted chopped walnuts, toasted (optional)

Chop the cranberries in food processor, add to sugar, stir and set aside. Combine boiling water with gelatin and cinnamon in large bowl, stirring 2 minutes until thoroughly dissolved. Stir in cold water and chill in refrigerator 1 to 1¼ hours until thickened but not set. Stir in cranberries, oranges and nuts. Spray 6-cup mold with non-stick cooking spray and pour in the gelatin mixture. Chill until set. Unmold when firm.

Old Fashioned Potato Salad

So, you were invited to a picnic and you are supposed to bring a dish to pass. Here's a great way to help yourself maintain your low-sodium commitment while eating away from home and introduce others to a tasty way to control their salt intake, too.

Serves 6 at 81 milligrams sodium each

5 potatoes, cooked and cooled
3 eggs, hard cooked
1 cup chopped celery
1/2 cup chopped onion
1/2 teaspoon dried thyme (add as much as you like)
1/4 teaspoon garlic powder

1 tablespoon prepared mustard
Ground black pepper to taste
1¹/₂ cups no-salt mayonnaise (see recipe this section)

Bring a large pot of unsalted water to a boil. Add potatoes; cook until tender but still firm, about 15 minutes. Drain, cool, peel and chop. Place eggs in a saucepan and cover with cold water. Bring water to a boil; cover, remove from heat, and let eggs stand in hot water for 10–12 minutes. Remove from hot water, cool, peel and chop. In a large bowl, combine the potatoes, eggs, celery, onion, thyme, garlic powder, mustard, pepper, and mayonnaise. Mix together well and refrigerate until chilled.

Avocado and Mango Salad

This combines creamy avocado and sweet mango with a tart lime and spice dressing.

Serves 4 at 12 milligrams sodium each

2 medium ripe mangos
2 medium firm but ripe avocados
Romaine or leaf-lettuce leaves
Lime dressing:
4 tablespoons Key lime juice
1 pinch (to your taste) cayenne pepper
1 tablespoon sesame oil
3 tablespoons light oil such as canola

Peel and cut mangos up into ¹/₂- to ³/₄-inch cubes. Halve avocado, remove pit and peel and chop into ¹/₂- to ³/₄-inch cubes. Gently whisk dressing ingredients in medium bowl. Add mango and avocado pieces and toss gently in dressing. Serve on lettuce leaves.

Italian Pasta Salad

Makes 4 hearty servings of a very traditional salad.

Serves 4 at 40 milligrams sodium each

4 ounces corkscrew pasta (rotini)
¹/₂ small zucchini
2 ounces reduced-fat provolone cheese, grated
¹/₂ cup broccoli florets, chopped
¹/₂ cup finely chopped sweet red peppers
¹/₂ cup finely chopped green peppers
¹/₂ small red onion, sliced
3 tablespoons grated Parmesan cheese
3 tablespoons snipped fresh parsley
¹/₂ cup homemade low-sodium Italian salad dressing
¹/₂ teaspoon dried oregano or 1¹/₂ teaspoons fresh oregano, minced
2 tablespoons homemade low-sodium Italian salad dressing (if necessary)

Cook the pasta according to the directions on the package, without the salt, of course. Drain well. Transfer the pasta to a large bowl. Cut the zucchini lengthwise into quarters, then thinly slice it (you should have about ¹/₂ cup). Add the zucchini to the pasta. Then add the provolone cheese, broccoli, red and green peppers, onion, Parmesan cheese, and parsley. Add the ¹/₂ cup dressing, then toss until the pasta mixture is coated. Sprinkle with the oregano. Cover and chill for at least 2 hours to blend the flavors. If necessary, add the 2 tablespoons dressing to moisten the salad. Gently toss.

Waldorf Salad

Makes 4 large servings.

Serves 4 at 26 milligrams sodium each

2 cups chopped apples
1¹/₂ teaspoons fresh lemon juice
¹/₃ cup chopped celery
¹/₄ cup raisins
3 tablespoons chopped walnuts
¹/₃ cup vanilla yogurt
¹/₄ cup frozen whipped topping, thawed
¹/₂ teaspoon grated lemon peel
¹/₈ teaspoon ground nutmeg

Place the apples in a medium bowl. Sprinkle with the lemon juice, then toss. Add the celery, raisins and walnuts. Place the yogurt in a small bowl. Add the whipped topping and gently fold in. Then gently fold in the lemon peel and nutmeg. Add the dressing to the apple mixture. Gently fold in until the apple mixture is coated.

Herb Vinegars

One last thought before we leave the subject of salad. All those herbs make great herb vinegar and it's simple to make your own. Use wine vinegar for the best flavor and warm it some in a saucepan. Although there are those who would say this step isn't needed, I find I extract more flavor this way. Decant it into jars or bottles that are very clean. Add washed-and-dried bunches of the herb you want to use. I usually chop up the herb for better extraction once again. Later I strain it well through cheesecloth and return it to the jar with a single sprig of the herb used. It's a pretty gift this way too. Use stronger herbs such as basil or oregano in red wine vinegar and more delicate ones such as tarragon or thyme in the white wine vinegar. Even if you never use it, it will look pretty on a kitchen windowsill.

Thank goodness fruit is not naturally salty, nor do we normally find it salted. Cans of fruit are exempt from the never-open-one rule that applies to most canned foods. But crazy as it sounds, once it gets added to a recipe, we have to be mindful of the sodium we will consume with that fruit. Case in point: crisps, cobblers, pies, and tarts all involve the addition of toppings, biscuits, pie crust, and the like, made with sodium-containing ingredients such as baking powder, baking soda, and the ubiquitous salt. Bam! We need work-arounds. In this section, I have developed a few recipes that will meet our needs for delicious ways to eat fruit and keep it low sodium.

Herbed Summer Peaches

Enjoy this delicious taste of summer with very little work.
Serves 4.

None. Nadda. Zero. Zip.

4–5 medium peaches (nectarines work here, also) peels on, sliced into wedges

1/2 cup white wine, not a dry one, Riesling is about right for this, or use apple juice

1/3 cup, packed, fresh basil leaves, no need to chop

2 tablespoons sugar

Whole basil leaves for garnish

Set aside half the peach wedges. Chop the other half and place in medium saucepan with the wine, basil and sugar (use less sugar if peaches are very sweet). Bring to a boil, reduce heat and simmer 12–15 minutes until slightly thickened. Remove and discard cooked basil. Pour remaining cooked peach mixture into food processor or blender; process until smooth. Stir processed warm peaches with reserved wedges of uncooked peaches. Garnish with fresh basil.

Fresh Peach Tart

What could be easier? This combines a cookie dough crust and a no-bake, fresh as summer filling. Use peaches that are at their peak of ripeness. As an alternative, use canned peaches, but spice them up a bit with a grating or two of fresh nutmeg over the top.

Serves 6 at 120 milligrams sodium each

1 cup flour

1/2 cup sugar

2 teaspoons grated fresh lemon zest (1 teaspoon if using dried)

1/3 cup unsalted butter

1 egg yolk

4 medium fresh peaches, peeled and sliced

2 tablespoons orange juice

1 8-ounce package cream cheese, softened

2 tablespoons powdered sugar

3 tablespoons half-and-half (or substitute peach-flavored liqueur for 1 tablespoon)

1/2 teaspoon freshly grated nutmeg

1/2 teaspoon vanilla

Whipped cream

Mint sprigs

In a medium bowl, combine flour, sugar, and zest. Cut in butter until crumbly. Stir yolk in with a fork. Press into bottom and sides of a 9-inch tart or quiche pan with removable sides. Bake 15 minutes in a 375° oven until golden brown. Cool completely. About 15 minutes

before serving, place peach slices in a bowl and stir gently with orange juice. Let stand 10 minutes. In a medium mixer bowl, combine remaining ingredients; beat until smooth. Remove rim of tart pan. Pour cream cheese mixture into shell and spread evenly. Top with peaches using slotted spoon to remove from bowl and arranging in a spiral pattern. Top each slice with a little dollop of real whipped cream and garnish with a sprig of mint if desired.

Poached Pears

Nothing could be easier and so yummy. Be sure to use unsalted almonds.

Serves 6 at 15 milligrams sodium each

1 29-ounce can pear halves in their own juice, drain pears, put keep the juice

2 tablespoons sugar

2 tablespoons brown sugar

1/2 teaspoon grated nutmeg (freshly grated if you can)

1/2 teaspoon almond extract

1/3 cup sliced almonds

Stir together pear juice, sugar, brown sugar and nutmeg in large skillet. Bring to boiling; reduce heat to medium and cook and stir until sugar dissolves. Remove from heat and stir in almond extract and pears. Let rest 4–5 minutes. Serve sprinkled with almonds. Goes beautifully with vanilla yogurt or ice cream, just remember to count the sodium content in anything you serve with the pears and sauce.

Strawberry Tart

Here's one place that just needs a few grains of salt. It teaches us to use careful restraint.

Serves 6 at 120 milligrams sodium each

1 1/4 cups flour

1/3 cup sugar

1/2 cup unsalted butter, cold and cubed

1/4 teaspoon salt (this really goes against my desire, but the crust tastes too flat without it, so measure carefully and don't think it doesn't count—it definitely does)

8 ounces cream cheese, softened

1/4 cup sugar

2 pounds strawberries, topped and halved

1/4 cup currant jelly, melted

In processor, pulse flour, sugar, butter and salt till crumbly. Press into 9-inch tart pan with removable bottom. Dot with fork, then freeze 15 minutes. Bake in preheated oven, 350° for 25–30 minutes. Cool.

Whisk together cream cheese and sugar. Spread on bottom of cooled tart. Arrange strawberries over filling, pressing gently into cheese. Paint berries with melted currant jelly to give it that bakery-shop shine. Keep chilled.

Blueberry Cobbler

I wait every year for blueberry season; I can't get enough. This is a great way to enjoy these sweet and healthy little juicy tidbits of wonderfulness! And yes, you can use frozen—don't let them thaw. Toss in frozen, reduce water to 3 tablespoons, and enjoy. If you add ice cream, remember to count the sodium in each scoop.

Serves 6 at 120 milligrams sodium each

$1/2$ stick unsalted butter, melted
1 cup flour
$1^1/2$ teaspoons baking powder
$1/4$ cup sugar
$3/4$ cup milk
2 cups fresh blueberries
$1/3$ cup water
$1/2$ cup sugar

Preheat oven to 350°. Pour melted butter into a shallow $1^1/2$-quart baking dish. In a mixing bowl, combine flour, baking powder, sugar, and milk. Pour evenly over the butter. In the same bowl, combine berries, water and sugar. Spoon evenly over batter, but do not stir in. Bake 40–45 minutes. Watch the batter rise to make a buttery crust.

Fruit Salad Hawaiian

Remember, cans of fruit are the only safe cans to open when controlling sodium; can you still find the old can opener?? How would that look on the plate next to Mahi-Mahi on an Island Vacation, (page 103) maybe some Islands of Love for dessert, (page 156) and sip some Grown-Up Hawaiian Punch (page 61) while you dine? Oh, baby, light the tiki and get out the grass skirt! What size coconuts do you wear?

Serves 6 at 35 milligrams sodium each

2 (15 ounce) cans mixed tropical fruit, drained
1 (11 ounce) can Mandarin orange sections, drained
1 ripe banana, sliced
$1^1/4$–$1^3/4$ cups vanilla whole-milk yogurt, however "dressed" you like it (sodium count rises as you come down in fat content, doesn't that just figure?)
1 teaspoon coconut extract
$1/4$ cup sweetened coconut flakes
$1/4$ cup toasted, chopped hazelnuts

Combine fruit in a bowl. Stir coconut extract into vanilla yogurt then fold into fruit. Sprinkle with coconut flakes and nuts. Refrigerate.

Grilled Pineapple

Here's a flexible fruit prepared in many flexible ways! Use your outdoor grill or a grill pan on the kitchen stove. Top with ice cream or whipped cream; serve with pound cake, or just as they are (be sure to count the sodium of whatever you add to these slices). Fresh or canned work equally well. Adjust ingredient amounts to the number of pineapple slices you want to grill.

Serves 2 at 12 milligrams sodium each

4 $1/2$-inch thick pineapple slices
2 tablespoons honey
1 teaspoon ground cinnamon

If using your outdoor grill, prepare grates by scraping clean and lightly oiling them; heat grates to a medium hot level. Indoor grill pan should also be lightly oiled and pre-heated. Lay pineapple slices out on paper towels and brush tops with half the honey. Sprinkle with half the cinnamon and place honey side down on hot grill. Reduce heat to medium and grill 2 or 3 minutes. Honey side will begin to caramelize. Brush tops with remaining honey and sprinkle with remaining cinnamon. Flip and grill on this side another 2 or 3 minutes to caramelize but don't let them cook so much that they fall apart on you. No reason you can't sprinkle with brown sugar instead of honey or cardamom or even nutmeg instead of cinnamon. A pinch of coconut would be a nice way to change it up. Experiment with flavors you like.

All-American Fruit Salad

Red, white and blue fruits make a great salad for any family or patriotic holiday get-together, or just a nice little salad for one or two! Works for breakfast too. Tell me that's not terrific!

Serves 2 at 8 milligrams sodium each

1 medium ripe banana, sliced
1 cup sliced fresh strawberries
$1/2$ cup fresh blueberries
1 tablespoon honey, any flavor you like
Juice of half a lime
2 tablespoons slivered almonds or pine nuts, preferably toasted

Combine fruits, drizzle with honey and lime juice and stir in gently. Sprinkle with nuts.

Fried Cinnamon Apples

The perfect quick and easy side dish for pork.

Serves 2 at 12 milligrams sodium each

3 tablespoons unsalted butter
2 large apples, peeled, cored, and sliced
1/4 cup ground cinnamon
2 tablespoons brown sugar
1/4 cup raisins

Melt butter in large frying pan on medium-high heat. Add apples and fry until golden. Meanwhile, combine cinnamon and sugar. Sift onto apples when they are finished cooking. Add raisins; cook 1 minute more, or until sugar is melted. Serve hot.

Banana Applesauce

Here's a scent that will bring them to the breakfast table a little faster!

Serves 8 at 7 milligrams sodium each

8 medium apples, peeled and cubed
1 medium ripe banana, thinly sliced
3/4 cup orange juice
1/2 cup packed brown sugar
1/4 cup honey
1/4 cup unsalted butter, melted
2 teaspoons ground cinnamon
1 small lemon

Place the apples and banana in a 3-quart slow cooker coated with cooking spray. In a small bowl, combine the orange juice, brown sugar, honey, butter, and cinnamon; pour over apple mixture. Cut ends off lemon. Cut into six wedges and remove seeds. Transfer to slow cooker. Cover and cook on high for 3–4 hours or until apples are soft. Discard lemon. Puree. Serve warm.

Apple Chips

Looking for a handy but healthy snack to have around? The sodium content for the whole recipe is under 5 mg.

Entire recipe is less than 5 milligrams sodium!

1/4 cup sugar
2 teaspoon ground cinnamon
2 large apples

Preheat oven to 250°. In a small bowl, combine the sugar and cinnamon. Using a serrated knife or mandolin, thinly slice apples crosswise, discarding the seeds and ends. Arrange in a single layer on parchment-paper-lined baking sheets; sprinkle with the cinnamon sugar. Bake the apple slices, turning every half hour for two hours or until dry. Remove to racks to cool. Store in an airtight container.

Cran-Apple Relish

Serve with pork or poultry. The small amount of chili powder gives it just a tiny bit of zip. You did make your own chili powder, right? (see page 53)

Entire 1-cup recipe is less than 5 milligrams sodium!

1 Granny Smith apple, finely chopped
1/4 red onion, finely chopped
2 tablespoons lemon juice
1/2 cup dried sweetened cranberries, chopped
1 teaspoon chili powder
2 teaspoons honey
1/2 teaspoon ground cinnamon

Combine all ingredients. Mix well. Chill until cold.

Spicy Cranberries

Makes 3/4 cup, just right for 2.

Entire recipe is less than 5 milligrams sodium!

1/4 cup water
1/2 cup sugar
2-inch cinnamon stick
1 cup fresh cranberries

Combine water and sugar in a small saucepan. Toss in the cinnamon stick and crank up the heat. Bring mixture to a boil and stir until sugar dissolves. With heat on high (be careful not to get splashed), add the cranberries and keep stirring until the berries all pop, about 2 minutes. Serve warm or cool, then chill. Remove cinnamon stick before serving. Looks pretty in hollowed out orange halves.

Baked Apples

Do one or a dozen!

At 12 milligrams sodium each, you might want to bake a couple.

1 medium baking apple
1 tablespoon raisins
A few pecans or walnuts if you like, unsalted, of course!
1 tablespoon apple or orange juice
1 tablespoon packed brown sugar
pinch of cinnamon

Core the apple but leave ½ inch of bottom in apple. Pierce skin in few places with point of sharp knife. Place in apple in shallow baking dish. Stuff center with raisins and nuts. Combine juice with sugar and cinnamon and pour over apple. Bake at 350 degrees for 30–35 minutes until soft basting with juices occasionally during baking.

Poultry, especially chicken and turkey, is the most versatile meat I know. It lends itself to almost any cooking method; blends with almost any flavors, sauces, or vegetables; and cooks up fancy or simple.

Let's talk turkey for a minute. Those pre-basted birds are a wonder of modern eating, it's true. But what's in that pre-basting solution they get injected with? Fat and salt, mostly. That's why fresh or frozen without additives of any sort is very important to you. Otherwise you could be quickly over-salted and a guest at the hospital instead of the dinner party. Want a great way to have a moist, tasty bird without all that salt? Read on, Macbeth—and everyone else.

One concern I want to be sure to highlight here is about those recipes you see in magazines from soup companies that want you to make it fast and simple by putting it all together in some kind of casserole or one-dish-skillet with a can of their condensed soup. Okay, it's fast, it's simple, but it's loaded with that poison called sodium! Even one humble serving made this way will put you over your safety margin. It goes back to the things I mentioned earlier about canned food. Nothing changes in the sodium column just because we mix it in a frying pan with chicken breasts and rice. Don't sacrifice your health for a speedy meal. Let's look at some other poultry ideas:

Apple Pecan Chicken Roll-Ups

This is easy but pretty enough to serve company or for special occasions.

Serves 4 at 87 milligrams sodium each

$1/2$ cup apple juice (in the fall, try cider when it's at its best)

$1/2$ cup instant brown rice

$1/4$ cup unsalted pecans, chopped

3 tablespoons green onion, chopped

4 skinless, boned chicken breasts, about a pound total

1 tablespoon olive oil

$1/2$ cup unpeeled apple, finely chopped

Preheat oven to 400°. In small saucepan, bring apple juice to a boil. Add rice, cover, reduce to simmer for 8–10 minutes or until liquid is absorbed. (It will scorch if not watched carefully). Stir in apple, pecans and onions. Remove from heat. Pound each breast to $1/4$ inch thick between waxed paper. Place $1/4$ of the rice mixture on each and roll up tucking in edges. Secure with toothpick. Heat oil in medium skillet over medium high heat. Add chicken and cook 4–5 minutes or until lightly browned. Place in shallow baking pan and bake 20–25 minutes or until no longer pink. Carefully pull out toothpicks before serving.

Bowtie Chicken and Vegetables

Ever come home from work tired with no idea what to cook? Looking for something fast, easy, cheap, and that will meet the taste demands of everyone at your table without knocking your sodium restraint off kilter? Here it is!

Serves 4 at 168 milligrams sodium each

3 tablespoons flour

$1/4$ teaspoon pepper

1 cup milk

1 cup salt-free chicken broth

$1/2$ cup Parmesan cheese, grated, divided

3 cups bowtie pasta, uncooked

2 cloves garlic, minced

2 chicken breast halves, 4–6 ounces each, boned and skinned

2 cups of your favorite vegetables, uncooked, in bite-sized pieces, frozen or fresh

In $1\frac{1}{2}$-quart saucepan, combine flour, pepper and milk. Stir in broth. Cook over medium stirring often until thick and bubbly. This would be a good time to throw in a bit of a favorite herb if you're so inclined. Add $1/4$ cup Parmesan cheese and cook 2 minutes more. Meantime cook pasta, (no salt in the water, please), in $2\frac{1}{2}$-quart saucepan. After about 6 minutes, add vegetables and cook 3 minutes more. Drain. Cut chicken into $3/4$-inch pieces. Cook garlic and chicken in skillet until chicken is done, 5–6 minutes. Combine chicken, sauce, pasta and vegetables. Garnish with remaining cheese.

Chicken Cacciatore

You see, chicken really is versatile. This is another quick, easy, inexpensive, and tasty way to please the crowd and keep the salt intake under control. Serve with pasta, but remember not to salt the cooking water.

Serves 4 at 110 milligrams sodium each

1 pound skinless, boneless chicken pieces, cut up

$1/2$ cup onion, chopped

1 medium green pepper, cut in strips

1 clove garlic, minced

2 tablespoons unsalted butter

28-ounce can no-salt-added whole tomatoes

8-ounce can no-salt-added tomato sauce

$1/2$ teaspoon oregano

$1/2$ teaspoon basil

$1/8$ teaspoon ground red pepper

Cook and stir chicken with onion, pepper and garlic in hot butter in large skillet until lightly browned. Add tomatoes, sauce and seasonings. Bring to a full boil. Reduce heat and cover. Simmer 5 minutes or until chicken is done and vegetables are crisp-tender. Serve with rice.

Chicken in Creamy Herb Sauce

You don't have to feel deprived just because you're cutting salt. This is easy and tasty.

Serves 4 at 97 milligrams sodium each

4 medium chicken breasts, about one pound total, pounded thin with meat mallet between sheets of wax paper

3–4 tablespoons flour

4 tablespoons unsalted butter

10-ounce package sliced mushrooms (you could substitute any favorite mushroom; portobello works well here)

1 shallot minced

$1/4$ teaspoon pepper

$1/3$ cup salt-free chicken broth

1 tablespoon tarragon chopped (if you really love another herb, try using that one instead)

$1/3$ cup heavy cream

Lightly dip chicken in flour. In 12-inch skillet, melt 2 tablespoons butter over medium-high heat and brown chicken in two batches. Remove and set aside. In same skillet, melt remaining 2 tablespoons butter and add mushrooms, shallot and pepper. Cook over medium heat stirring frequently about 4 minutes or until mushrooms are golden and tender. Stir in broth and tarragon; bring to a boil. Return chicken to skillet. Reduce heat to low and simmer, covered, 5 minutes or until chicken is no longer pink. Stir in cream. Bring just to simmer without boiling and cook 1 minute. Great served over noodles.

Hickory Smoked Chicken

Love to grill out? Me, too. Here's one for a lazy Sunday afternoon with wonderful flavor.

Serves 6 at 93 milligrams sodium each

3 cups hickory wood chips
5 pounds roasting chicken
1 teaspoon sage
2 teaspoons chopped fresh rosemary
1 orange, sliced
2 medium celery ribs, chopped
3 onions, quartered
1 tablespoon chopped fresh rosemary
$1/2$ cup unsalted butter, melted

Soak wood chips in water 30 minutes. Thoroughly rinse and pat chicken dry. Rub cavity of chicken with sage and 2 teaspoons rosemary. Fill cavity with orange slices, celery and onions. Fasten opening with skewers. Tie or skewer legs securely to bird. Arrange hot coals around edge of grill. Place foil drip pan under grilling area. Drain half of the wood chips; add to hot coals. I've found that they smoke best if they're put in a little metal box nestled in among the coals so they don't dry out fast. Once dry they just burn up quickly like any wood. Stir 1 tablespoon rosemary into melted butter. Place chicken, breast side up, on grill over drip pan about 4 inches from medium coals. Cover; grill 3 to 3½ hours adding more coals and wood chips every 30 minutes or as needed and basting occasionally with rosemary-butter until done. Meat thermometer should read 180°. Smells as good cooking as it tastes done. Lock the gate, the neighbors will be over. You can actually use this smoking wood chip grilling technique with any meat, of course.

Chicken with Tomatoes and Mushrooms for the Crockpot

Putting the chicken in frozen is a good method, I've learned. It gives everything a chance to cook through without ending up with mushy chicken. I've put this on at 6 AM and served it at 6 PM that way.

Serves 4 at 210 milligrams sodium each

2 medium onions, thinly sliced
2 pounds chicken, (8–10 pieces), drums and thighs work well for long-time simmering.
2 cloves garlic, minced
16-ounce can unsalted whole tomatoes
10-ounce package fresh button mushrooms or your favorite fresh mushrooms
$1/4$ teaspoon fresh ground pepper
1 bay leaf
$1 1/2$ teaspoons dried oregano (or about 4 teaspoons fresh to taste)
$1/2$ teaspoon basil (or $1 1/2$ teaspoons fresh to taste)
$1/4$ cup dry white wine

Layer ingredients into your crockpot in the order listed, onions first. Simmer low 6–8 hours, longer if starting with frozen chicken. It's a real treat: smells great to come home to after a long day of work and it's so nice knowing dinner's ready!

South Seas Chicken and Vegetables

So you bought that turmeric and the fresh ginger and you don't know what to do with the rest? Try this.

Serves 4 at 135 milligrams sodium each

4 chicken quarters or one whole chicken, about 3½ pounds
1 tablespoon unsalted butter, melted
$1/2$ teaspoon grated fresh gingerroot
$1/4$ teaspoon paprika
$3/4$ pound fresh or frozen (no salt) Chinese pea pods
$1/2$ cup chopped onion
$1/2$ teaspoon ground turmeric
$1/4$ teaspoon fresh grated gingerroot
1 tablespoon unsalted butter
8 ounces whole small fresh mushrooms (if small ones are not available use medium, and halve or quarter them; don't even think canned)
2 teaspoons fresh lemon juice
8 cherry tomatoes, halved

Truss, tie, or skewer whole chicken if that's what you are using. Place chicken breast up if whole, skin up if quartered on rack in roasting pan. Combine butter, ½ teaspoon gingerroot and paprika. Brush evenly over chicken and place uncovered in oven preheated to 375°. Roast ¾ to 1 hour for quarters or 1 to 1¼ hours for whole chicken until done. Meantime, rinse and remove strings of pea pods if needed. Cook onion, turmeric and remaining gingerroot in melted remaining butter in large skillet over medium heat until onions are almost tender. Stir in pea pods, mushrooms and lemon juice.

Cook uncovered 5–7 minutes, stirring occasionally until crisp tender. You could toss in a handful of unsalted cashews here if you like. Stir in tomatoes and heat through. Serve with chicken.

Rosemary Chicken Thighs with Sweet & Sour Orange Dipping Sauce

Sodium content per serving of 2 large pieces chicken plus 2 tablespoons sauce per serving: 126 mg. each!

Serves 4 at 126 milligrams sodium each

1 tablespoon plus 1 teaspoon minced fresh rosemary

2 teaspoons dark brown sugar

1 teaspoon freshly ground black pepper

1 teaspoon crushed red pepper flakes

2 tablespoons vegetable oil; more for the grill

1 3/4 to 2 pounds boneless, skinless chicken thighs (about 8 large, 10 medium, or 12 small), trimmed of excess fat

1 cup orange marmalade (the kind with a little Irish whiskey works very well here)

3–4 tablespoons rice or white wine vinegar

In a small bowl, mix 1 tablespoon rosemary with the brown sugar, pepper, and red pepper flakes. In a shallow pan, drizzle the oil over the chicken and toss to coat. Sprinkle the chicken evenly with the rosemary mixture. Warm the marmalade, vinegar, and remaining rosemary in a small saucepan over low heat until just warm; set aside in a warm spot.

Prepare a hot charcoal fire or heat a gas grill with all burners on medium high for 10 min. Clean the hot grate with a wire brush and then lubricate it with an oil-soaked paper towel. Put the chicken on the grate and grill (covered on a gas grill or uncovered over a charcoal fire) until one side has dark grill marks, 5 to 6 minutes for large thighs or 4 to 5 minutes for medium and small thighs. Turn and continue to grill until well marked on the other sides and cooked through, 5 to 6 minutes longer for large thighs or 4 to 5 minutes for medium and small thighs.

Move the thighs to a platter and let rest 4 to 5 minutes. Serve hot, warm, or at room temperature with individual bowls of warm marmalade dipping sauce.

Herb Roasted Chicken

I like to roast 2 of these birds on my day off to give us "leftovers" to build on a busy workday or make a sandwich from for lunch boxes. The aroma as this chicken roasts is wonderful.

Serves 6 at 70 milligrams sodium each

One 3 1/2- to 4-pound chicken, giblets removed, rinsed inside and out, and skin patted dry with paper towels

1/4 cup Citrus, Garlic, and Herb Oil (see page 143)

2 tablespoons minced fresh oregano

2 tablespoons minced fresh basil

1 tablespoons minced fresh thyme

1 teaspoon freshly ground black pepper

Combine Herb Oil with additional fresh herbs; reserve stems from herbs. Loosen skin from breast on both sides of chicken and work 1/3 of herb mixture under skin on each side, reserve remaining third of herb mixture. If you have fresh lemon, cut it up and put into cavity with broken-up, reserved, herb stems. Tie drumsticks together. Place on roasting pan and into 400° oven for 20 minutes. Reduce heat to 325° for an additional hour. Brush bird with reserved herb oil and return to oven until breast meat registers 165° on meat thermometer. Remove and tent with foil, allowing to rest 10–15 minutes before carving.

Oven-Fried Chicken

Lower in fat than traditional, but still crispy.

Serves 4 at 395 milligrams sodium each

1 cup water plus 4 tablespoons buttermilk powder

2 eggs, well beaten

1 teaspoon of your favorite salt-free herbs and spices

2 cups crushed crispy rice cereal (for cornflakes add 70 mg. more sodium per serving)

3 pounds chicken breast halves, thighs and drumsticks rinsed and patted dry with paper towels

1/4 cup unsalted butter, melted

Grease a 13x9-inch pan lightly and preheat oven to 400°. In a shallow dish or pie plate, combine water, buttermilk powder, eggs, and herbs and spices. In another dish, place crushed cereal. Dip chicken pieces, one at a time, into milk bath, then roll in cereal. Arrange in baking pan. Drizzle butter over all. Bake, uncovered 45 to 50 minutes until tender, juices are clear, and meat reaches 165° on meat thermometer.

I use buttermilk powder and reconstitute it as needed rather than remembering to buy it and then to use it up before it turns bad, plus 1 cup made this way saves sodium. To substitute 1 cup buttermilk for the 1 cup water plus 4 tablespoons buttermilk powder, add 25 mg. sodium per serving.

Curried Orange Chicken

Strike out into the realm of new flavors. Make your own curry and show off your prowess at combining flavors that will make you forget about salt. The sauce is unique and will make you think you're dining in 5-star restaurant.

Serves 4 at 217 milligrams sodium each

About 3 pounds chicken parts (if including breasts, be sure they are split into 2 pieces)
1 teaspoon curry powder (see curry recipes p. 54)
1/2 cup orange juice (plus another 1 or 2 tablespoons, maybe), any kind works
1/4 cup honey (any will do, but how about orange-blossom honey?)
1 tablespoon prepared mustard (plain old yellow is perfect)
2 tablespoons cornstarch
4 tablespoons cold water
1 orange—cut two thin slices out of the middle and reserve for garnish, then remove and toss the rest of the peel; cut the pulp into large chucks and hold onto all the juices that leak out for the sauce

Sprinkle and rub chicken with curry powder. Arrange skin side down in baking dish prepared with a couple good shots of cooking spray. Combine 1/2 cup orange juice, honey, and mustard in a microwave-safe container. Heat just till it bubbles, about a minute and a half on full power. Pour over chicken and place in 375° oven. After half an hour, turn the chicken pieces over, baste with juices, and return to oven another 20–30 minutes until done.

Remove chicken to serving plate, cover with aluminum foil and keep warm. Pour juices from roasting pan into medium saucepan and bring up to simmer. Combine cornstarch and water thoroughly (a small whisk is very handy here) and stir into bubbling juices. Keep stirring until thickened, about a minute. Stir in peeled orange pieces and juices collected. Heat through. If the orange wasn't very juicy so the sauce ends up too thick, add a tablespoon or two of orange juice and stir in to blend. Pass the sauce with the chicken.

Fruit 'n' Honey Chicken

So quick to put together and a nice switch when you're craving something a little sweet.

Serves 2 at 75 milligrams sodium each

2 small, boneless, skinless chicken breasts
1 tablespoon olive oil
3 tablespoons apricot preserves
2 tablespoons orange juice
1 tablespoon honey (any flavor you like)

In medium skillet, brown and sauté chicken on both sides until juices run clear, about 7–8 minutes. Combine remaining ingredients and pour over chicken, continuing to cook gently another minute or two until heated through. Great with carrots and an herby potato for the contrast in flavors.

Quick and Tangy Chicken

The bite from the small dose of cayenne is nicely balanced by honey and brown sugar.

Serves 2 at 110 milligrams sodium each

1/3 cup flour
1/4 teaspoon cayenne pepper
2 small chicken breasts cut into strips
1 tablespoon unsalted butter
2 tablespoons fresh lime juice (1 lime should do it)
2 tablespoons honey
1 tablespoon brown sugar
1 teaspoon Worcestershire sauce

Combine flour and cayenne in resealable plastic bag. Toss chicken strips in a few at a time to coat. Melt butter in medium skillet and brown chicken on all sides. Combine remaining ingredients and pour over chicken in skillet, cooking another minute or two to be sure sauce is hot through and chicken is done.

Spicy Chicken Tenders

Very fast and moderately spicy, adjust the red pepper flakes to your taste.

Serves 2 at 95 milligrams sodium each

1 tablespoon water
1/4 teaspoon crushed red pepper flakes
1/4 teaspoon curry powder
1/8 teaspoon each: ground turmeric, ginger, cinnamon, and paprika
1/2 pound chicken tenders

Combine water and seasonings. Brush each side of each tender with mixture. Chill 15 minutes to absorb flavors. Place chicken on broiler pan sprayed with cooking spray. Broil 4 inches from heat about 3 minutes on each side until juices are clear.

Chicken Parmesan

If you're careful to use only no-salt-added tomato sauce, tomatoes, and 5-milligrams-sodium-per-slice bread for your crumbs, you can stuff yourself here.

Serves 2 at 443 milligrams sodium each

1 small onion, chopped
4 garlic cloves, minced
1 tablespoon olive oil
1 can (15-ounce) no-salt tomato sauce
1 can (14 1/2-ounce) stewed no-salt tomatoes
1 teaspoon each: dried basil, thyme, and oregano
1/4 teaspoon pepper
1/4 milk
1/2 cup flour
1 egg, lightly beaten
1/4 cup seasoned salt-free bread crumbs
2 tablespoons grated Parmesan
2 teaspoons dried parsley
2 boneless, skinless chicken breast halves
2 tablespoons unsalted butter
1/2 cup shredded mozzarella
Hot cooked spaghetti boiled with NO salt in the water

In medium saucepan, sauté onion and garlic in olive oil until softened; stir in tomato sauce, stewed tomatoes, herbs, and pepper. Reduce heat, cover and simmer for 20 minutes. Meanwhile, place milk, flour, and egg in three separate shallow dishes. In a fourth, combine bread crumbs, Parmesan, and parsley. (I use a paper plate for the dry ingredients to save dirty dishes.) Dip chicken in milk, roll in flour, then dip in egg and roll in crumbs. In a medium skillet, brown chicken in butter over medium heat until golden and juices run clear. Sprinkle with mozzarella, cover and cook 2–3 minutes more until cheese is melted. Serve over spaghetti topped with sauce.

Chicken with Herbs and Vegetables

What garden doesn't have an abundance of zucchini and little tomatoes? Not yours? I bet you have a friend, neighbor, or acquaintance with so much they're looking for someone to give some to. Here's a way to enjoy using them.

Serves 2 at 90 milligrams sodium each

2 medium skinless, boneless chicken breast halves
Fresh ground pepper
2 tablespoons olive oil
1/4 of 9-ounce package refrigerated pasta
1 small clove garlic, minced
1 medium green or yellow zucchini or yellow summer squash sliced 1/4-inch thick
1/2 cup apple juice or salt-free chicken broth
1 short sprig fresh rosemary, minced, or 1/2 teaspoon dried, crushed
2 tablespoons dry white wine, or more salt-free chicken broth

2 teaspoons cornstarch
1/2 cup halved cherry or grape tomatoes

Cook pasta according to instructions on package (but don't add salt). Meanwhile, season chicken with pepper; brown in olive oil over medium heat and cook 8–10 minutes until cooked through. Remove chicken and cover, keeping warm. Add garlic to skillet, stir and cook 30 seconds. Add zucchini, apple juice, and rosemary. Bring to boiling; reduce heat. Cover and simmer for 2 minutes. Include the tomatoes as well, if you like them cooked, or reserve and add fresh at the end. In a small bowl or cup, stir cornstarch into wine; add to skillet. Cook and stir until thickened and bubbly about 3–4 minutes. If not already added, stir in tomatoes. Serve chicken over a bed of pasta and vegetables.

Cumin-Sauced Grilled Chicken

Grill out, on your stove, under the broiler, whatever works. Prepare the marinade the night before and put the chicken parts in a zipper plastic bag. When you get up, add the marinade to the bag o' chicken and when you get home from work or finish cleaning the basement, mowing the lawn, and so on, its ready for the heat.

Serves 2 at 122 milligrams sodium each

1 pound chicken legs, thighs, or breasts, bone-in

Marinade
1/4 cup "No Soy Sauce" (see page 142)
Zest and juice of one lime
1 teaspoon minced garlic (about 1 large clove)
1 tablespoon olive oil
1 teaspoon ground cumin
1/2 teaspoon paprika, regular or smoky
1/2 teaspoon dried oregano
Few grinds fresh black pepper

Combine all marinade ingredients thoroughly and put into plastic bag. Add chicken and massage to work flavor into the meat. Seal bag and let sit in fridge 8 hours. Grill over indirect heat or on a stovetop grill (I have used a heavy grill pan on a large burner with success here) until meat reaches 165° on meat thermometer. Is it snowing out your window? No built-in grill on your range? (Me, either.) Go ahead and run this chicken under the broiler. Make lemonade and Corn Salad (page 134) and pretend it is mid-July!

Tarragon Chicken and Leeks

Serves 2 for 150 milligrams sodium each using light cream or 200 milligrams with evaporated milk.

Serves 2 at 150 or 200 milligrams sodium each

2 skinless, boneless chicken breast halves, about 6–8 ounces each
1 tablespoon unsalted butter
1/2 cup sliced leeks (about 1 medium, rinse thoroughly first)
1/2 cup light cream or evaporated milk
2 teaspoons finely chopped fresh tarragon (or about 3/4 teaspoon dried if you must)
1 teaspoon cornstarch

Spray a medium skillet with cooking spray. Over medium heat, cook chicken gently so it doesn't dry out but cooks through, about 12–14 minutes, turning once and watching for clear juices. Remove from pan, but cover with foil and keep warm.

Melt butter in same pan. Toss in leeks and sauté, stirring frequently until just softened, about 3 minutes. Combine remaining ingredients in small bowl and whisk well to blend cornstarch thoroughly. Immediately stir into leeks (if you have to set it down after you blend it, re-stir when ready to add so cornstarch is redistributed and not left in the bottom of the bowl—it loves to separate out). Bring to a gentle boil, stirring constantly. Boil and stir about a minute until thickened. Return chicken and any juices to skillet and stir through just to return to eating temperature. I like to serve it over something that will help me soak up the sauce, maybe rice or noodles. Of course you'll cook those in unsalted liquid, riiiiiight?

Fruit and Chicken Curry

Here's a great chance to mix and match your favorite dried fruits and experiment with herbs and spices.

Serves 2 at 250 milligrams sodium each

2 chicken breasts, skin and bones removed
2 tablespoons unsalted butter
1/4 cup chopped onion
1 bay leaf
2 teaspoons curry powder—you can use one you have combined yourself (see page 54 for ideas) or substitute 1 teaspoon ground coriander, 1/2 teaspoon cumin, and 1/2 teaspoon cardamom
1 pinch crushed red pepper flakes
3/4 cup very hot water
1 cup dried and snipped or diced dried fruit—create your own combo or try one of these: 1/2 cup dried chopped apples with 1/4 cup snipped dried apricots and 1/4 cup raisins
OR
1/2 cup snipped dried pineapple with 1/4 cup dried cherries and 1/4 cup dried currents
1 tablespoon sugar

1 teaspoon salt-free chicken bouillon granules or 1 salt-free chicken bouillon cube
1 teaspoon lemon juice, fresh is best, but not mandatory
Hot cooked rice (maybe made with chopped, unsalted peanuts and fresh parsley?)

Brown chicken breasts in butter over medium heat 3–4 minutes on each side until light golden brown but not cooked through. Remove to plate, but leave drippings in pan. Add onion, bay leaf, curry powder or spices you are substituting, and red pepper flakes to drippings in pan, stirring and cooking over medium heat 3–4 minutes until onion is soft. Add water, dried fruit you have selected, sugar, salt-free chicken bouillon granules, and lemon juice to pan; stir bringing to a simmer, 1 or 2 minutes. Return chicken and any collected juices to the pan; cover, and simmer another 10 minutes or until chicken is done. Serve over hot rice (that you made without salt).

So-Easy Chicken in Citrus Butter

You can change this anytime you like by changing the citrus juice—lime, lemon or orange. Yep, you could also do it in grapefruit juice, maybe ruby red?

Serves 2 at 37 milligrams sodium each

2 boneless, skinless chicken breasts or one large cut into two pieces, each about 4 ounces (if you feel energetic, pound the breasts to thin them down, it tenderizes and makes them cook quicker) Works with turkey tenderloin, too.
2 or 3 turns of the peppermill
1–2 tablespoons olive oil
3 tablespoons unsalted butter
2–3 teaspoons of your favorite citrus juice
1/2 teaspoon dill, sage, or tarragon, whatever you have fresh
1/2 teaspoon minced chives

Sprinkle chicken with pepper. Heat oil in medium skillet and brown and cook chicken over medium heat until done. Remove and tent with a piece of foil to keep warm. In same skillet, melt butter and stir in juice and herbs. Drizzle over the chicken.

Roast Turkey (This one's for you, Anne.)

Stuffing is usually bread, sometimes croutons. Croutons are usually salted when they are made commercially. Bread and croutons soak up fluids, in this case the turkey's juices. That's where dry turkeys are born. To avoid dry turkeys, especially at holidays when we want to serve our very best, we often resort to those salty birds pre-basted with chemicals we don't need. A simpler, healthier, more flavorful solution is to think about stuffing in a totally new way. No bread. Yup. Make your bread stuffing, sure, but make it separately in a casserole with no salt added of course. Stuff your formerly feathered friend with flavor:

One 4-oz. serving is 37 milligrams sodium

12-pound fresh or fresh-frozen turkey (in any event, naturally unbasted)

Several good sized sprigs fresh parsley

1 large handful fresh sage, or if that's not possible, 2 teaspoons dried

Nice sprig of rosemary

Small bunch thyme (okay, you caught me. Do you think Simon and Garfunkle will want royalties on this?)

2 onions, quartered (you can leave the peels on, you won't be eating this stuffing)

2 apples, quartered, seeded

2 oranges, sliced, peels on

2 celery stalks with leaves intact

Chop up herbs a bit and celery, too. Rinse the bird and pat it dry. Combine all stuffing ingredients and stuff it into bird. Truss, tie, or skewer it the way you would have with bread stuffing in it. Now, if fat and cholesterol are not your issues (ya, right), you can take a tablespoon or two of softened, unsalted butter and rub it all over the bird's skin. But spraying the dried turkey all over with a spray olive oil or butter flavored cooking spray gives you great results without salt and with very little added fat to worry about. Put turkey on rack in roaster pan big enough to contain juices, but not high-sided. High sides interfere with browning. Pop it in preheated oven at 450°, (no that isn't a typo) for 15 minutes. Turn the heat down to 325° without opening the door to peek. It should take about 18 minutes per pound, so a bird of 12 pounds should be done in about 3½ hours. Take its temperature after about 2¾ hours. The bird is ready to exit the oven and meet its adoring public when the thermometer placed in the thickest part of the thigh says 185° and juices run clear. If it browns too quickly, cover it loosely with an aluminum foil tent, but remove it for the last 20–30 minutes for final crisping. The turkey should stand at room temperature for 15 minutes or so before carving to let the juices soak back into the meat. Otherwise they all run out when you slice it. During cooking, if you feel compelled to baste, go ahead and use the drippings in the roasting pan to do so. A 4-oz. serving of turkey roasted this way will cost 79 milligrams of sodium. The pre-basted way robs you of more than five times that amount.

Easy Mini-Turkey Pot Pies

As you will see, this is a very adaptable recipe—use up leftovers, mix and match, add what you love, subtract what you don't. As long as your veggie choices stay true to the

no-salt rule, each of these four pies will run you about 347 mg. sodium each. And you can bake them all at once, or freeze and bake next week or next month. What could be easier or tastier?

Serves 4 at 347 milligrams sodium each

1 small onion, diced

1 large carrot, diced (or use ½ to ¾ cup frozen)

½ cup peeled, diced potato (1 medium)

1 rib celery, diced

¼ cup diced red bell pepper

¼ cup unsalted butter (half a stick)

⅓ cup flour

Parsley: ½ teaspoon dried, or 1½ teaspoons chopped fresh

Rosemary: ¼ teaspoon dried, or ¾ teaspoon minced fresh

Sage: ¼ teaspoon dried, or ¾ teaspoon minced fresh

¼ teaspoon fresh ground pepper

1 cup milk

1 cup sodium-free turkey or chicken broth

2 cups cubed cooked turkey (chicken will work well here, too)

½ cup frozen peas, corn, or green beans

1 sheet refrigerated pie pastry at room temperature

In a large saucepan, sauté vegetables in butter until tender, not brown. Add flour, herbs, and pepper; stir to blend well. Slowly whisk in milk, a little at a time, whipping constantly to keep smooth. Stir in broth. Bring to a boil, reduce heat to steady simmer and cook and stir about 2–3 minutes until thickened and bubbly. Stir in turkey and peas. Divide mixture among four ungreased 5-inch pie plates.

Divide pie pastry into 4 even portions and roll lightly to reshape into 6-inch circles. Cover turkey with pastry; flute or crimp edges; cut small vent slits in top. If you wish, cover tightly and freeze up to three months. When you're ready for one or two, bring them out of freezer about a half hour before you want to bake them.

Place on a foil-lined baking sheet (some of that good gravy may bubble over). Cover loosely with another sheet of foil and bake at 375° for 30 minutes, take the foil off the top and continue baking another 15 or 20 minutes until brown and bubbly delicious. To bake unfrozen pie skip the foil cover and bake at 375° about 20 minutes.

Turkey with Fruit & Thyme Sauce

Adjust to what is in season at the market.

Serves 2 at 130 milligrams sodium each

1 turkey tenderloin (about 12 ounces)

2 tablespoons flour

2 tablespoons olive oil

1 tablespoon minced shallot (substitute sweet onion if you need to)

1/4 cup dry white wine or sherry

2 tablespoons salt-free chicken broth

1–2 tablespoons heavy cream

1/2 cup halved red grapes (the darker they are, the more antioxidants in them) or use sweet cherries, halved and pitted, or use 1/2-inch cubed mango, or use your imagination

2 teaspoons fresh thyme leaves

1 tablespoon cold unsalted butter in 4 pieces

Remove any silverskin on turkey and cut tenderloin into 2 servings. Pound each of them to about half an inch thickness between pieces of plastic wrap. Sprinkle flour over meat and press into surfaces on both sides of each piece. I find this easier to do over a paper plate or even just a sheet of paper towel. Heat the oil in a medium frying pan over medium-high. Sauté 2–3 minutes on each side until golden. Remove to a plate, cover in foil and keep warm. Add shallots or onion and stir, cooking about 2 minutes until softened but not browned.

Add wine carefully and stir, scraping up the brown bits of, what is it? Yes, FLAVOR!! Add broth and cream (I use the 2-tablespoon amount as I tend to cook it down quickly, if you are using a lower heat, or trying to cut even tiny amounts of fats, use 1 tablespoon) and bring up to a boil, then turn down to a simmer, cooking and stirring until reduced by half, a couple minutes. Stir in the fruit and thyme. Turn off the burner, and with the saucepan off heat, stir in the butter 2 cubes at a time until melted and blended. Sprinkle on a little pepper if you need it; try white or pink pepper since it is a white sauce and a delicately flavored dish.

Country Style Turkey

Here's a tasty way to use leftover cooked or uncooked turkey without canned soup that works with chicken, too.

Serves 4 at 165 milligrams sodium each

1 pound turkey cut into strips

1/2 cup chopped onion

2 tablespoons unsalted butter

2 cups milk

10-ounce package frozen mixed vegetables

1/2 teaspoon sage

1 1/2 cups instant cooking rice

Cook and stir raw turkey and onion in hot butter in large skillet until lightly browned. If using cooked turkey, sauté onion for 2 minutes before adding turkey.

Add milk, vegetables and sage. Bring to a full boil; stir in rice. Cover; remove from heat. Let stand 5 minutes. Fluff with fork and serve.

Curried Turkey Breast

Want something easy but a little exotic? Try this. There are several interesting flavors here that blend well.

Serves four at 110 milligrams sodium each.

2 large skinless turkey breasts

1/2 teaspoon coriander

1/2 teaspoon paprika

1/4 teaspoon turmeric

1/2 teaspoon cumin

1/4 teaspoon cayenne (red) pepper

1/4 teaspoon cinnamon

2 tablespoons fresh grated gingerroot (most produce sections carry this now)

1 tablespoon olive oil (use the good stuff)

2 tablespoons fresh lemon juice

1/2 cup plain yogurt

Chives or green onions chopped fine for garnish

Combine all ingredients except turkey and chives in a bowl or measuring cup. Place turkey in pan in single layer and spread with spice and yogurt mixture. Cover with plastic and chill at least 2 hours. Remove plastic and bake in oven preheated to 350° for 40 minutes. Baste with juices every 10 minutes or so. Slice and sprinkle with chives. Serve with juices.

Tarragon Turkey from Leftovers

Gotta love the leftovers!

Makes 4 hearty servings for 102 mg. sodium each

2 tablespoons unsalted butter

1 cup sliced fresh mushrooms

2 tablespoons flour

1 1/2 cups salt-free chicken or turkey stock

1/4 cup white wine

1/2 teaspoon dried mustard

1 tablespoons fresh, minced OR 1 teaspoon dried, crushed rosemary

4 cups cubed leftover turkey

Melt the butter over low heat in a large sauté pan. Add the mushrooms and sauté until soft, about 5 minutes. Whisk in flour and cook and stir a minute to lightly brown and cook out the raw taste. Increase the heat to medium high and whisk in the stock. Stir in wine, mustard and rosemary. Cook, stirring frequently until thickened, about 10 minutes. Stir in the turkey and simmer several minutes to heat through. Serve immediately over rice, noodles, or mashed potatoes.

McBalch's Healthy Chicken Nuggets

If you dip it into a sauce, be mindful of the sodium that will add.

Makes 4 servings for 73 milligrams sodium each

1 pound boneless, skinless chicken breast, sliced lengthwise

1 cup plain yogurt

1 cup coating mix—see directions

Make a healthy "bread crumb" coating using ¾ cup low-sodium, unsalted, plain bread crumbs and adding ¼ cup total, of a combination of wheat germ, flax seed, crushed corn flakes, or whatever works for a little crunch but no added sodium. Add or don't add herbs to taste.

Dip the chicken into the yogurt, then roll in the coating mixture. Spray a baking sheet with non-stick coating and place strips on sheet. Bake at 400° for 6 minutes, flip and bake another 6 minutes.

Garlic and Herb Chicken with White Wine Sauce

Serves 4 for only 89 milligrams sodium each

1 4-pound whole chicken, cut into eight parts

Freshly ground black pepper

2–3 whole heads of garlic cloves separated

Olive oil

1¼ cup dry white wine, such as a Sauvignon Blanc

3 large sprigs of fresh tarragon

3 large sprigs of fresh thyme

Lightly smash the garlic cloves with the side of a heavy chef's knife, just enough to break the cloves.

Trim the chicken pieces of excess fat. Pat them dry and sprinkle pieces generously with salt and pepper. Heat 3 tablespoons olive oil in a Dutch oven (or a large, thick-bottom pan with a tight fitting cover) on medium-high. Working in batches, brown the chicken pieces on all sides. Lay the chicken pieces on the hot oil; do not move until browned, then turn over to other side using tongs. Remove from pan when browned.

Add a little more olive oil to the pan if necessary. Add the garlic and sauté until golden brown, about 4 minutes. Add the wine and the herbs. Bring to a boil. Add the chicken pieces. Reduce the heat to medium low. Cover the pan and simmer until the chicken is cooked through. Move the chicken pieces from top to bottom every 5 minutes for about 20 minutes. Season to taste with pepper. Transfer chicken pieces to a platter; spoon garlic sauce over the chicken.

A Last Word on Poultry

Poultry. *Experiment with it. Poach it in wine and your favorite herb. Broil it and serve with a sauce, (see section on sauces for ideas). Pick a no-salt marinade to use with poultry and chill boneless pieces in it all day while you do other things; then alternate pieces with vegetables or even pineapple on skewers for the grill. Cut any poultry into little slivers and stir-fry with slivers of yellow, red, and green bell peppers and some minced shallots in olive oil with a little unsalted butter. Brown tenderloins lightly in a skillet then simmer several minutes with some apricot marmalade, fresh grated gingerroot, and maybe a bit of minced garlic. The point is that you are limited only by your imagination, not by a lack of salt. Open your old cookbooks. I'd bet there are a number of recipes you can adapt if you carefully check out the sodium content of the ingredients first.*

Fish—some people love it and some people hate it. I have members from both camps in my household. There are lots of great ways to cook fish without eating those pale bland square fillets we used to be faced with. I am very fortunate to live near a large supermarket with an excellent fish market inside. I've also bought fresh delicious fish at, of all places, the farmers' market. It doesn't have to be a frozen, breaded brick. And remember what you read before, salt-water fish does not mean high sodium content. The salt comes from what people do to the fish after they catch it. Crab and lobster, however, are mostly out of our sodium budget, if not our financial one. A few shrimp, cooked and eaten conservatively, are not completely off the menu, though. Try these:

Jason's Fish Fry

My younger son loves to fish and cook what he catches. He has invented a few recipes, but the beauty of this one is the cornmeal. It has essentially no sodium where the same amount of bread crumbs would be prohibitive. I used flounder because it's easy to come by if you fish at the market. If you use another fish, refigure the sodium content because most fish I've checked out have less (yes, less) sodium than flounder, except sole. Something else you can do is drop the chili powder and use a favorite herb (mine is lemon thyme and is great for fish). It will change the whole character of the recipe and give your cooking more variety. Made as presented here, there are 4 servings at 137 milligrams sodium each; one pound of flounder is 420 milligrams sodium, the rest of the ingredients add up to 126 milligrams total in case you want to substitute another fish.

Serves 4 at 137 milligrams sodium each

$1/2$ cup cornmeal
2 teaspoons chili powder
$1/4$ teaspoon pepper
1 egg, lightly beaten
1 pound flounder fillets
$1/4$ cup olive oil
1 tablespoon unsalted butter

Combine dry ingredients in shallow dish. Dip fish in egg then in dry ingredients. Shake off excess. In large skillet heat oil and butter over medium high heat until hot. Sauté fish until lightly browned on both sides, 3–4 minutes. Drain on paper towels before serving.

Shrimp with Basil Lemon Sauce

Here is another quick recipe that doesn't sacrifice taste or blow your sodium budget. Mince your garlic and chop your basil (see page 41 for easy chiffonade instructions) before you start cooking and have your sides ready because this is done in a flash.

Serves 6 at 154 milligrams sodium each

4 tablespoons unsalted butter
1 clove garlic, minced
$1^{1}/2$ pounds shrimp, peeled and deveined
3 tablespoons fresh basil, chopped
2 tablespoons fresh lemon juice

Melt butter in large heavy skillet over medium heat. Add garlic and cook until soft. Do not brown. Add shrimp and basil and sauté over medium high stirring constantly for 2 minutes. Add lemon juice, stirring constantly. Continue cooking another 2–3 minutes. Serve immediately. Outstanding taste.

Grilled Herbed Fresh Catch

This will only cost you 185 milligrams sodium per fish in spite of the bacon! The bacon doesn't crisp up, it's just there to flavor and baste the fish so take it out and toss it to save some of each slice's sodium, (85 milligrams per slice of Oscar Mayer Lower Sodium).

Serves 6 at 185 milligrams sodium each

6 10-ounce fresh whole fish(I used rainbow trout for the sodium calculations at about 100 milligrams dressed, each. You can use whatever you catch; try pike— mmm!)
6 slices Oscar Mayer Lower Sodium bacon
6 sprigs fresh dill
1 medium onion, cut in sixths (I've also used 6 cleaned, whole green onions instead)
1 small lemon, cut into pieces

Rinse and pat fish dry after cleaning, boning and butterflying; leave skin on to keep fish moister. Place a slice of bacon, a sprig of dill and a piece of onion in the cavity of each prepared fish. Place in fish-grilling basket sprayed first with non-stick cooking spray. It's okay to spray the fish skin, too; it will help crisp it without drying out the fish. Grill over medium coals about 10 minutes, 5 on each side, until flesh is opaque and done through. Fish generally takes 10 minutes for each inch of thickness measured at the thickest point. Toss the bacon, (as in toss it out), and serve the fish with fresh lemon and more fresh dill if desired. Great at a campsite or just in the backyard.

Grilled Halibut

Don't marinade all day, it will make fish mushy. If you have stems of the herbs (you are growing herbs, right?) toss them on the grill and let the aroma flavor the fish.

Serves 6 at 61 milligrams sodium each

2 tablespoons light olive oil
2 tablespoons fresh lime juice
$1/2$ teaspoon dried thyme
$1/2$ teaspoon dried basil
$1/8$ teaspoon dried rosemary
6 4-ounce halibut fillets

Place fish fillets in a large, shallow glass baking dish. Whisk together olive oil, lime juice, and herbs. Pour marinade over fish, cover, and refrigerate 2 to 4 hours. Preheat barbecue or gas grill. Oil grilling rack, and adjust height to between 4 to 6 inches from heat. Remove fish from marinade, and place on grill. Cook 10 minutes per inch of thickness, or until fish flakes with a fork. Turn once to brown both sides.

Crunchy "Oven-Fried" Fish

Here's another that takes advantage of other low-salt methods of breading fish.

Serves 6 at 55 milligrams sodium each

1 pound catfish fillets (I used farm-raised to calculate the sodium content)
$1/4$ cup flour
$1/4$ teaspoon lemon-pepper
1 egg white
$1/4$ cup Progresso unseasoned bread crumbs
$1/4$ cup cornmeal
$1 1/2$ teaspoons lemon peel
$1/2$ teaspoon basil

Combine flour and lemon-pepper and place in shallow dish. Beat egg white till frothy. Combine remaining ingredients in another shallow dish. Dip one side only of each fillet into flour mixture, then egg white, then crumbs. Spray pan with non-stick cooking spray and place fish in pan coating side up. Tuck under any thin edges. Bake 450° 6–12 minutes or till done.

Favorite Swordfish Steaks

Here's my favorite way to cook swordfish.

Serves 4 at 160 milligrams sodium each

4 6-ounce swordfish steaks, 1 inch thick
4 tablespoons unsalted butter
8 6-inch sprigs fresh thyme or lemon thyme

Melt the butter in a large saucepan. Lay 4 sprigs thyme in the butter and top with 4 swordfish steaks. Top each steak with the last 4 sprigs thyme. Sauté about 5 minutes on medium watching to be sure thyme crisps but doesn't burn. Turn steaks being sure cooked thyme comes up and uncooked thyme is down. Cook another 5 minutes until done and thyme is crispy. If you love thyme like I do you can eat the sautéed thyme along with the swordfish. If not, discard cooked thyme and garnish with fresh. Delicious!

You can do the same thing with any meaty, thick fish such as salmon and change the herb if you like. I've never tried it, but it might work well with chicken breast, too. Experiment!

Trout Amandine

These servings are generous!

Serves 4 at 212 milligrams sodium each

4 pan-dressed trout (about 1 pound each)
$1/2$ teaspoon pepper

2 eggs
$1/2$ cup half-and-half cream
$1/2$ cup all-purpose flour
$1/2$ cup slivered almonds
3 tablespoons unsalted butter, divided
3 to 4 tablespoons lemon juice
$1/2$ teaspoons dried tarragon
$1/4$ cup olive oil

Sprinkle pepper in the cavity of each trout. In a shallow bowl, beat eggs and cream. Dip trout in egg mixture then roll in flour. In a small skillet over low heat, sauté the almonds in 2 tablespoons butter until lightly browned. Add lemon juice and tarragon; heat through. Remove from heat and keep warm. Meanwhile, in a skillet over medium heat, combine oil and remaining butter. Fry trout for 8–10 minutes; carefully turn and fry 8 minutes longer or until it flakes easily with a fork. Top with almond mixture.

Salmon Baked with Yogurt, Mustard, and Herbs

This is such a great dish. Not only is it super easy and quick, it offers the benefit of antioxidant-rich salmon. Feel free to increase or decrease seasonings as you like. The cooking method and ingredients will work with other fleshy fish, too.

Serves 4 at 248 milligrams sodium each

1 pound salmon
4 ounces plain whole milk yogurt
2 tablespoon Dijon mustard
$1/4$ teaspoon freshly ground pepper
1 small handful dill, minced, about 2 tablespoons
1 small handful parsley, minced, about 2 tablespoons

Rinse and pat salmon dry with paper towels. Place in baking pan coated with cooking spray. Combine remaining ingredients, spread over salmon and bake 15–30 minutes in 400° oven.

Cold Poached Salmon with Cucumber Dill Sauce

Excellent on a buffet or cocktail party table or just because it's delicious.

1 large salmon fillet, about 24 oz.
Water to cover the bottom of the pan, about $1 1/2$ cups
6 peppercorns
1 bay leaf
1 tablespoon lemon juice
1 cup plain yogurt

1/2 cup cucumber peeled and diced
1 tablespoon lemon juice
2 tablespoon fresh dill chopped fine

Check the salmon fillet for bones and remove any you find. Bring the water, peppercorns, bay leaf and lemon juice to a boil in a skillet large enough to hold the fillet lying flat. The liquid should be about a half inch deep, enough to cover the fish partially. Place the fish in the liquid. When it returns to a boil, turn down the heat so that it continues to simmer gently, cover loosely and poach for about 10 minutes, or until the fish is tender and cooked through. Put the yogurt and cucumber in the canister of a blender or food processor and blend until the cucumber is pureed. Add the lemon juice and dill and blend a few seconds to mix. Put the fish on a platter, pour some of the sauce over it and garnish with a few whole sprigs of dill. Serve the rest of the sauce in a bowl.

Once again, try to make up your own recipes, and adapt ones you have. You could try something like poached fillets in water and white wine with lemon slices and handfuls of herbs. Try parsley or tarragon for a change. Serve poached, steamed, or broiled fish with a home-made sauce. (Check out the ones a few sections up ahead.) Again, it's not the fish; it's what we do to it that raises the sodium content.

Coconut Shrimp

Be careful about your measuring and portioning. You deserve a tasty change from time to time, but don't let the sodium in the ingredients get out of hand. One serving is 6 shrimp. You may want to dip them in a fruity sauce: try thinning orange marmalade with a little orange juice.

Serves 4 at 260 milligrams sodium each

24 large shrimp
1 egg
2/3 cup beer
1 1/2 teaspoons baking powder
1/2 cup flour
1 cup coconut shreds (be aware, that, for some reason I can't figure out, sweetened coconut is higher in sodium. Since this isn't a dessert, I calculated based on unsweetened)

Beat egg, beer, baking powder, and flour; place in shallow bowl. Place coconut in second shallow bowl. Over medium-high, heat enough oil in a skillet to cover the bottom of the pan. Pat shrimp dry and dip first into beer mixture, then coconut. Place shrimp in hot oil and pan-fry till cooked through and lightly browned, turning once, about 4–5 minutes. Don't over cook shrimp here or in any recipe; it makes them tough and chewy.

Easy Tropical Salmon Bake

Lots of great flavor and healthy eating.

Serves 4 at 95 milligrams sodium each

1 1/2 pounds fresh or frozen and thawed salmon
1 tablespoon olive oil
2 teaspoons fresh grated lemon zest, divided
Fresh-ground pepper to taste
2 cups cooked white or brown rice
Fruit of one mango, peeled and chopped
1 tablespoon chopped cilantro
Lemon wedges, if desired

Rinse fish and pat dry with paper towels. Place in greased 3 quart baking dish. Drizzle olive oil over fish and sprinkle with one teaspoon fresh grated lemon zest, and freshly grated pepper (here's a good place for fruitier pink peppercorns, see discussion on pepper, page 39). Combine rice, mango, cilantro, and remaining lemon zest. Spoon around fish. Bake, uncovered, in preheated 425° oven for about 15 minutes. Cut fish into four servings and serve with rice and lemon wedges, if desired.

Jerk-Spiced Shrimp

No, you shouldn't serve this just when your jerk brother-in-law comes to dinner. It's too good for him!

Serves 4 at 255 milligrams sodium each

1 tablespoon sugar
1 tablespoon paprika (you pick—plain, smoky, or hot)
1/2 teaspoon garlic powder
1/4 to 1/2 teaspoon ground red pepper (cayenne)
1/4 teaspoon ground thyme
1/8 teaspoon ground allspice
2 tablespoons olive oil
1 1/2 pounds shrimp, deveined and shelled (Go for the 16 to 20 per pound size so you can figure 24 to 30 for the recipe and 6 or 8 per serving—because size matters.)

Preheat the grill or the broiler. Combine all the spices, set aside. Rub all those beautiful shrimp around well in the oil. Sprinkle on the spice mixture and toss around to coat evenly. Thread shrimp onto skewers (If wooden skewers are used, be sure to soak in water for 30 minutes first; don't want them going up in flames and dumping shrimp between the grates!) Be sure to oil grates or coat broiler pan with cooking spray. Grill or broil 3–4 minutes per side; don't over cook.

Dilled Shrimp and Rice

Quick to make especially if you buy your shrimp already peeled and deveined, and carrots shredded.

Serves 4 at 195 milligrams sodium each

2 tablespoons unsalted butter, divided
1 pound raw shrimp, peeled and deveined
1 cup shredded carrot (2 medium or buy shredded carrots for convenience)
1 cup sugar snap peas or snow peas
3 green onions (scallions) sliced (about $1/3$ cup)
2 cups cooked rice
1 teaspoon grated lemon peel
$3/4$ cup salt-free seafood or chicken broth
1 tablespoon fresh, minced dill or 1 teaspoon dried and crushed

Melt one tablespoon butter in large skillet. Stir in shrimp and cook over medium high 3–4 minutes until pink and just cooked through, don't overcook or shrimp become tough. Remove and keep warm. Melt remaining butter and stir in carrots, peas, and green onions. Cook and stir over medium-high 3 minutes until crisp-tender. Stir in shrimp, rice, lemon peel, and broth; heat through. Stir in dill and serve.

Fish My Way

Want my favorite way to prepare salmon, or most other fleshy firm fish, for that matter?

Serves 4 at 95 milligrams sodium each

Fish fillets or steaks (Go for the best. Wild-caught salmon is seasonal and costs more, but it's totally worth the splurge occasionally. Try this with catfish, perch, snapper or whatever your heart desires—make this Your Way!)

Per about a pound of fish combine:
1 teaspoon coriander powder
1 teaspoon brown sugar
$1/4$ teaspoon fresh ground pepper

Put a tablespoon of olive oil and a tablespoon of unsalted butter in a sauté pan and heat till butter foams. Meantime, pat the fish dry. Sprinkle half the coriander, brown sugar and pepper on each side of the fish and gently massage it in. Gently lay it on the pan and sizzle gently for 3–4 minutes and flip. Cook the other side another 3–4 minutes. Don't over cook and watch your heat: don't want it to burn and brown sugar will burn. Serve and eat it NOW! Don't wait for anything; it's just too good. So easy, and easy to change and make it yours. Have fun.

Herb-Crusted Red Snapper

Don't you just love easy, tasty, and fast? All that great flavor with so little sodium at a fast-food speed. Adjust the proportions of the spices and herbs to suit your taste. Try toasting your fennel seeds first. Just toss them into the heavy skillet you're going to cook the fish in over moderately high heat and keep them moving for just 2 or 3 minutes. Don't let 'em burn. You will be amazed at how this takes the flavor up another notch.

Serves 2 at 85 milligrams sodium each

1 tablespoon dry bread crumbs from low-sodium bread (5 milligrams per slice)
1 teaspoon dried basil
1 teaspoon paprika
$1/2$ teaspoon fennel seeds
$1/2$ teaspoon dried thyme
$1/2$ teaspoon dried oregano
$1/4$ teaspoon pepper
$1/4$ teaspoon crushed red pepper flakes
2 red snapper fillets (5 ounces each), skinned
2 tablespoons olive oil

Rinse fillets and pat dry; set aside. In food processor, combine the bread crumbs and seasonings; process until fennel seed is finely ground. Transfer to paper plate and dip fillets into mixture coating both sides. In heavy skillet over medium high heat, cook fillets in hot oil 3–4 minutes on each side until done.

Mahi-Mahi on an Island Vacation

Can you hear the surf and the rustle of the palm fronds as you sip something citrus from a coconut? Maybe this will help—it's the perfect flavorful getaway. Try this with salmon, trout, grouper, snapper…

Serves 2 at 140 milligrams sodium each

1 pound Mahi-Mahi steaks or fillets
2 tablespoons brown sugar
1 tablespoon chili powder (see my recipe, page 53)
1 teaspoon ground cumin
$1/2$ teaspoon ground cinnamon
1 tablespoon unsalted butter
1 tablespoon olive oil

Rinse and pat fish dry with paper towels. Combine rub ingredients and rub over both sides of each piece of fish. Cover and let flavors penetrate flesh in refrigerator for half an hour or so. Melt butter with oil in large skillet that will allow you to place all fish pieces without touching each other. Crowding will steam not sauté. Place fish skin side down in medium-hot pan and sauté 5–6 minutes on each side being careful not to burn. Alternatively, spray a baking pan with cooking spray and lay fish in pan, skin side down, not touching, and bake at 375° 20–25 minutes until done.

Sole and Asparagus Bake

Yummy way to use the batches of sauces you make up yourself!

Serves 2 at 196 milligrams sodium each

1 small bunch fresh asparagus, cleaned, cooked and drained, or a 10-ounce package frozen with no sodium added, cooked and drained
1/4 cup Tartar Sauce (see page 141, if you're going to make a batch, might as well use it)
2 frozen sole fillets, thawed, 4 ounces each
2 tablespoons Chili Sauce (see page 53, another good use for this tasty homemade)

Place asparagus in small, shallow baking dish. Dot tartar sauce over asparagus. Top with fillets. Spoon chili sauce over fish. Bake at 350° for about 30 minutes or until done.

Cajun-Seared Catfish

Quick and easy!

Serves 2 at 102 milligrams sodium each

2 tablespoons olive oil
1 teaspoon paprika
2 teaspoons fresh thyme, minced (substitute a scant teaspoon of dried if you don't have fresh at the ready, rub it between your hands to activate the flavor as you add it to the spice mix)
1/2 teaspoon cayenne pepper
1/4 teaspoon freshly ground pepper
2 catfish fillets (about 6 ounces each) or substitute a nice piece of snapper (for about the same sodium count)

Place a large skillet on medium high heat and warm the oil in the pan. Combine the spices and herbs (I just dump it all on a clean paper towel rather than dirty a bowl for this) and transfer to a plate: pie or paper work well. Gently pat the fish fillets dry with paper towels (you'll get a better crust formation this way) and dredge

in the spice mixture rubbing it into the fish on both sides. Place fillets in hot oil. Cook 3 or 4 minutes on each side. Serve immediately.

Mediterranean Sea Bass

So flavorful!

Only 126 milligrams sodium for each of 4 servings

Paste
3 tablespoons extra-virgin olive oil
1 tablespoon finely chopped fresh basil
1 tablespoon finely chopped fresh thyme
2 teaspoons dried lavender
1 teaspoon minced garlic
1/4 teaspoon freshly ground black pepper

4 skinless Chilean sea bass fillets, about 6 ounces each and 1 inch thick
Lemon wedges

To make the paste: In a small bowl whisk together the paste ingredients.

Pat fish dry with paper towels. Spread the paste evenly on both sides of the fish fillets. Grill over direct high heat until the flesh is opaque throughout and starting to flake, 5 to 7 minutes, turning once halfway through grilling time or use grill pan on kitchen stove. Serve warm and garnish with lemon wedges, if desired.

Hook a Good Catch

Works well with flounder, cod, sole, orange roughy; try new types.

Serves 2 at about 250 milligrams sodium each

1/2 cup cornmeal
2 teaspoons salt-free chili powder (see page 53)
1/4 teaspoon pepper
1 egg lightly beaten
1 pound fish fillets, whatever fish is on sale today
1/4 cup olive oil

Combine dry ingredients in shallow dish. Dip fish in egg then in dry ingredients. Shake off excess. In large skillet heat oil over medium-high until hot. Sauté fish until lightly browned on both sides, 3–4 minutes. Drain on paper towels before serving.

It was a bit of a surprise to me that meat has so much natural sodium. That makes it a little more challenging to eat red meats and keep the sodium down, but it can be done.

Red meats have robust flavors of their own requiring stronger seasonings as a rule in order to avoid bland food. Garlic and onion, more potent herbs such as sage, oregano, coriander, and thyme; spices like cloves, red pepper flakes, and paprika; veggies like bell peppers and broccoli; and other flavors like vinegars and red wine will all add great flavors and enticing aromas. Next, vary the cooking method such as grilling, roasting, and stir-frying, and before you know it, salt has no meaning!

Beef Stroganoff

If you do it like this, it's 6 servings at only 105 milligrams sodium each. This assumes you use your homemade beef broth or the equivalent.

Serves 6 at 105 milligrams sodium each

1 1/2 pounds sirloin steak, cut in thin strips
5 tablespoons flour, divided
6 tablespoons unsalted butter, divided
3 tablespoons olive oil
1/2 pound mushrooms, sliced
1/2 cup onion, chopped
1 clove garlic, minced
1 1/4 cups no-salt beef broth
1 cup sour cream
4 tablespoons dry red wine

Coat beef strips with 2 tablespoons flour. Brown beef quickly in 3 tablespoons butter and the oil and remove from skillet. Add mushrooms, onion, and garlic; sauté for 4 minutes and remove. Add remaining butter and blend in remaining flour. Stir in broth and cook, stirring over medium heat until thickened. Return meat and onion mixture to skillet. Stir in sour cream and wine. Heat through without boiling. Great served over noodles.

Swiss Steak for the Crockpot

This is a real time saver if you have a crockpot, if not you can still do it in a Dutch oven.

Serves 8 at 118 milligrams sodium each

2 pounds round steak, 1 inch thick
1/4 cup flour
2 carrots, chopped
1 cup celery, chopped
1/4 cup chopped onion
1/2 teaspoon Worcestershire sauce
8 ounces salt-free tomato sauce

Cut steak into 8 serving-sized pieces. Dredge in flour. Put vegetables and tomato sauce into crockpot first, then top with steak. Sprinkle with Worcestershire sauce, (measure accurately, it's not sodium free). Simmer on low for 8–10 hours.

Easy Burgundy Stew

This is a tasty way to feed a bunch on a cool evening. Freezes well, too, so you can put some away for another day.

Serves 8 at 100 milligrams sodium each

2 pounds beef roast, (get the one on sale: bottom or top round, tip and chuck all work well. Get it boneless, that's easier to measure and serve). Trim the fat well and cut into one-inch cubes.
2 cups carrot slices
1 cup celery slices
2 sliced onions
2 cups fresh sliced mushrooms (half a pound)
3 tablespoons flour
1 tablespoon chopped fresh thyme (or a teaspoon dried)
1/2 teaspoon mustard powder
1/4 teaspoon fresh ground pepper
1 cup water
1 cup dry red wine (you can substitute homemade salt-free beef broth)
1 can (16 ounces) salt-free tomatoes, coarsely chopped, in the juice

Heat oven to 325°. Combine meat cubes and vegetables in oven-safe Dutch oven or large casserole. Combine flour, thyme, mustard, and pepper; stir into meat mixture. Mix in remaining ingredients including juice from canned tomatoes. Cover and bake 4 hours or until tender and thickened. Wait till you smell this one cooking!

Speedy Italian Beef Stew

Hearty, quick, economical, and nutritious meal.

Serves 2 at 155 milligrams sodium each

3/4 pound fairly tender beef such as cube steak, or sirloin, fat trimmed, cubed
2 teaspoons olive oil
1 cup water
1 (8-ounce) can no-salt-added tomato sauce or 1 cup homemade
1 potato, peeled and cubed
1 large carrot, peeled and sliced
1/2 small onion, sliced
1/2 small sweet red pepper, chopped
1 envelope Herbox or other no-salt beef bouillon
1/2 teaspoon crushed dried oregano
1/2 teaspoon crushed dried basil
1/4 teaspoon garlic powder
1/2 cup frozen peas

In large saucepan, heat oil and brown beef on medium-high 5 minutes. Stir in remaining ingredients except the peas. Bring just to boil. Reduce heat to simmer, and cook uncovered 45 minutes. Stir in peas and simmer 15 more minutes.

Easy Beef Stir-Fry

Be sure you have a batch of "No Soy Sauce" (found on page 142) ready.

Serves 2 at 80 milligrams sodium each

$1/2$ pound beef sirloin sliced $3/4$-inch thick, then cut the strips in half lengthwise and crosswise so you have 3-inch x $1/8$-inch x $3/8$ inch strips, or there about, don't sweat the details. It helps to have the pieces evenly sized to keep cooking even.

2 tablespoons water

2 cups fresh (or frozen with out sodium) stir-fry veggie blend (carrots, snap peas, broccoli, onion)

$1/4$ of a red bell pepper sliced into thin strips

2 teaspoons olive oil

$1/2$ teaspoon crushed red pepper

Marinade

1 tablespoon "No Soy Sauce" (page 142)

1 clove garlic, minced

$1^1/2$ teaspoons grated fresh ginger (more if you love it like I do)

1 tablespoon dry sherry

$1/2$ teaspoon sugar

1 teaspoon cornstarch

Combine marinade ingredients and stir in beef strips. Set aside at room temp while preparing other ingredients. Put water, vegetable blend, and peppers into large non-stick skillet (use a wok if you have one!). Cover and cook 4–5 minutes till crisp-tender with intensified color. Drain and keep warm. Working in two batches is important here because if you crowd the meat into the pan it will steam and be an ugly gray color. Spreading the beef out in the pan lets it stir-fry and brown quickly keeping color, flavor, and eye-appeal. Helps keep it from getting tough, too. So into the still-hot pan put 1 teaspoon oil and half the crushed red pepper. Add half the meat and marinade to the sizzling pan and stir while it cooks quickly, 1–2 minutes, cooking just till pink is gone. Remove from pan and repeat with remaining oil, crushed red pepper, and beef and marinade. Toss the other batch of meat and the veggies back into the pan. Heat through and serve.

Do NOT give in to temptation, you can do this! Serve with some good brown rice, ok, any sodium-free rice you like, but it doesn't hurt to go for the nutritious stuff. Toast a few peanuts and throw them on top, unsalted, of course! It's kinda hard to buy half-pound pieces of beef, so think about buying a more available one-pound portion of the beef and use half for this recipe, and freeze half. Tah dah, no leftovers today and you have beef waiting for your next recipe. This pulls together quickly, so it's great on a busy day.

Old Fashioned Rump Roast

I got this from a newspaper column once and must admit it's one of the best ways I know to do a beef roast. Generous Sunday-dinner-sized servings.

Serves 12 at 118 milligrams sodium each

5 pounds rump roast, trimmed

Freshly ground black pepper

3 tablespoons olive oil

$1^1/2$ cups chopped onion

3 cloves minced garlic

1 cup water

2 bay leaves, broken

$1/2$ teaspoon dried thyme

$1/2$ teaspoon dried sage

5 tablespoons flour

5 tablespoons water

Season meat with pepper. Brown on all sides in hot oil using tongs, not fork to turn. This should take about 15 minutes. Remove from pot and reduce heat to medium low. Cook and stir onions and garlic until softened. Add water to pot and scrape up brown bits. Return meat to pan and add herbs. Cover and transfer to oven. Simmer 2½ hours at 350°. Add water every 30 minutes as needed. Meat is done when fork tender and dark brown. Remove meat to platter and keep warm. Shake flour and water in jar until well mixed. Simmer juices in pot on stove. Remove bay leaves and slowly whisk in flour mixture. Cook gravy whisking often until thick and bubbly.

Pepper Steak

This is especially delicious at peak time for ripe tomatoes and bell peppers. A little red wine makes it extra special. If you want your steak to be very tender, use sirloin. Skip that bland, tasteless fast cooking rice. Try a nice Jasmine or Arborio; they aren't hard to cook up and will make the meal even tastier.

Serves 4 at 121 milligrams sodium each

1 pound round steak

2 tablespoons olive oil

2 medium onions, thinly sliced

1 large clove garlic, minced

$1^1/2$ cups salt-free beef broth

$1/2$ cup dry red wine

2 teaspoons Worcestershire sauce

2 teaspoons fresh chopped basil

$1/2$ teaspoon fresh ground black pepper

2 small bell peppers cut in strips

2 tablespoons cornstarch

$1/4$ cup water

2 nice, ripe, red tomatoes, cut in eighths

4 servings hot cooked rice

Cut meat into strips about $1/4$-inch wide by 2–3 inches long by $1/4$-inch thick. Heat oil in 12-inch skillet over medium-high heat until drop of water sizzles on it. Tilt skillet to coat with oil. Add meat, onions separated into rings, and garlic. Cook for 6–7 minutes or until onion is tender, stirring often. Stir in broth, wine, Worcestershire sauce measured carefully, basil, and pepper. Bring to a boil; reduce heat to medium low; cover and simmer 30 minutes. Stir in pepper. Cover and simmer 5 minutes or until meat is tender. Combine cornstarch and water, mixing until smooth. Stir into meat mixture. Cook and stir over high heat 3 minutes, until thickened and bubbly. Reduce heat to medium low and add tomatoes. Cover and heat 3–4 minutes until heated through. Serve over hot cooked rice.

Stuffed Peppers

When peppers are at their peak, why not make 4 and freeze a couple?

Serves 2 at 132 milligrams sodium each

2 small peppers, red, orange, yellow, purple, even green
1/2 pound low-fat ground beef
1/4 cup quick-cooking rice, uncooked
Dash of pepper
Pinch of your favorite herb
1/2 teaspoon (measure carefully!) Worcestershire sauce
1 tablespoon finely chopped onion (or a teaspoon of dehydrated onion flakes, but be sure there's no sodium in them)
1 egg, beaten slightly
1 (8-ounce) can no-salt-added tomato sauce or 1 cup home prepared without salt

Cut tops off peppers, remove seeds and membranes. Precook peppers in boiling water 5 minutes and drain, or cook a couple minutes in the microwave until slightly softened. Combine remaining ingredients except use only half the tomato sauce. Mix well and stuff into peppers. Stand them upright in a small oven proof dish or pan and pour the remaining sauce over the tops. Cover and bake at 350° 45–50 minutes removing cover last 10 minutes. Baste peppers with sauce 2 or 3 times during cooking.

A couple thoughts here: green peppers aren't "ripe," and once they turn color, they have much more flavor, nutrition, and are easier to digest.

Crockpot Stuffed Peppers

I love coming home from work to the smell of these simmering, especially when I've used peppers from my own garden.

Serves 6 at 80 milligrams sodium each

6 bell peppers*
1/3 cup uncooked quick-cooking rice

1 1/4 pounds lean beef ground
2 teaspoons chopped fresh oregano
1 tablespoon chopped fresh parsley
1 teaspoon garlic powder
1 medium onion, finely chopped
16-ounce can salt-free tomato sauce
1/2 cup water

Cut off tops of peppers, seed, and rinse. Combine beef with rice and seasonings. Stuff peppers and stand in crockpot. Combine sauce and water. Pour over peppers. Simmer low 8–10 hours.

*Use tall, thin peppers so they fit in pot better. If you have a smaller crockpot, adjust the recipe to the number of peppers you can fit into it.

Pot Roast Dinner

Very tasty.

Serves 2 at 150 milligrams sodium each

3/4 pound boneless beef chuck roast
1 teaspoon olive oil
3/4 cup water
2 large carrots, peeled and halved
1 small onion, peeled and quartered
2 medium potatoes, peeled and quartered

In a heavy skillet, brown meat on all sides in oil. Add water, cover, and simmer an hour; add more water as needed. Add the carrots, onion, and potatoes. Continue to simmer 45–60 minutes until meat and veggies are tender.

American Rice

The sage and fennel seeds together with the beef will give you the taste of sausage without all the salt. Ample servings.

Serves 2 at 88 milligrams sodium each

1/2 pound ground beef
1 teaspoon minced fresh sage or a scant 1/2 teaspoon dried and rubbed between your hands before tossing it in
1/2 teaspoon fennel seeds (taste best if lightly toasted before adding, see Herbs and Spices section)
2 tablespoons chopped onion
2 tablespoons chopped celery
2 tablespoons chopped bell pepper
1 clove garlic, minced
1 cup water
1/3 cup uncooked long grain rice
1/2 teaspoon paprika, Hungarian, smoky, or plain

Pinch red pepper flakes, more to taste

16-ounce can no-salt-added tomatoes, diced (You can buy canned, no-salt-added, or whole tomatoes if it's hard to find no-salt diced; just dice yourself by dragging a sharp knife through them a bunch of times right in the can. Use with all the juice.)

In saucepan, cook ground beef, sage, fennel, onion, celery, bell pepper, and garlic until vegetables are soft and meat is no longer pink. Add a tablespoon of oil if meat is too lean to produce enough fat for cooking the vegetables in. Add water, rice, paprika, and red pepper flakes. Bring up to a boil, then cover and reduce heat to simmer until rice is tender, about 20 minutes, stirring once. Add a little water if mixture gets too dry before rice is done. Uncover; stir in tomatoes. Heat through.

Old-Fashioned Meatloaf

Memorable.

Serves 8 at 144 milligrams sodium each

$2/3$ cup skim milk

2 large eggs

2 slices good, dense bread, like whole wheat, cut into $1/2$-inch cubes

$1/4$ cup diced onion

1 clove garlic, minced

1 tablespoon Worcestershire sauce

1 teaspoon dried oregano

3–4 grinds fresh ground pepper

$1/2$ pounds lean ground chuck

$1/4$ cup, no-salt-added ketchup (such as Hunt's)

1 tablespoon balsamic vinegar

It will be a whole lot easier to get the meatloaf out, and to wash the pan, if you line a 2-quart baking dish or loaf pan with foil. Now combine the milk and eggs in a large bowl and beat to loosen the eggs. Stir in bread cubes, onion, garlic and Worcestershire sauce. To release more flavor, take the dry oregano into your hands and rub them together over the bowl so the oregano is crushed as it falls into mixture. What's it all about? FLAVOR!! Grind in the pepper and give it a stir. Smoosh in the ground beef until it's all thoroughly mixed; using your hands here just makes sense. Form it into a loaf shape and transfer to pan. Bake at 350° for about 45 minutes. Take it out and drain fat. Combine ketchup and vinegar (I do love good balsamic—it really pumps up the flavor without making food taste tart or sour) and spread over the top of the meatloaf. Return it to the oven another 10–15 minutes to set the topping and finish cooking the meat. Let stand a few minutes, pour off any fat, and transfer to platter for slicing.

Heavenly Homemade Hash

Cringing at the thought of sodium-laden hash? If you are, I'm proud of you—it means you're thinking hard! But I have good news if you crave it. This is easy and will satisfy your craving at 85 milligrams sodium for each of the 2 servings here. It's a good way to use up the rest of the Sunday roast beef. No, you can't do this with corned beef that would be disastrous, but you could use leftover turkey.

Serves 2 at 85 milligrams sodium each

1 tablespoon unsalted butter

1 cup cubed cooked beef

$1/2$ cups chopped raw potato

2 tablespoons chopped onion

$1/4$ cup beef broth, homemade, or from salt-free bouillon

Melt butter in medium skillet. Add the rest of the list and stir well. Cover and cook over low, stirring often until potatoes are tender. Uncover and cook 5 minutes longer.

Meaty Rigatoni Bake

It's a little work, but worth the trouble when you think about all the sodium in the usual recipe. Using beef with fennel and sage fools the tongue into believing you put sausage in this dish, but you wouldn't really do that. This makes two very hearty servings. Measure the cheeses carefully; that's where most of the sodium is.

Serves 2 at 446 milligrams sodium each

1 cup uncooked rigatoni, ziti, or other tube pasta

$1/2$ pound lean ground beef

$1/2$ teaspoon fennel seed

$1/2$ teaspoon sage

$3/4$ cup fresh mushrooms, sliced

$1/2$ cups homemade Spaghetti Sauce (see page 116)

$1/2$ cup shredded mozzarella

2 tablespoons grated Parmesan

Cook pasta according to directions on package WITHOUT the salt in the water! In medium skillet, stir together beef, fennel seeds, sage, and mushrooms; sauté over medium until no pink remains in beef. Stir in sauce. Drain pasta and stir into beef and sauce in skillet. Transfer to baking dish sprayed with cooking spray. Sprinkle cheeses on top. Bake at 350° for 30 minutes until hot.

Apricot-Sauced Pork Chops

Don't be put off by the snipping of dried apricots. I find it's faster to do with kitchen shears but you may want to use

a chef's knife instead. Just keep rinsing it under hot water to reduce the stickiness after each cut. You can easily cut this recipe in half or down to a third for 2 servings—it will also make the snipping process go more quickly.

Serves 6 at 62 milligrams sodium each

3/4 cup orange juice
1/4 cup sugar
1/2 cup dried apricots, snipped (this can be tedious)
1/4 teaspoon cloves
6 3/4-inch-thick lean pork chops
1 tablespoon olive oil

In small saucepan, combine juice, sugar, apricots, and cloves. Bring to a boil, cover, and simmer 20 minutes or until apricots are tender. Trim meat well and brown in oil. Place chops in 8x13-inch baking dish and spoon apricot mixture over them. At this point, chops can be covered and refrigerated up to 24 hours if needed. When ready, cover with foil and bake 45 minutes at 350°.

Winey Pork Chops

Okay, I think this is a good place to quote that saying, "I love to cook with wine. Sometimes I even put it in the food." You'll love the rich flavor.

Serves 4 at 79 milligrams sodium each

4 1-inch-thick pork chops, well trimmed
1 cup dry red wine
1 clove garlic, crushed
1/2 cup onion, minced
1/4 cup olive oil
1/4 cup balsamic vinegar
1 teaspoon rosemary
Fresh ground pepper

Combine marinade. Place chops in plastic bag, add marinade and support in dish in refrigerator for 4 hours to overnight. Discard marinade and grill or broil 15–20 minutes or until juices run clear.

Slow Cooker Country-Style Spareribs

This method loads in the flavor and makes the process so much easier than all that boiling, roasting, and grilling that is just too time consuming for me.

Serves 6 at 203 milligrams sodium each

6 pounds spareribs
1 onion, chopped
1 green bell pepper, chopped
2 stalks celery, chopped

2 (8-ounce) cans no-salt tomato sauce
3 tablespoons brown sugar
2 tablespoons white wine vinegar
4 tablespoons lemon juice
2 teaspoons Worcestershire sauce

Season ribs with pepper to taste. In a large skillet, over medium-high heat brown ribs on all sides. Place half of the onion, green pepper, and celery in the bottom of a slow cooker. Place half of the ribs on top the vegetables then repeat with the remaining vegetables and ribs. In a medium bowl, combine the tomato sauce, brown sugar, vinegar, lemon juice, and Worcestershire sauce. Pour mixture over the top of the ribs. Cook on high for 1 hour. Reduce to low and cook for another 8–9 hours.

Pan Pork Chops with Broccoli Rabe

Deglazing with wine is the key here. Once you've browned those chops up nice you'll see all that flavor stuck to the bottom of the pan. Carefully pour in the wine and like magic you can loosen and stir up all that flavor.

Serves 4 at 55 milligrams sodium each

2 tablespoons oil
Freshly ground pepper to taste
4 nicely trimmed pork chops
1/2 cup white wine
1 cup salt-free chicken stock
1 big bunch broccoli rabe, trimmed and chopped into 2- to 3-inch pieces
2–3 tablespoons golden raisins

Preheat oven to 375°. Heat a cast iron skillet on stove till hot; add oil. Sprinkle pepper over both sides of chops and place in hot oil. Brown 2–3 minutes, turn, and repeat. Remove chops and deglaze pan with wine, scraping all the flavorful bits up. Add stock. Top with rabe and raisins. Place in oven uncovered for 10–12 minutes until chops are done and rabe is crisp-tender.

Pork Tenderloin with Apples

Coating the pork with spices then serving with sautéed apples boosts the flavor without the sodium.

Serves 4 at 90 milligrams sodium each

1/4 teaspoon ground coriander
1/4 teaspoon freshly grated black pepper
1/8 teaspoon ground cinnamon (use the good Ceylon stuff here, see discussion on these spices page 52)
1/8 teaspoon ground nutmeg (grind it yourself if you have the stuff, if you don't, why not?)

1 pound pork tenderloin cut crosswise into 12 equal
    pieces (note when buying pork tenderloin that the
    packages often contain two)
Cooking spray
2 tablespoons unsalted butter
2 red-skinned good cooking apples, peel left on, sliced
    thinly
1 medium shallot, sliced thinly
1/4 cup apple cider
1 teaspoon fresh thyme leaves

Heat a skillet over medium high heat. Combine coriander, pepper, cinnamon, and nutmeg. Sprinkle evenly over pork medallions. Coat skillet with cooking spray and add pork. Cook 2–3 minutes on each side just till done. Remove from skillet, tent with foil to keep warm. Melt butter in same skillet. Add apples and shallots and sauté about 4 minutes until apple slices start to brown. Add apple cider to pan and bring up to simmer. Cook until apples are crisp-tender. Stir in thyme and scrape up any flavorful bits stuck to bottom of pan. Serve with pork.

My Favorite Pork Chops

These are amazing—loaded with flavor, almost no sodium. I've never served this to anyone who didn't love it, and no one has looked for a salt shaker. Sweet cherry season is relatively brief—don't miss out on this delicious, low-sodium feast.

Each of 4 servings is 90 milligrams sodium.

4 tablespoons olive oil
4 3/4-inch-thick pork chops, about 10 ounces each, plus
    or minus
6 tablespoons good raspberry vinegar
2 tablespoons honey, pick your favorite flavor, I use laven-
    der, yep, but clover and orange blossom work well—
    what? Never thought about getting flavor out of
    honey? Flavor is what it's all about; take any chance
    that offers a way to cut the sodium use!
1 cup dark, sweet cherries, halved and pitted (oh, it's
    worth it, honest)
1–2 tablespoons minced fresh rosemary leaves
4 tablespoons cold unsalted butter, each in 4 cubes for 16
    total—cold is important, so cut it up before you start
    cooking and stash in the chiller till you need them.

Heat oil over medium-high and place chops in pan. Cover, cooking 7–8 minutes. Flip and cook another 7–8 minutes or until fully cooked. Remove to a plate, cover with foil and keep warm. Pour vinegar into hot pan, scraping up those delicious, brown, flavorful bits, then add the honey and stir in well. Bring it to a boil and stir until it thickens some. Stir in the cherries and rosemary, and simmer until cherries are softened but not falling apart. Sweet cherries give up little juice, unlike

sour, so the sauce should stay at the syrupy consistency you had before they were added. Now take the pan off the burner and drop in 2 or 3 cubes of butter at a time, stirring until they melt and blend in. Keep going until all the butter is blended in and the rich sauce is shimmering and delicious. Enjoy sauce spooned over the chops.

Pork Chops with Apple-Pecan Butter Sauce

In the mood for something with a mildly sweet glaze? This is it. And it goes perfectly with a side of squash or sweet potatoes. So low in sodium that you can eat two chops.

Serves 4 at 55 milligrams sodium each

4 3/4-inch-thick boneless pork chops
Fresh ground pepper
2 tablespoons unsalted butter
1 medium apple, cored and sliced in thin wedges, skin
    left on
1/4 cup chopped pecans
2 tablespoons packed brown sugar

Trim any excess fat from chops, season with pepper. In large skillet, melt butter over medium heat. Add apples, cook a minute, and flip over; move to side of skillet. Add chops and cook 4 minutes. Flip chops. Stir apples and spoon over chops. Sprinkle pecans and brown sugar over chops and apples. Cover and cook another 5–6 minutes until chops are done; remove to plates and spoon apples and sauce over chops.

Sweet 'n' Spicy Pork Chops

Tasty with a side of cole slaw.

Serves 2 at 75 milligrams sodium each

2 nice 3/4-inch-thick pork loin chops, 6 ounces or so each
4 quick grinds of the pepper mill
2 tablespoons brown sugar
1 tablespoon minced onion
1 teaspoon chili powder (take it up a little if you dare. You
    can find a recipe for this on page 53)
1/2 teaspoon garlic powder
1/2 teaspoon prepared mustard (not Dijon)

Hit each side of each chop with a grind of pepper and toss them on a foil-lined broiler pan. Broil about 6 minutes on one side about 5 inches from the heat. Meantime, combine remaining ingredients. Flip the chops and spread with brown sugar mixture. Broil another 6–8 minutes until done.

Beer Chops

You can use root beer if you like that better. It will make it sweeter but it also makes it (big) kid friendly.

Serves 2 at 154 milligrams sodium each

3/4 cup dark beer or root beer
1/2 cup no-salt ketchup
2 teaspoons Worcestershire sauce
1 teaspoon brown sugar (skip if using root beer)
1/2 teaspoon salt-free chili powder (see recipe page 53)
2 tablespoons olive oil
2 tablespoons flour
1/2 teaspoon onion powder
1/2 teaspoon freshly ground black pepper
1/4 teaspoon garlic powder
2 pork loin chops

Combine beer, ketchup, Worcestershire sauce, brown sugar, and chili powder in small bowl; set aside. Heat oil in large skillet. In a zipper-lock plastic bag, combine flour, onion powder, pepper, and garlic powder. Drop one chop at a time into bag and shake to coat, then place in hot oil. Brown, then flip and brown other side. Pour beer mixture into skillet with chops. Bring to a boil, cover, and reduce heat to simmer. Cook 10–15 minutes until tender, turning once. Remove chops and keep warm. Boil sauce to reduce by half. Serve sauce over chops.

Spicy Herb Pork Chops

Here's a place where you can certainly play with the flavor and make it your way—try marinating the chops in a little lime juice for an hour first. Use red onions or scallions if that's what you like or have handy. Switch the mint to apple mint or lemon mint. Change out the sage for cilantro if you like it. The flavors of the salsa really develop if they can have an hour or two in the fridge before serving time.

Serves 2 at 65 milligrams sodium each

2 pork loin chops
1 tablespoon olive oil

Salsa

1 medium plum tomato, chopped
2 tablespoons chopped onion
1 tablespoon minced fresh mint
1 teaspoon minced jalapeño pepper
1 tablespoon lime juice
1 large sage leaf, minced

Combine salsa ingredients; refrigerate till ready to serve. Heat oil in skillet and brown then cook chops until done, 4–5 minutes on each side. Serve with salsa. Recipe easily doubles if you have guests!

Faux Sausage

None. Nadda. Zero. Zip.

Dying for the taste of sausage, but you just can't risk it? Congratulations, you go to the head of the class! Most sausages get their flavor from fennel seeds and sage. Try cooking up some ground turkey or lean beef, adding some of these herbs. It may satisfy the craving.

Lamb Rosemary

This is so full of flavor and aroma that you'll have the neighbors coming over to see what smells so good! Don't substitute fast-cooking rice.

Serves 4 at 75 milligrams sodium each

4 lean sirloin or shoulder lamb chops, well trimmed
1 cup raw regular long-grain rice
1 cup sliced fresh mushrooms
2 cups water
1 clove garlic, minced
1 tablespoon chopped fresh rosemary
1 teaspoon mustard powder
1/4 cup chopped fresh parsley
2 tablespoons pine nuts

Brown chops in medium skillet sprayed with non-stick cooking spray over medium-high heat just until browned on both sides. Drain. Combine rice, mushrooms, water, and garlic in same skillet; place lamb on top of rice mixture. Sprinkle evenly with rosemary and mustard. Bring to boil, reduce heat, and cover. Simmer 14 minutes; do not peek or stir. Remove from heat and let stand 10 minutes covered. Remove lamb; stir parsley and pine nuts into rice, and serve lamb with rice.

Braised Lamb Shanks

Old fashioned flavor, easy on the budget, and light on the sodium. Skim the fat and serve the sauce over a side of fluffy mashed potatoes.

Serves 2 at 100 milligrams sodium each

2 tablespoons flour
Dash fresh ground pepper
2 medium lamb shanks
1 tablespoon olive oil
1/2 cup chopped onion
1 small clove garlic minced
3/4 cup water
1 tablespoon fresh chopped parsley (or 1 teaspoon dried)
1/4 teaspoon curry powder (if you aren't crazy about curry, substitute dried oregano)

Combine flour and pepper. Coat shanks with mixture and brown evenly in hot oil. Stir in onion and garlic;

cook until tender but not brown. Add remaining ingredients. Cook, covered over low heat, about 1¼ hours or until tender, turning meat occasionally.

Lamb Patties with Creamed Peas and Onions

This is a very economical dish that feels like comfort food. It goes together quickly and works nicely with a side of mashed potatoes. Be sure to use catsup without salt.

Serves 2 at 332 milligrams sodium each

2 tablespoons milk
2 tablespoons catsup
¹⁄₂ slice white bread made into fresh crumbs, or minced up with a knife
¹⁄₂ teaspoon dried oregano, crushed between your hands before adding to the mixture
3 grinds fresh black pepper
¹⁄₂ pound ground lamb
2 tablespoons olive oil
¹⁄₂ medium sweet onion, thinly sliced but not chopped
2 tablespoons unsalted butter
2 teaspoons flour
¹⁄₂ cup milk
1 cup frozen peas, thawed

In a medium mixing bowl, combine milk, catsup, crumbs, oregano, pepper. Add lamb and combine thoroughly. Form into two patties about ¾-inch thick. Heat oil in a medium skillet and sauté patties over medium heat until done, about 5–6 minutes each side, flipping once. Set patties aside, covered with foil, and keep warm. Wipe out any fat in pan. Melt butter in same skillet and cook onion over medium heat until softened, but not browned. Blend flour into butter and onions in pan. Cook 1 minute, then add ¹⁄₂ cup milk. Stir in peas. Cook and stir until sauce is thickened and bubbly. Return patties to pan, cover. Heat through and serve.

Garlic Lamb

Garlic is a traditional flavoring for lamb. So is mint. I love mint jelly on the side with this dish. It balances and compliments the lamb perfectly. You could also add some chopped mint (only a teaspoon or so) to the garlic puree for a change.

Serves 10–12 at 100 milligrams sodium each

6 pounds boneless leg of lamb
10 cloves garlic, smashed with flat side of chef's knife blade
1 cup olive oil
1 teaspoon black pepper

1 cup red wine
1 cup salt-free chicken stock

Place smashed cloves of garlic in blender with oil and pepper. Blend slowly then turn to high until puree is pasty. Spread over lamb in a pan that can withstand direct heat of the burner as well, such as an aluminum baking pan. Roast at 400°, about 2 hours or until 135° on meat thermometer. Remove from pan, cover, and keep warm while making sauce. Place roasting pan over burners on medium heat and deglaze with wine. Scrape all the good bits from the bottom of the pan. Add stock and increase heat to slow boil to reduce volume of sauce by about half. Pour through sieve into serving cup. Serve hot with lamb.

Want to get all this flavor but not have all that leftover lamb in the fridge to deal with? Use a smaller cut of boneless lamb. You can also ask your butcher to cut a large roast into approximate 2-pound roasts and freeze some. Then make half the puree and what you don't use on your smaller lamb roast can be kept in a tightly closed container in the fridge and used on chops, chicken breasts, whatever you like.

Marinated Leg of Lamb for Grill or Broiler

Here's another great way to use herbs. If you want to add fresh instead of the dried in the recipe, simply triple the amount. Don't be shy, it's just a marinade. Have the lamb "butterflied" by the butcher. That will flatten it out so it cooks evenly. This is wonderful on the barbecue.

One 4-oz. portion is 80 milligrams sodium

6 pounds boneless leg of lamb
¹⁄₂ cup white wine vinegar
1 cup olive oil
1 teaspoon oregano
3 teaspoons dried mint flakes
2 cloves garlic
2 tablespoons dried thyme
2 tablespoons dried rosemary

Combine vinegar, oil and seasonings. Process in blender until emulsified. Prick meat all over with tip of knife. Put meat in zipper bag and pour marinade over. Set bag in a dish in case of leaks and refrigerate 8–24 hours turning often. Discard marinade (do not reserve any marinade that has been in contact with raw meat) and bring meat back to room temperature. Transfer to grilling rack or broiler pan. Takes about 12 minutes on grill over hot coals for medium-rare, but check it with a meat thermometer. It should register 140° for rare, 160° for medium. Let rest on cutting board 10 minutes and cut thinly across the grain.

Sweetly Spiced Pork

A very tasty and speedy way to have a healthy pork meal.

Serves 4 at 85 milligrams sodium each

1 pound pork tenderloin, cubed
1 tablespoon olive oil
Pepper to taste
1/2 teaspoon ground cinnamon
1 cup butternut squash, cubed
1 onion, chopped
1/2 teaspoon ground cloves
1/4 teaspoon ground mace
2 tart apples, peeled, cored, and chopped
1 cup dried cranberries
2 tablespoons brown sugar
1/2 cup apple juice
1/2 cup chopped toasted walnuts
Pepper to taste

Heat oil in a large skillet over medium heat. Add pork and saute until lightly browned, about 3 to 4 minutes. Stir in cinnamon and season with pepper to taste. Remove pork from skillet and set aside. To same skillet add squash and saute for 4 minutes. Add additional oil if needed. Stir in onion and saute until soft. Stir in the cloves, mace, apples, cranberries and brown sugar. Saute for 4 to 5 minutes. Stir in the apple juice, reduce heat and simmer until apples are tender. Stir in reserved pork and cook for about 5 more minutes. Add chopped walnuts just before serving.

Grilled Pork Tenderloin with Orange Glaze

Serves 4, which is good because the neighbors are going to smell this on the grill want a taste. By the way, the marinade here has only 3 or 4 milligrams of sodium in the batch, in case you were thinking of trying it with other foods. And if you were, congratulations. Love it when my patients get so motivated. Be alert to measuring accurately; the marmalade and mustard in the glaze are the real sodium sources here.

Serves 4 at 145 milligrams sodium each

Marinade

1 cup orange juice
1/4 cup cider vinegar
1 tablespoon fresh ginger, finely grated
1 teaspoon orange peel, finely grated
1 pound pork tenderloin

Glaze

1 cup orange marmalade
Fresh ground pepper to taste
1 tablespoon fresh ginger, finely grated
2 tablespoons "No Soy Sauce" (see page 142)
2 tablespoons cider vinegar
1 tablespoon French-style mustard

Combine first 4 ingredients in zipper-style plastic bag. Add pork; remove air and seal. Marinate in refrigerator at least 4 hours or overnight.

When ready to cook meat, prepare glaze. Melt marmalade in small saucepan. Stir in remaining ingredients; reduce heat to low. Cook 10 minutes. Reserve ¼ cup for brushing on meat. Place remaining glaze in small bowl to serve with pork. Remove pork from marinade. Oil hot grid to help prevent sticking. Grill pork on covered grill, over medium coals 18–25 minutes or until 155° on meat thermometer. Turn and brush with reserved glaze last 10 minutes of cooking. Let pork stand 5–10 minutes before slicing.

Meat Tenderizer

Oh, a word about meat tenderizer. I know, you think the word I'm going to say is DON'T or NO or STOP or TRASH or POISON—well yes, but what if the word was papaya? One of the main active ingredients in meat tenderizer is an enzyme from the papaya called papin. The rest of the ingredients of meat tenderizer are poison. How can we get the good papin without the poison? Dice up a papaya, spread it on all sides of the cut of meat you want tenderized and place in a plastic, resealable bag. Massage the fruit into the meat and marinate in fridge 30 minutes, more if it's a big cut or a very tough cut. Wipe off the papaya and proceed as usual. Violá!

A Final Word About Meats . . .

These represent only a fraction of the things you can do as you improve your detective skills. Find where sodium is lurking and flush it out; replace it with real flavor. Take a look at the section on sauces a little further on for some marinade, gravy, and sauce ideas for your meats, too. There is nothing wrong with a plain, broiled, or baked chop or burger, it's what you put on top that can put your sodium counts over the top.

Try using whole-grain pastas to increase the nutritional value of your meal . . . if you like the texture. One of the nice things about pasta is that it is so absorbent. That makes it easy to soak flavor into it. You know, like when you used to add salt to the boiling water to cook the pasta in, but now you don't, because you don't want to let that salt raise your daily sodium intake and keep you from eating things you really want. One of the things pasta soaks up best is tomato sauce, and that's something you can make—and even buy—without salt. Now let's flavor that up, too . . .

Spaghetti Sauce

Here's a basic sauce for making all things pasta. Tinker with it as long you don't accidentally add something with sodium in it. Don't like bell peppers in it? Drop them. Love garlic? Double it! Like it juicier? Increase the no-salt tomato sauce. Enjoy it as you like it, just adjust the sodium content for anything else you add. And please, no sausage. It's not the fat I'm thinking about, it's the heavy sodium load.

Makes 6 cups at 68 milligrams sodium per cup

1 pound lean ground beef
2 medium onions, chopped
1 green pepper, seeded and chopped
2 cloves garlic, minced
1 tablespoon sugar
2 teaspoons dried crumbled basil
2 teaspoons dried crumbled oregano
1/8 teaspoon crushed red pepper
2 cans (16 ounces each) no-salt-added tomatoes with juice, chopped coarsely
1 (8-ounce) can no-salt tomato sauce
1 (6-ounce) can no-salt tomato paste

Brown ground beef and drain well. Add remaining ingredients, stir well and simmer for a couple hours or until as thick as you like. This can also simmer in a crockpot on low for 10–12 hours or on high for 5–6 hours. It keeps well and freezes well, too.

Baked Ziti

Regular cheese is generally laden with sodium. Low-salt cheese tastes like, well, blah. So this is calculated on regular mozzarella. Please measure carefully.

Serves 4 at 193 milligrams sodium each

8 ounces uncooked ziti
26-ounce can no-salt tomato sauce
1 pound lean ground beef
6 ounces mozzarella cheese, grated
8 ounces mushrooms, sliced
2 teaspoons fresh oregano, chopped
2 teaspoons fresh basil, chopped

Cook ziti in unsalted water until tender but still firm in the middle (al dante). Drain. Brown beef and mushrooms over medium heat in large skillet until done. Drain fat. Combine ziti and beef mixture with sauce and half the cheese. In medium greased casserole, bake, covered at 350° for 45 minutes. Uncover. Sprinkle on remaining cheese and herbs. Bake uncovered another 10–15 minutes until cheese melts and browns.

American Goulash

Four generous servings of one of America's comfort foods.

Serves 4 at 107 milligrams sodium each

2 cups uncooked elbow macaroni
1 pound lean ground beef
1 cup sliced fresh mushrooms
1 medium onion, chopped
1 cup celery slices
1 teaspoon dried basil
1/2 cup no-salt ketchup
1 (16-ounce) can no-salt-added tomatoes with the juices, coarsely chopped
1/4 teaspoon freshly ground pepper

Cook the macaroni al dante (so the center is still firm) without salt in the water. Brown beef together with mushrooms and onions. Drain fat. Combine all ingredients in a Dutch oven and simmer, covered for 45 minutes to an hour.

Shrimp and Pasta Salad

I can't tell you how many times I've taken this to a party and brought home an empty dish.

Serves 16 at 56 milligrams sodium each

SALAD
16-ounce package orzo, uncooked
2 cups broccoli flowerets
2 cups carrot, thinly sliced
1 cup celery, coarsely chopped
3/4 cup red onion, chopped
1 pound shrimp, cooked, cleaned, and shelled

DRESSING
16 ounces sour cream
16 ounces plain low-fat yogurt
2 tablespoons chopped fresh thyme
1/2 teaspoon pepper

Cook pasta according to package directions and drain. Rinse with cold water and drain well. In very large bowl combine pasta and all remaining salad ingredients; set aside. In medium bowl, stir together all dressing ingredients. Pour over salad and stir to mix well. Cover; refrigerate at least 2 hours.

NOTE: Two 7-ounce packages uncooked, dried pasta rings can be substituted for the uncooked dried rosamarina pasta (orzo).

Eggplant Lasagna

Reminds me of Eggplant Parmesan but with much less sodium.

Serves 6 at 232 milligrams sodium each

4 cups milk
2 tablespoons cornstarch
1/4 teaspoon freshly grated nutmeg
1/8 teaspoon freshly ground pepper
1 (8-ounce) package lasagna noodles
1 medium eggplant (about a pound, peeled if you like)
1 (8-ounce) cup ricotta cheese
2 eggs + 2 egg whites
1/2 cup chopped onion
1/2 cup shredded mozzarella

Stir cornstarch into cold milk to dissolve in medium saucepan and add nutmeg and pepper. Heat just until it boils then reduce heat to medium. Continue cooking 8–10 minutes until thickened, stirring frequently. Set aside but keep warm. Cook noodles in boiling water without salt, 5–6 minutes until softened but not cooked through. Rinse and drain. Cut eggplant in half then crosswise into 1/4-inch slices. Combine ricotta cheese, eggs and egg whites and onions. Spray a 13x9-inch baking dish with non-stick cooking spray. Spread about a half cup of the sauce in the pan. Top with 4 noodles, then top with half the eggplant. Sprinkle 2 tablespoons of the shredded mozzarella over the eggplant and top that with half the ricotta and egg mixture. Top with 3 more noodles, another half cup of sauce, the remaining eggplant, then the rest of the ricotta and egg mixture. Finish with the remaining noodles, then sauce and the last of the cheese. Bake uncovered 50–60 minutes until done through and bubbling. Let stand a few minutes to firm up a bit before trying to cut.

Pasta with Chicken and Asparagus

If you hate asparagus, try changing it to a veggie you do love. 2 cups of raw broccoli florets will only raise your sodium count by 10 mg. per serving.

Serves 4 at 275 milligrams sodium each

1 pound pasta (penne works well)
1 pound asparagus, woody ends snapped off and spears cut into 2-inch pieces
4 boneless, skinless chicken breasts, cut into bite-sized pieces
2 tablespoons olive oil
1 tablespoon of your favorite herb (oregano and basil work well here)

1/2 cup grated Parmesan cheese
2 tablespoons white wine
1/2 cup heavy cream

In boiling water without salt, cook pasta al dante, about 8 minutes. Add asparagus pieces for last 3 minutes or so of cooking time. While pasta cooks, sauté chicken pieces in olive oil in large pan just till done, about 3 or 4 minutes. Stir in herbs, cheese, and wine. Cook one minute and add heavy cream, heat through but don't boil. Drain pasta and asparagus and add to the chicken; stir and serve hot.

Macaroni and Cheese

Miss the taste of cheese? You can still enjoy it if it's planned carefully. For women particularly, it's important to get adequate calcium. This can be very difficult, if you're cutting out dairy to cut down sodium. This may seem like a lot, but with planning it can fit into your diet from time to time, especially if you like comfort foods occasionally.

Serves 8 at 306 milligrams sodium each

1 (8-ounce) package uncooked elbow macaroni
1 cup ricotta cheese
1 cup shredded mozzarella cheese
1/2 cup shredded cheddar cheese
2 eggs, beaten
3/4 cup evaporated skim milk
2 tablespoons finely chopped onion
1/2 teaspoon dry mustard
1/8 teaspoon white pepper
Paprika
1 teaspoon Parmesan cheese
1/2 cup homemade low-sodium toasted croutons

Preheat oven to 350°. Cook macaroni according to package directions but without salt. Drain. In a large bowl, combine ricotta, mozzarella and cheddar cheeses with eggs, milk, onion, Worcestershire sauce, mustard and white pepper. Mix until blended. Fold in cooked macaroni. Spoon mixture into a 2½-quart casserole dish sprayed with non-stick cooking spray and sprinkle with paprika and Parmesan. Top with a handful of croutons. Bake 20 to 30 minutes, or until bubbly.

Garden Pasta

Here's a way to use up all that garden zucchini.

Serves 2 at 115 milligrams sodium each

4 ounces dried spaghetti, or other favorite pasta or 9-ounce package refrigerated pasta
1 green or yellow zucchini or yellow summer squash halved and sliced 1/4-inch thick

2 teaspoons olive oil
1 tomato in 1/2-inch wedges
4 tablespoons homemade pesto (see page 145)

Prepare and drain pasta according to instructions on package, but without salt. Meanwhile, cook zucchini in olive oil over medium heat until just tender. Transfer pasta to serving bowl and toss with zucchini, tomatoes, and pesto.

Homemade Alfredo Sauce

Be judicious. Even homemade, it's a hefty sodium dose because of the cheese.

Makes 2 1/2 cups at 170 milligrams sodium per 1/4 cup

1 1/4 cups heavy cream
1 cup salt-free chicken broth
1 tablespoon cornstarch
Several turns of the fresh black pepper grinder
Large pinch ground nutmeg (you do grind this fresh yourself, right?)
1 tablespoon olive oil
4 cloves garlic, minced (about 2 teaspoons)
1/2 cup grated Parmesan cheese

Stir together cream, broth, cornstarch, pepper, and nutmeg. Set aside. In medium saucepan, heat oil over medium heat; add garlic; cook and stir for 20–30 seconds just till fragrant. Add broth and cream mixture, stirring and cooking for 2–3 minutes until thickened and bubbly. While still cooking, add Parmesan and stir till melted into cream mixture. Serve immediately or refrigerate up to 3 days, or freeze in individual 1/4-cup portions for up to 3 months. Thaw before warming and heat gently to keep from curdling.

Gingered Garlic Shrimp and Pasta

Quick and delicious!

Serves 2 for 387 milligrams sodium each

1 tablespoon fresh gingerroot, minced
2 cloves garlic, chopped
2 tablespoons unsalted butter
2 tablespoons olive oil
2 plum tomatoes, sliced
3/4 cup salt-free chicken broth
3 teaspoons fresh parsley, minced
3 teaspoons fresh basil, minced

1 1/2 teaspoons cornstarch
1 tablespoon cold water
1/2 pound shrimp uncooked, peeled, deveined
2 cups hot cooked angel hair pasta (cooked without salt in the water)

In large skillet, sauté ginger and garlic in butter and oil for 2–3 minutes or until tender. Stir in the tomatoes, broth, half the parsley and basil. Combine cornstarch and cold water until smooth; add to the skillet. Bring to a boil; cook and stir for 2 minutes or until thickened.

Reduce heat; add shrimp. Simmer uncovered for 2–3 minutes or until the shrimp turn pink. Add the pasta and remaining parsley and basil; toss to coat.

Herb Couscous with Saffron and Zucchini

Did you realize that couscous is actually a pasta? It is made from semolina like many other familiar pastas and is a popular staple in the cuisines of Northern African nations. Often served with a stew type dish over it, here it becomes a delicious side dish.

Serving 8, made exactly like this, each serving contains 5 milligrams sodium. What a bargain!

1 1/2 cups salt-free chicken stock
1/2 teaspoon freshly ground black pepper
1/4 teaspoon ground cumin
1/2 teaspoon saffron threads
2 tablespoons olive oil
2 tablespoons unsalted butter
2 zucchini, large dice
1 1/2 cups plain, dry couscous (10 ounces)
1 cup chopped basil leaves
1 cup chopped parsley leaves

Bring the chicken stock to a boil in a small saucepan, and turn off the heat. Add the pepper, cumin, and saffron threads and allow to steep for at least 15 minutes.

Meanwhile, heat the olive oil and melt the butter in a sauté pan. Add the zucchini and cook for 5 minutes, or until lightly browned. Bring the chicken stock just back to a boil. Place the couscous in a large bowl and add the cooked zucchini. Pour the hot chicken stock over them. Cover the bowl tightly with plastic wrap and allow to stand at room temperature for 15 minutes. Add the basil and parsley. Toss the couscous and herbs with a fork, and serve warm or at room temperature.

I've thought long and hard about this chapter. By now, you are accustomed to my tongue-in-cheek approach in this book, but allow me a serious moment to philosophize.

We all have ideas about what makes good eating, based on how we were raised, or more specifically, by what was on our tables growing up. The foods of our heritage are important to us at family dinners, gatherings for holidays, and other special occasions, and just anytime we want to cook or eat food that has a familiar ring, an inherent flavor. Defining ethnicity in food is no simpler than defining it in terms of geography, religion, or culture. Boundaries are blurred. There is little to use as the central base by which to compare. We could say, since my typical (though not exclusive) reader lives in the U.S., that American food is our "norm" and all other is "ethnic." But within accepted norms of "American" cuisine are many variations all across the country: New England, Southern, Northern Pacific regional, Mid-western, and West Coast styles to name a few. Within these are influences that flavor (sorry, couldn't avoid one pun) the regional cuisine. For example, you folks who identify yourselves as "southern" in lifestyle or gastronomic desire, have areas of even more focused influence within those margins as well—soul food, Louisiana French, and Cajun styles of cooking are major examples. Another is the influence of Mexican styles and flavors in southwest Tex-Mex cooking, and so on. And many regional styles come from locations where the flavors and cooking methods developed as a direct result of what was readily available to the cooks: fish along the Atlantic seaboard, coconut and pineapple in Hawaii, or, going back to the immigrant origins of our menu items, lamb in the middle east, olive oil of the Mediterranean, meatballs Swedish-style, Irish potatoes, Jewish deli foods, and so on.

America is a melting pot, they say (who are "they," anyway?). And so we count ourselves fortunate that we can draw from so many sources to vary our diets and keep our taste buds from becoming bored and cantankerous! As a result, we can take the best ideas from many resources and make them ours. What foods did you grow up with? What did your mom and gramma serve? Often they knew the ingredients and instructions by rote because the foods, ingredients, and cooking styles came from their childhoods. Did you have special menus for Sunday dinner at Gramma's house? Do you crave those tastes? Then recreate them! A few simple adjustments will pull them into the acceptable sodium range for your needs and the taste of Mama's good cookin' becomes a pleasure on your palate again.

While I have chosen not to break this chapter down by trying to group recipes together suggesting common heritages for them, I have not avoided national or regional identities in their titles or ingredients. This is not to say that my approach is to see "ethnic foods" as bound in one category, lumping them together and implying that they are somehow "different" or "not normal." In fact, they remind us of our roots and families, our histories, and as such, give us comfort. These recipes are taken from friends, family, and patients with varying ethnic backgrounds, so except for de-sodium-ization, (yes, I made that word up) they are authentic. Run your eyes over the recipes that follow. If your taste buds quiver, then go for it! If you've been looking for something that tastes like the homeland, I hope you find it here. Bon appetit! Buon appetito! Guten Appetit! Mahlzeit! Buen apetito! Smaklig måltid! Thokoleza ukudla!—or however your ethnicity would articulate it . . .

Pork Chops Mexicana

Chocolate played an important part in the history of Mexican cuisine. Initially, it was served as an unsweetened beverage. The word "chocolate" is derived from the Aztec word xocoatl, and the drink was often flavored with, yes, chili pepper. Cinnamon arrived with the Spaniards. The marriage between cinnamon and the native chocolate was made in culinary heaven. Try it here.

Serves 2 at 115 milligrams sodium each

2 boneless pork chops, ½-inch thick (about 4 ounces each)

¾ cup Onion Salsa (page 64) or Sharon's Southwest Mango Salsa (page 125)

½ teaspoon unsweetened baking cocoa

Pinch of cinnamon

2 tablespoons chopped fresh cilantro or green onions

Spray medium non-stick skillet with cooking spray and sauté chops over medium-high for 2–3 minutes on each side until browned on both sides. Combine salsa, cocoa, and cinnamon; spoon over chops and reduce heat to medium low. Simmer 5 more minutes until center of chops are no longer pink and sauce thickens slightly, turning once and stirring sauce after 3 minutes. Sprinkle with cilantro or green onions. Olé! (Actually the cocoa makes it "mole," pronounced like "olé" with an "m," and it's a traditional Mexican flavor.)

West African Ribs

Love peanuts? Love ribs? Here's a way to enjoy them that incorporates two favorite flavors of West Africa, peanuts, also called groundnuts, and chilies. (Be sure your peanut butter is no salt added, or make your own just by processing unsalted peanuts in a food processor. I do it all the time and love the fresh flavor it gives me. If it's too tight, loosen with just a couple drops peanut oil while processing.)

Serves 4 at 145 milligrams sodium each

2 pounds pork back ribs
1 onion, chopped
2 cloves garlic, chopped
2 tablespoons olive oil
1 tablespoon ground coriander
2 tablespoons lemon juice
2 teaspoons red chili pepper flakes
1/2 cup creamy, salt-free peanut butter
Fresh ground pepper to taste

Place ribs in shallow baking pan. Combine remaining ingredients in a blender or food processor and process until smooth. Spread on ribs and roast at 350° 1½ hours until tender.

Thai Chicken with Lemongrass

Hmmm, new flavor? Good! That's what we want to offset the old drive for salt, right? Lemongrass is very fragrant and will fit nicely with tropical flavors such as coconut, ginger, and citrus. It's found commonly in Thai food, especially in Thai curry paste. Look for the short spikes without the unneeded leaves. The flavor is in the canes. If you don't have access to a large produce section, look for it in a squeeze tube. I find many less-common herbs this way. It makes it easy to keep some on hand without endless searching and wasting when all you need is a little bit.

Serves 2 at 75 milligrams sodium each

1/4 cup coarsely chopped fresh cilantro (don't avoid the short, tender stems), extra for garnish if desired
2 tablespoons coconut milk (it comes in a can and may look almost solid when you open it. Just stir it and it'll smooth out. Look for other recipes that use coconut milk as long as you are opening the can!)
1 teaspoon chopped lemongrass or equivalent in lemongrass paste (buy this in the produce department)
2–3 fresh basil leaves (Thai basil?)

1 teaspoon (or more to taste), minced jalapeño or other moderately hot pepper (try Thai bird chilies but be cautious—these are powerful)
1 small clove garlic, minced
1/2 teaspoon packed brown sugar (yes, it's tiny, but it balances the heat nicely)
1/8 teaspoon (big pinch will due) ground coriander
Several grinds fresh black pepper
2 boneless, skinless chicken breasts
1 lime, quartered

In a small processor, combine cilantro, coconut milk, lemongrass, basil, jalapeño, garlic, brown sugar, coriander, and pepper and process to a smooth puree. Spread puree over chicken breasts to cover all sides and marinate in refrigerator 2–24 hours. Grill over medium-hot coals, on medium-hot grill pan for the stove, or broil until done, 5 minutes or so on each side. Rest 5 minutes and serve with lime wedges. Sprinkle with extra cilantro, if desired.

Moroccan Lamb Tagine with Raisins, Almonds, and Honey

One of my very favorites! Make couscous with some of the juices in the pot. Amazing!

Serves 6 at 118 milligrams sodium each

2 teaspoons Moroccan spice blend such as Ras-el-Hanout (see spice section—there's a recipe for this blend)
3/4 teaspoon black pepper
3/4 teaspoon ground ginger
1/4 teaspoon crumbled saffron threads
3 cups water
3 lb. boneless lamb shoulder cut into 1-inch cubes (if you can't find lamb shoulder, except as chops, use a leg of lamb instead. The cost of enough should chops for this recipe is just ridiculous!)
1 large red onion chopped small
2 garlic cloves finely chopped
2 (3-inch) cinnamon sticks
1/2 stick (1/4 cup) unsalted butter, cut into pieces
3/4 cups raisins
3/4 cups whole, blanched, unsalted almonds
1/2 cup honey

Whisk together Moroccan spice blend, pepper, ginger, saffron, and 1 cup water in a 5-quart heavy pot. Stir in lamb, remaining 2 cups water, onion, garlic, cinnamon sticks, and butter and simmer, covered, until lamb is just tender, about 1½ hours (if cutting recipe back and/or using small pieces of meat from shoulder chops, cut time to under an hour).

Stir in raisins, almonds, and honey, and simmer, covered, until meat is very tender, about 15–30 minutes more. Uncover pot and cook over moderately high heat, stirring occasionally, until stew is slightly thickened, about 15 minutes more.

Make couscous with some of the juices in the pot before uncovering for last cooking time. I use half juices, half water, and it is perfect!

Asian Chicken Soup

The herbs and spices common in Asian cooking surprised me when I saw that the list included many I expected from very different cuisines. For example, Asian, especially Southeast Asian food is commonly flavored with chili peppers. Cinnamon, coriander, ginger, star anise, cardamom, cloves, cumin and turmeric are all frequent flavorings. Here we focus on the citrus bite of lemongrass.

Serves 4 at 36 milligrams sodium each

Handful of fresh cilantro
4 cups sodium-free chicken stock
1 fresh lemongrass stem, bruised
1 small fresh red chili
Grated peel and juice of half a lime
Freshly ground pepper
8 ounces boneless chicken breast, diced
1 cup snow peas, cut diagonally into thin strips
1 carrot, shaved into ribbons
4 green onions (scallions) sliced thinly

Separate cilantro leaves from stems. Set leaves aside and add stems to 4-quart pot. Pour on stock; stir in lemongrass, chili, and lime peel. Bring to a boil, reduce heat to simmer and cover. Simmer 15–20 minutes. Strain through cheesecloth; discard seasonings and herbs; return stock to pot. Add lime juice and a few grinds of fresh pepper. Toss in the chicken chunks and bring back to a boil. Reduce and simmer for 5 minutes. Add vegetables and simmer another couple minutes until chicken is cooked and vegetables are tender. Chop cilantro leaves and toss into pot with ¾ of the sliced green onions. Stir and simmer one minute. Serve with more green onion sprinkled on top.

Asian Trout

The cuisines of Asia, in particular, Thailand, Viet Nam, Laos, and Cambodia, are full of great flavors with a wide range of sweetness and spiciness.

Serves 4 at 85 milligrams sodium each

4 trout fillets, 6–8 ounces each
4–6 tablespoons chili oil
2 tablespoons lime juice
1 garlic clove, minced

1 tablespoon grated fresh ginger
1 tablespoon grated fresh lemongrass
1 tablespoon minced fresh cilantro

Preheat broiler to high heat. Rinse trout and pat dry. Brush both sides of fillets with chili oil and arrange on foil-covered broiler pan. Combine remaining ingredients and spread over the fish. Broil 5–6 minutes, turning once, until cooked through. Arrange on plate and pour collected cooking juices over fish before serving.

Moroccan Red Snapper

Influenced by both North African flavors, such as those of Algeria, and the Spanish influences across the Gibraltar, Morocco has blended many great spices and flavors.

Serves 4 at 171 milligrams sodium each

4 garlic cloves
¾ cup fresh cilantro
2 teaspoons paprika (smoky or hot as you like it)
2 teaspoons ground cumin
¼ teaspoon chili powder
⅔ cup olive oil
¼ cup lime juice
4 cleaned and ready-to-cook red snapper fillets, about 12 ounces each (8 6-ounce fillets will also work)
Lime wedges and cilantro leaves for garnish, if desired

Using food processor, make a Chermoula: combine garlic, cilantro, paprika, cumin, and chili powder. With processor running, gradually pour in oil, and then lime juice. Process thoroughly to a loose pasty consistency. Cut 3–4 diagonal slits into the flesh of the fillets and rub Chermoula into them and over surface of fish. Lay on plate or baking dish and cover. Refrigerate to marinate for about an hour. To grill, preheat gas grill, or prepare charcoal grill and oil grates. To broil, preheat broiler to high. Broil or grill 4–5 minutes on each side until done. Garnish with lime wedges and cilantro and serve immediately.

Chicken Spiced the Middle Eastern Way

Middle Eastern cuisines boast many spices, but also other flavors that you'll find wipe out a craving for the salt shaker. And all the great native veggies and the couscous will make you feel like you're on a magic carpet.

Serves 4 at 127 milligrams sodium each

3 cups sodium-free chicken stock
4 6-ounce chicken breasts, boned and skinned
4 tablespoons unsalted butter

4 tablespoons olive oil

1 yellow onion, sliced thinly

2 pounds fresh, or two 14½-ounce cans no-salt-added tomatoes

1 small fresh chili, ribs and seeds removed, finely chopped

¼ cup chopped fresh cilantro

1 teaspoon ground ginger powder

1 teaspoon ground saffron

½ teaspoon ground nutmeg

1 eggplant, ¾ pound, cut into bite-sized pieces, peel on

3–4 carrots, peeled and diced

4 small zucchini, chopped

1 pound dried chickpeas that were rinsed, soaked and simmered until tender (or canned if you have a sodium-free resource)

1¾ cups water

10-ounce box plain, unprepared couscous (be careful, read the label, you don't want anything added, like flavors, and cheeses, and stuff that makes it salty. It shouldn't have more than 5 mg. sodium per 1 cup cooked.)

Bring stock to boil in large pot. Add chicken, reduce heat and simmer gently for 20 minutes. Remove chicken and set aside. Set stock aside. Melt half the butter with the oil in another large pan over medium heat. Stir and cook onion for 3 minutes. Add tomatoes, chili, cilantro, and spices. Cook and stir 1 minute. Stir in eggplant, carrots, zucchini, reserved stock, and the chickpeas. Bring to boil, reduce heat and simmer, covered, for 20 minutes. Wipe out first pot and add water and remaining butter. Bring to boil. Stir in couscous and remove from heat. Let stand 10 minutes. After 8 minutes, add chicken to the vegetables and simmer 2 minutes to heat through. Serve chicken and vegetables over couscous. Pour on any juices remaining in pot. Garnish with cilantro or parsley leaves.

Slow-Roasted Italian Pork

This takes a little planning, but what a great main dish for when the family crowd descends. Mine loves it. The flavor is actually infused into the meat by tucking slivers of yumminess directly into slits in the fat and meat and marinating it for hours. You won't look for the shaker and you'll want to squirrel away some for a sandwich the third day!

Serves 16 at 100 milligrams sodium each

1 pork shoulder, about 8–9 pounds

3 cups sliced onions

2 oranges sliced, including peels

2 tablespoons (about 5–6 cloves) minced garlic

1 tablespoon toasted fennel seeds

Freshly ground black pepper to taste

Day before serving

Cut hatch marks ½-inch into fat layer on top of roast. Layer slices of onion and orange on bottom of roasting pan. Place roast over slices and rub garlic and fennel into slits and over the fat and meat. Cover and marinate in refrigerator 12–24 hours.

Day of serving

Preheat oven to 275° and bake roast, uncovered 7–8 hours. Remove to platter and tent to rest. Pour off juices, discarding or separating onions and oranges. Remove fat from pan drippings, thicken for gravy or serve au jus with onions if reserved. (Leftovers make a great sandwich with a slice of provolone—yep, ya gotta count the sodium in the cheese at about 125 mg. per pre-packaged slice; check your package label.)

Chicken and Chili Enchiladas

Very authentic flavors in a scrumptious and easy to make dish. Dial up or down the green chili spiciness as you like it. Stick to fresh cilantro, it really makes a difference. Be sure to measure the salty cheese carefully.

125 milligrams sodium per enchilada

Vegetable oil

3 fresh hot green chilies such as jalapeño or Serrano, seeded and chopped

1 Spanish onion, chopped

2 garlic cloves, chopped

2 tablespoons chopped fresh cilantro

2 tablespoons lime juice

½ cup sodium-free chicken stock

2 beefsteak tomatoes, peeled, seeded, and chopped

Pinch of sugar

1 pound cooked chicken, shredded

3 ounces cheddar cheese, grated (yes, ya gotta measure or it'll get ya. It should be about ¾ cup if you don't try to pack in extra!)

2 teaspoons chopped fresh oregano

8 corn tortillas (skip those flour tortillas, whew!)

Preheat oven to 350°. Oil a large ovenproof dish with vegetable oil; set aside. Put two of the chilies, the onion, garlic, cilantro, lime juice, chicken stock, and tomatoes into food processor and pulse a few times until well blended. Scrape into a medium pan and simmer over medium heat ten minutes or until thickened. Mix the remaining chili with the chicken, ½ cup of the cheese, and oregano. Stir in half the sauce. Heat the tortillas in a dry, heavy-bottomed skillet, or in the microwave according to package directions. Divide the chicken mixture evenly among the tortillas, spooning it down the centers, then roll up and arrange, seam-side down, in the prepared dish. Pour the remaining sauce over the enchiladas and sprinkle with remaining cheese. Bake in preheated oven 20 minutes. Serve immediately.

Swedish Meatballs

My source tells me there are many recipes for "authentic" Swedish meatballs, but this is her favorite. Sauces also vary from none to brown to white. Use what you like. Just be sure the sodium is minimized and accounted for! I'm told that the traditional way to serve these is with a side bowl of lingonberry sauce. Ya, they're tiny. If you want dinner-sized, make a dozen and charge yourself 33 milligrams each. Remember, sauce is extra.

Makes 48 at 8 milligrams sodium each

1 tablespoon unsalted butter
1 tablespoon minced onion
$1/3$ cup fine dry bread crumbs from low-sodium bread
$1/2$ cup salt-free beef broth or water
$1/2$ cup half-and-half cream
$3/4$ pound ground 90% fat-free ground beef
$1/4$ pound ground pork
$1/4$ teaspoon finely ground white pepper
$1/4$ teaspoon ground mustard
Pinch fresh grated nutmeg

White Sauce

$1/2$ cup hot water
1 teaspoon salt-free chicken bouillon
2 tablespoons unsalted butter
2 tablespoons flour
$1^1/2$ cups half-and-half
1–2 teaspoons minced fresh dill

Blend all ingredients, then beat (yes, beat the mixture with an electric mixer) until very smooth. Form into small $3/4$- to 1-inch balls (I use a melon baller for consistency). Place on rimmed, lightly greased baking sheets and bake at 450° for about 10 minutes. Stir gently into sauce, if you are using one. You can panfry them, but I find they resemble something other than balls no matter how careful I try to be. They keep well for a couple days in the fridge, or freeze them spread out on a clean baking sheet and store in a freezer bag or container; just take out what you need, thaw and rewarm at 350° for 10 or 15 minutes. This easily doubles, and there's no rule that says you can't make them any size you want, just adjust the sodium count and cooking time. Since this is my book, I can be biased and tell you about my favorite sauce for these little knobs of wonder:

Drain the fat from the baking pan after the meatballs are done, but keep the tasty stuck-on stuff where so much flavor is. Stir in water and bouillon. Stir and scrape to loosen the good stuff. Meantime, melt butter in a medium saucepan and stir flour into it, being sure to whack the lumps and keep it smooth. Keep it warm as you work and stir, and let it cook a minute or two, so it cooks off the raw flour taste, but don't let it brown. Then whip the chicken-brown bits mixture into the flour/butter mixture. Again, be careful to keep it smooth (it's ok to whirl this in a blender for a jiffy to smooth it out, then return to pan). Turn up the heat, let it come to a boil, and then take it down to a simmer. Stir half-and-half into the saucepan, keep it moving so it doesn't scorch, and simmer till thickened a bit. Here's where I like to add the dill. Now pour this over those meatball babies and pass the fancy toothpicks! All the sodium is in the half-and-half which, at 6 mg. per tablespoon, doesn't sound bad (unless you're counting fat and cholesterol . . .).

Frikadellen

A German-style cross between a meatball and a fancy hamburger.

Serves 4 at 160 milligrams sodium each

2 slices low-sodium bread, cubed
Cream, about 3 tablespoons or so
1 pound ground meat (a combination of beef and pork works well here)
1 medium onion, finely chopped
1 egg, lightly beaten
2 teaspoons chopped fresh parsley (or 1 teaspoon dried)
2 teaspoons chopped fresh oregano or marjoram, (or 1 teaspoon dried)
Couple grinds of black pepper
1 tablespoon prepared mustard (German style is best, but plain yellow is good)
1 tablespoon unsalted butter
1 tablespoon vegetable or olive oil

Soak the bread cubes in the cream, but only use enough to thoroughly moisten them, not make them soggy; they need to hold the meat together. Combine with remaining ingredients except butter and oil, and form into 4 thick patties.

Heat butter and oil in large frying pan over medium heat. Fry Frikadellen about 6–7 minutes, turn and fry another 6–7 minutes until golden and cooked through. Serve sprinkled with more chopped fresh parsley, if desired.

Duck a l'Orange

A 4-pound duck will give you about 2 pounds of meat. Since most of the measurable sodium in this recipe comes from the duck meat, figure about 160 mg. sodium per 8-oz serving.

Serves 4 at 160 milligrams sodium each

2 carrots in 1-inch chunks
2 shallots, cut into quarters
1 bay leaf
1 medium orange, quartered
1 duck, 3^1/$_2$ to 4 pounds

Sauce

^{1}/$_2$ cup sugar
2 tablespoons water
Zest of 2 oranges
1 cup fresh-squeezed orange juice (no need to strain any pulp)
5 tablespoons (^{2}/$_3$ stick) unsalted butter
2 tablespoons orange liqueur
1 medium orange, very thinly sliced

Preheat oven to 350°. Place carrots and 6 pieces of shallots centered in bottom of medium roasting pan. Squeeze juice from 2 orange quarters over vegetables. Put remaining 2 shallot quarters and 2 orange quarters into duck cavity. Place duck in pan so it sits directly over the carrots and shallots. Roast about an hour and a quarter basting 3–4 times with drippings in pan until done.

Remove duck to warm platter, cover, and keep warm. Press vegetables in pan to remove all juices and discard the mashed vegetables. Combine sugar and water in medium saucepan. Without stirring (any utensil used at this point will likely crystallize the sugar; makes fair candy but kinda messes up the fancy sauce), swirl the sugar over low heat, allowing it to come to a slow boil, bubbling for 2 minutes. It will begin to caramelize. Now watch it closely and as soon as it becomes a dark golden brown, remove from heat and add the reserved duck juices, orange zest, and juice carefully, so as not to be splattered and burned. (Don't worry, it really will all be worth it in the end!) Put saucepan back on the burner over medium-high and simmer 15 minutes to reduce and thicken somewhat.

Grind a little pepper over the sauce, and then gradually stir in the butter with a whisk. Remove from heat to add the orange liqueur (it's flammable, don't take the chance), and stir in the orange slices. Return to the burner and warm through very gently. Carve the duck and pass the sauce. Pat yourself on the back; you are now a French chef and you got all that flavor without salt. P.S. Now you can really ramp up your cooking by making a stock from the duck carcass!

Slow-Cooked Beef Bavarian

Mellow spices and apple blend to make this hearty and satisfying version of the pot roast.

Serves 6 at 102 milligrams sodium each

2 pound boneless top round roast
1 cup cider or unsweetened apple juice
^{1}/$_2$ cup no-salt-added tomato sauce
^{1}/$_2$ cup chopped onion
1 tablespoon cider vinegar
2 teaspoons ginger root grated from the piece you keep frozen (see spices and herbs section page 35)
1 teaspoon ground cinnamon (probably should save the expensive, good Ceylon stuff for another recipe, see discussion in spice chapter page 52)
2 tablespoons cornstarch
^{1}/$_4$ cup water

Brown the beef on all sides in a little olive oil before you pop it into a 3-quart slow cooker (One of those liners made for slow cookers is a big help here.). Combine cider, tomato sauce, onion, vinegar, gingerroot, and cinnamon. Pour over roast. Cook on low 6 hours. You can do this in the oven at 300°, covered tightly, for the same length of time. Combine the cornstarch and water and stir into the juices. Cook an additional hour till thickened. I like serving it with noodles.

Sharon's Southwest Mango Salsa

Truly southwest taste.

20 milligrams sodium in the entire bowlful!

1 ripe mango, peeled, pitted, and diced (about 1^1/$_2$ cups)
^{1}/$_2$ medium red onion, finely diced
1 jalapeño pepper, minced (include the ribs and seeds depending on how hot you like it)
1 small cucumber, peeled and diced (about 1 cup)
3 tablespoons fresh cilantro leaves, chopped
3 tablespoons fresh lime juice
Diced ripe avocado if you like, and as desired (sodium content is negligible)

Combine in a bowl and serve with anything you like! You can substitute diced peach for half the mango and adjust the cilantro up or down to taste.

Fadge (Real Irish Potatoes)

I got this recipe from a sweet elderly Irish lady direct from the old sod. Except for removing the salt, I left it just the way she recited it to me.

Serves 6 at 18 milligrams sodium each

2 pounds potatoes, unpeeled
1 egg, beaten
1/2 cup unsalted butter
3 tablespoons flour
1 1/2 tablespoons parsley
1 1/2 tablespoons chives
1 1/2 tablespoons lemon thyme (you can get by with plain thyme)
Milk
Pepper
Extra flour
Extra unsalted butter

Use "old" potatoes. Boil potatoes in their jackets, pull off the skins and mash straight away. Add the egg, butter, flour and herbs and mix well. Season with pepper. Add a little creamy milk if mixture seems too thick. Shape into 1-inch-thick rounds and cut into 6 pieces. Dip in seasoned flour. Bake on a griddle over an open fire or fry in melted butter on a gentle heat. Cook the fadge until crusty and golden on one side, then flip it over and cook it on the other side, about 4–5 minutes on each side. Serve with a blob of butter melting on top. (Please note, I did not even consider calculating the cholesterol content here!)

Guacamole

Here's a deal: there is so little sodium in the whole batch made this way, that you don't have to count it at all. Of course you do have to count the sodium in whatever vehicle you are using to get the guacamole to your palate. Give my Corn Chips a try (page 64).

None. Nadda. Zero. Zip.

2 large ripe avocados
Juice of one lime
2 teaspoons extra virgin olive oil
1/2 sweet or red onion, finely chopped
1 fresh green chili, ribs and seeds removed, finely chopped
1 clove garlic, finely minced
1/4 teaspoon ground cumin
Cilantro, enough for 1 tablespoon chopped and sprigs for garnish
Fresh black pepper

Halve, pit, peel, and chop avocados coarsely. Place in glass or plastic bowl. Sprinkle on lime juice and olive oil. Mash with fork to desired consistency. Toss on onion, chili, garlic, cumin, cilantro, and a few grinds of black pepper. Stir to combine thoroughly. Serve immediately, as it will discolor over time. Decorate with fresh cilantro leaves.

Vegetable Curry

Healthy and delicious.

Serves 4 at 16 milligrams sodium each

2 tablespoons canola or grape seed oil (these handle the higher heat well)
1 teaspoon cumin seeds, toasted (if you aren't going to toast it, you will lose out on lots of flavor)
1 medium onion, chopped (white, yellow, or red all work well)
2 cloves garlic, minced
1 full inch fresh ginger, grated or minced (peel it if you like)
1 green chili, seeded and minced (ok, 2 if you insist)
1 tablespoon ground cumin
1 tablespoon ground coriander
1/2 teaspoon turmeric
1 14 1/2-ounce can no-salt-added diced tomatoes
1 small, thick-sliced zucchini
1 small eggplant, cut in 1-inch pieces
1 handful cauliflower florets
1/2 cup sliced okra
OR
Mix and match vegetables that you like. Aim for about 4 cups in all; have them all cut up and waiting for their call to the pan.
2–4 tablespoons chopped fresh cilantro for garnish according to your taste (for my taste it's zero! I know, people either love it or hate it. If you love it, dump it on! No sodium to worry about)

Heat oil over medium-high heat a minute, then toss in cumin seeds. Let 'em dance until they get toasty but not burned. Add onion and stir until softened but not all the way to browned; add the garlic, ginger, and chili(s), stirring and cooking another minute or so. Don't let the garlic brown; it turns it bitter. Stir in ground cumin, coriander, and turmeric; stir and cook another minute or so. Add tomatoes and cook a few minutes until the juiciness is closer to sauciness as it cooks down some. Add remaining vegetables, cooking and stirring till it cooks through but isn't mushy.

Depending on what veggies you use, toss them into pot in staggered additions according to how much cooking time they need so, they all reach the desired degree of tenderness simultaneously in the end.

Sprinkle with that smelly cilantro stuff and serve hot with basmati rice.

Vegetable Couscous

Very filling!

Serves 4 at 51 milligrams sodium each

2 Tablespoons vegetable oil
1 large onion, coarsely chopped
1 carrot, chopped
1 turnip, chopped
2 1/2 cups sodium-free vegetable stock
1 cup plain dry couscous
2 tomatoes, peeled and quartered
2 zucchini, chopped
1 red bell pepper, seeded and chopped
scant 1 cup green beans, chopped
grated rind of 1 lemon
pinch of ground turmeric
1 Tablespoon finely chopped fresh cilantro
fresh ground pepper to taste
Fresh cilantro or parsley for garnish

Heat oil in large pan over medium heat. Add onion, carrot, and turnip and cook, stirring frequently, for 3–4 minutes. Add stock and bring to boil. Reduce to simmer, cover and cook 20 minutes.

Put couscous in medium bowl and moisten with a little boiling water. Stir until grains have swollen and separated. Add tomatoes, zucchini, red bell pepper, and green beans to pan and stir. Stir lemon rind into couscous, then add the turmeric and mix thoroughly. Put couscous in cheesecloth-lined steamer or strainer and set over pan of vegetables. Simmer vegetables so couscous steams 8–10 minutes. Season couscous to taste with pepper, then pile onto warmed plates.

Ladle vegetables and some of the juice over the top. Scatter cilantro over and garnish with fresh leaves. Serve immediately.

Spiced Indian Eggplant

Makes 4 tasty sides. Don't you just love eggplant?

Serves 4 at 5 milligrams sodium each

Spices

2 1/2 teaspoons Garam Masala (see discussion in Spices chapter on page 54)
2 teaspoons ground coriander
1/2 teaspoon turmeric
3 tablespoons unsalted butter (if you're a purist, use ghee. You can make it yourself from unsalted butter, but be sure that's what you use or the sodium cost ratchets up)
2 medium eggplants, skin left on, cut into 3-inch random-shaped chunks.

Sauce

1 1/2 cups water
2 tablespoons sugar
2 tablespoons red wine vinegar
1/4 cup chopped fresh cilantro

Combine spices and set aside. Combine sauce ingredients and set aside. Melt the butter in a large skillet over medium heat. Add spices and stir for 30 seconds. Stir in eggplant and pour on sauce ingredients. Stir just to distribute evenly. Cover and cook 10 minutes at a simmer. Uncover and cook another 10 minutes to reduce sauce. If not quite done, cover and give it another gentle 5 minutes or so until cooked to your liking. Serve hot.

Baklava

Who would think of a sweet ending such as this in terms of its sodium content? Interestingly, salt gets into all kinds of sweets. The experts say it enhances the flavor. But it all counts, so we look for ways to build flavor in a dessert without adding salt. Here's a good one.

Serves 4 at 182 milligrams sodium each

Scant 1 1/2 cups unsalted shelled pistachios, finely chopped
1/2 cup toasted hazelnuts, finely chopped
1/2 cup blanched hazelnuts, finely chopped
Grated rind of 1 lemon
1 tablespoon soft, light brown sugar
1 teaspoon pumpkin pie spice
1 stick plus 3 tablespoons unsalted butter, melted, plus extra for greasing pan
16 sheets frozen phyllo pastry, thawed
1 cup water
2 tablespoons honey
1 tablespoon lemon juice
1 1/2 cups superfine sugar
1/2 teaspoon ground cinnamon

Preheat oven to 325°. Put all nuts, lemon rind, brown sugar, and pumpkin pie spice into bowl and mix well. Grease a round 8-inch-diameter, 2-inch-deep cake pan with softened unsalted butter. Cut whole stack of phyllo sheets the same size as the pan. Keeping the stack covered with damp kitchen towel, lay one circle on the base of the pan and brush with melted butter. Adding one sheet at a time, layer and brush 6 more sheets each with melted butter. Spread one-third of the nut mixture over the buttered sheets. Add three more sheets one at a time, brushing each with melted butter. Spread another third of the nut mixture over these layers. Top with three more sheets, each brushed with melted butter. Spread remaining nut mixture over this layer. Add last three sheets one at a time, brushing each with melted butter. Cut into wedges (trust me, it's easier now). Bake one hour. Meanwhile, put the water, honey, lemon juice, superfine sugar, and cinnamon in pan. Bring to a boil stirring constantly. Reduce to a simmer and let cook undisturbed for 15 minutes. Cool. Remove baklava from oven at end of cooking time and immediately pour syrup over all. Let set before serving.

Authentic Irish Beef, Pea and Potato Soup

This is as close as I can get to a fantastic soup I savored on my tour of Ireland. Plan ahead so you have time to soak the dried peas.

Serves 4 for 188 milligrams. sodium each

2 lbs stew beef, in 1^1/$_2$-inch cubes
2 tablespoons olive oil
3 quarts water or salt-free beef stock
^{1}/$_2$ cup split peas soaked for 12 hours overnight
^{1}/$_2$ cup barley
1 bay leaf (optional)
1 onion, thinly sliced
1 leek, thinly sliced
2 carrots, thinly sliced
1 turnip, thinly sliced
1 parsnip, thinly sliced
1 celery stalk, thinly sliced
White pepper, to taste
^{1}/$_2$ head cabbage (regular, Savoy, or Nappa all work)
3 lbs. potatoes

Brown beef in hot oil in soup pot or Dutch oven. Browning helps deepen the beef flavor so don't skip this step. After all, what do we want? FLAVOR! Meantime, wash, peel, and chop all vegetables except potatoes and cabbage; set them aside for now. Wash barley. Put everything but the potatoes and cabbage into the pot and cover with salt-free vegetable or beef stock. Bring to a boil for 1 minute; reduce heat to low and simmer over low heat for 3 hours.

While the soup is simmering, wash the cabbage, remove the core, and shred using the slicing blade of a food processor, a large sharp knife, a mandolin, or the slicing side of a box grater. When the soup has been simmering for 2½ hours or about 30 minutes before serving, stir in the shredded cabbage. Now is the time to peel the potatoes and quarter them. (If you want to prepare them earlier, be sure to submerge in cold water to prevent them from turning brown due to air exposure while they wait.) Boil or steam them separately from the soup until fork tender. Drain them well; return them to the hot pan and shake over heat to dry out.

Put the potatoes in soup bowls with vegetables and broth to serve. Sprinkle with a pinch of finely chopped fresh parsley over each bowlful.

Cilantro Lime Rice

Great as a side dish (serves 4 at 3 milligrams sodium each) or toss in cooked shrimp or cooked poultry (be sure to add the extra sodium) and make it a 2-person meal. What a deal!

Serves 2 at 6 milligrams sodium each

1^1/$_2$ cups salt-free cooked long-grain white rice (brown will work, but it's not Mexican-authentic)
1 tablespoon vegetable oil
1 clove garlic, minced
Juice of one lime (about 2 tablespoons)
1 cup coarsely chopped cilantro

In medium skillet, heat oil over medium-low heat. Sauté garlic in oil one or two minutes till softened but not brown. Stir in remaining ingredients. Cook and stir until rice is heated through and cilantro just begins to wilt.

Spicy Okra

You will love this zesty okra dish.

Makes 6 side-dish servings for 4 milligrams sodium each

2 10-ounce packages frozen, cut okra (check labels—be sure it says 0 in the sodium column)
1 tablespoon vegetable oil
1 medium onion, coarsely chopped
1 14^1/$_2$-ounce can of no-salt-added diced tomatoes (again, watch that label)
1 fresh jalapeño pepper (or habañero chile), pierced 3 times with a fork
^{1}/$_4$ teaspoon black pepper

Rinse okra in a colander under hot water. Heat oil in a 10-inch heavy skillet over moderately high heat. Sauté onion for about 3 minutes. Add tomatoes (including juice) and chile; bring to a boil. Reduce to simmer and cook and stir the mixture for 8–10 minutes. Add okra and cook, gently stirring, until okra is tender, about 5 minutes. Stir in pepper and discard the chile. Mmmm.

There's a lot to be said for the lowly carrot; if I think of it before I finish writing this book, I'll let you know. But seriously, folks, vegetables can offer endless variety, lots of flavor on their own, and just plain look pretty on the plate. The key is to cook them without making mush out of them (unless that's your intention, but that works best with potatoes). Of course you cook them with no salt in the water. And any butter or margarine added is of the unsalted persuasion, right? Again herbs can play a big part here. I love carrots steamed with fresh mint; it doesn't take much but it sure wakes up my taste buds (there it is, something to be said for carrots, and so soon, too).

A couple interesting facts about veggies: carotenoid lycopene is a powerful antioxidant found in tomatoes and (drum roll ...) other red and pink produce. (Imagine that, watermelon has a redeeming quality above and beyond just being delicious!) Antioxidants help protect against cell damage and have been linked with decreasing risk of cancer and, wait for it, yes, you guessed it, heart disease! Lycopene isn't the only antioxidant, of course, but it's easy to get and tasty to eat. Research says it is absorbed by the body best when cooked (think spaghetti sauce) but imagine all those other yummy places tomatoes hang out that we don't even think about: ketchup, salsa, chili sauce. While you're imagining them, be sure your images of these sources are salt-free!

Wonder what oil is best to cook your sautéed veggie dish in? I choose olive oil. Not just for all the well-publicized reasons, but also because research says it aids in fat digestion and absorption of those veggie-vitamins A and K.

There are lots of ways to cook other veggies, too. They don't have to boil forever in a pot of water. You can steam, grill, bake, sauté, nuke, broil, you name it. Let your creative juices flow. Here's a few ideas you may want to try, but don't give up on recipes you've always made. Look for the sodium and replace it with any number of other goodies. Make your usual scalloped potatoes leaving out the salt and using unsalted butter. Please don't think that rinsing canned vegetables will remove the salt content. It won't. It's in there. Steam or boil fresh or frozen vegetables, and try adding something extra: a squeeze of fresh lemon in the asparagus-steaming water, unsalted almonds to the green beans, dried, minced onion to rehydrate as the peas cook, diced, red bell pepper in the corn, dillweed in the zucchini and summer squash, brown sugar, orange juice, and unsalted walnuts in the mashed sweet potatoes (then you can give it a fancy name of your own).

Don't forget those herbs. Toss them in wherever you'd like. Use just herb stems in the steaming water for flavor without visible leaves mixed into the food. Steam or boil them in your salt-free broth. Add chili powder or crushed red pepper to get a southwestern flavor. Pick almost any herb or diced vegetable to sauté with diced cooked potatoes. Mix chopped vegetables like onions, mushrooms and zucchini into couscous or brown rice, using a tablespoon of white wine and homemade salt-free broth to cook the rice or couscous in, and maybe sprinkle in a little curry. Fancy. Easy. Getting excited? Okay, maybe a little interested at least? Create. Have fun.

Glazed Carrots

(Since I brought them up in the introduction)

Serves 4 at 30 milligrams sodium each

4 8-inch carrots, peeled and trimmed
2 tablespoons brown sugar
2 tablespoons unsalted butter

Slice the carrots into thin "pennies." Place in steamer basket over rolling boiling water and cover. Steam until tender. Drain water and melt butter and sugar together in pot. Add carrots, stirring constantly until well glazed and all moisture has cooked off. Kids will eat these. You can also substitute granulated sugar and add ginger to taste. Mmmm.

Oven Tomatoes

You can't beat this fresh from the garden—anybody's garden.

Serves 4 at 8 milligrams sodium each

2 nice, red, ripe tomatoes, about 3 inches in diameter, cut in half
2–3 teaspoons extra good olive oil (garlic flavored works well here)
4 teaspoons finely chopped herbs—pick what you like: oregano and basil are classic; chives are good, too

Preheat the oven to 350°. Spray a muffin tin with nonstick cooking spray (the cupcake shape helps keep the tomato upright unless it's a small tomato. Small ones slip down into the cups and are hard to get out neatly). Balance the tomato halves on the edges of 4 muffin cups. Drizzle the olive oil on the cut surfaces and sprinkle with the herbs. You can even add a pinch of grated Parmesan or Romano if you're very stingy with your pinch. Check the tables beginning on page 22 to see how much sodium is in your pinch. Bake 20 minutes or so. The aroma is wonderful.

Snow Peas and Water Chestnuts

A quick and healthy way to add a little Asian flavor. If you have some fresh ginger around (you keep a "hand" of the ginger root in the freezer so it's handy, right?) slice of a couple very thin pieces and add them to the cooking water. Remove when serving. Garnish with some diagonally sliced scallion (green onion) tops.

Serves 4 at 7 milligrams sodium each

2 tablespoons peanut oil
10 canned water chestnuts, sliced $1/4$-inch thick
1 small onion sliced thinly
1 pound fresh snow peas
1 teaspoon fresh thyme leaves
1 tablespoon water

In hot oil in a large skillet with tight-fitting lid or in a wok, sauté water chestnuts and onion stirring frequently until onion is tender and translucent but not browned. Stir in snow peas, thyme, and water. Cover tightly and simmer until pea pods are crisp-tender, about 5 minutes.

Grilled Vegetables

You may remember my mentioning how much I love to grill out. Here's one of my favorites. Enjoy to your heart's content!

Serves 6 with sodium so low it can't be counted!

1 small zucchini, cut up into roughly 1-inch chunks
1 red bell pepper, seeded and chunked
1 yellow bell pepper, seeded and chunked
1 red onion, peeled and cut into bite-sized chunks
8–10 button mushrooms or 1 medium portobello mushroom, cleaned and cut into chunks
Olive oil
Herbs of your choice

Toss prepared vegetables with olive oil and herbs to taste. Place in grilling basket over hot coals and shake often, so they cook without burning. It should take 15–20 minutes to get them to crisp tender and delicious.

Packet Potatoes

This can be done in the oven, but, of course, it was originally engineered for the barbecue. I make them as single-serving

packets so I can vary the contents for the individual. Here's how mine usually looks:

Serves 1 at less than 20 milligrams sodium each

1 potato, sliced $1/4$-inch thick
1 small onion or 2–3 slices of a big one, can be any kind
1 tablespoon unsalted butter
1 teaspoon of whatever herb strikes your fancy at the moment

Cut a large enough piece of aluminum foil to contain the ingredients and spray lightly with non-stick cooking spray. Arrange ingredients on foil and fold over sealing well all around. There should be no breaks or openings. Toss on grill over medium-hot coals. Turn frequently with tongs taking care not to tear the foil. In about 20 minutes they should feel soft to the pressing finger. Even with a large potato, this is under 20 milligrams sodium. If you do it in the oven, place it in a baking dish in case you get a leak. Clean-up is a cinch.

Grilled Corn on the Cob

An ear of corn runs about 15 milligrams of sodium.

You can do something similar to Packet Potatoes (see recipe above) with corn on the cob, too. Husk and remove silk. Rinse. Wrap and seal each ear separately tossing in a little unsalted butter and some chopped herbs if you want. Turn frequently with tongs. They're done when the kernels have some "give" to them under gentle pressure, too. Usually takes 20–30 minutes. You can do this with the husks on and skip the foil. I just find it hard to husk and desilk the corn when it's hot. It doesn't seem practical to me. You can also do them in the oven at 350° for about a half hour.

Wild Rice with Leeks and Mushrooms

This hearty dish is a perfect complement for all types of game, meat, or fowl. Be sure to clean the leeks well, because they often have dirt between the layers. Trim off the green tops and tough outer leaves. Halve them lengthwise, slice and place in a strainer. Rinse well with cold water to remove any dirt. When purchasing wild rice, look for whole grains rather than broken pieces. Wild rice is often gritty, so it needs to be rinsed well with cold water.

Serves 8 at 26 milligrams sodium each

3 cups water
$1^1/2$ cups wild rice
$3^1/2$ cups salt-free homemade chicken broth
1 tablespoon olive oil

3 leeks, chopped
1 1/2 cups sliced mushrooms
1/4 teaspoon ground black pepper

In a large saucepan, combine the water and rice. Bring to a boil over high heat. Cover, remove from the heat and let stand for 20 minutes. Drain well and return to the pan. Add 3 cups of the broth. Bring to a boil over medium-high heat. Stir, cover, reduce the heat and simmer for 25 minutes, or until the rice is just tender and the liquid has been absorbed. While the rice is cooking, warm the oil in a large nonstick skillet over medium heat. Add the leeks and sauté for 3 minutes. Add the mushrooms; sauté for 3 minutes. Add the pepper and remaining 1/4 cup broth. Cover and simmer for 5 minutes. Set aside until the rice is ready. Add the rice to the pan and mix well.

Dilled Peas and Cauliflower

The only thing here with sodium worth noting is the cheese!

Serves 4 at 80 milligrams sodium each

1 tablespoon water
1 tablespoon unsalted butter or margarine
1 10-ounce package frozen cauliflower
1/4 teaspoon dillweed
1 10-ounce package frozen peas
4 tablespoons Parmesan cheese

Place water, butter, cauliflower and dill in 1 1/2-quart microwavable casserole. Cover tightly and microwave on high (100%) 4 minutes. Stir in peas. Cover and microwave until vegetables are tender, 5–7 minutes. Sprinkle with cheese.

Lemon Broccoli

This so light and fresh. The sauce adds lovely flavor and the whole dish just cries out to be served next to a fresh seafood catch of the day.

Serves 4 at 20 milligrams sodium each

3/4 pound fresh broccoli or 1 10-ounce package plain, frozen
1/4 cup chopped celery
1/4 cup thinly sliced green onion including tops
3 tablespoons unsalted butter
1 tablespoon lemon juice
1/4 teaspoon grated lemon peel

Rinse and trim fresh broccoli and cut into spears. Steam 10–15 minutes until crisp-tender in unsalted water. If using frozen broccoli, cook according to package directions without the salt. Drain well. In small saucepan, melt butter and cook celery and onion until tender but

not brown. Stir in lemon juice. Add hot steamed broccoli and toss to coat. Heat through. Serve sprinkled with grated lemon peel.

Saucy Brussels Sprouts

Here's one of my family's traditional Thanksgiving recipes. It's simple but looks fancy.

Serves 4 at 182 milligrams sodium each

2 pints or 4 cups rinsed and trimmed fresh Brussels Sprouts (it's fine to substitute frozen, if you're checking the label and rejecting packages that list salt in the ingredients)
1/2 cup chopped onion
2 tablespoons unsalted butter
1 tablespoon flour
1 tablespoon brown sugar
1/2 teaspoon dry mustard
1/2 cup milk
1 cup dairy sour cream

Cook sprouts in small amount boiling water until crisp tender. Drain well. Meanwhile in medium saucepan, cook onion in butter until tender but not brown. Blend in flour, brown sugar and dry mustard. Whisk in milk. Cook, stirring constantly until thickened and bubbly. Blend in sour cream. Gently stir in cooked sprouts, (halve them if large) and just heat through being careful not to boil.

Cranberry Rice Pilaf

The many flavors here blend well making this a go-with-anything side dish. Adjust the spices, cranberries or pine nuts as you wish.

Serves 4 at 35 milligrams sodium each

3/4 cup chopped celery
1/2 cup chopped onion
2 tablespoons unsalted butter
1 tablespoon olive oil
1 clove garlic chopped, not minced (tends to burn too quickly) or use 1/2 teaspoon salt-free garlic powder and add with other seasonings
1 cup uncooked long-grain rice (Basmati is my favorite, Jasmine works well, too)
2 1/2 cups salt-free chicken broth or stock
1/2 chopped fresh mushrooms
1/2 cup dried cranberries
1/2 teaspoon curry powder
1/2 teaspoon dried orange peel or 1 teaspoon freshly grated orange zest
1/2 teaspoon freshly grated pepper (here's a good place to use a white or pink pepper—see my discussion on pepper, page 39)

2 teaspoons fresh, minced parsley or 1 teaspoon dried, crumbled

3 tablespoons toasted pine nuts (to intensify their flavor, toast them on a baking pan in a 325° degree oven, stirring occasionally, until they're golden, 10–12 minutes). If you have no pine nuts on hand, but there are almonds in your pantry, use them instead, toasted and chopped.

In a large saucepan, sauté celery and onion in butter and oil until tender. Add garlic and rice; cook and stir 5 minutes until rice is lightly browned. Add broth, mushrooms, cranberries, and seasonings; if using fresh parsley, reserve till the end. Bring to a boil. Reduce heat and cover. Simmer 20 minutes or until all liquid is absorbed and rice is tender adjusting cooking time or adding a little more broth as needed. Stir in nuts and fresh parsley and serve hot.

Green Beans My Way

3 milligrams sodium per half cup

This is so fast and satisfies all the eaters who critique my cooking! Who'd believe it? Since fresh green beans have 3 mg. of sodium per half-cup, you can eat these till your eyes pop, or you aren't hungry anymore. Just be sure the label on the frozen beans says no sauces or butter added and the sodium content is about 3 mg. per half-cup serving or keep searching for a new brand. Of course, fresh is best. And we would never open canned, right? Prepared with fresh or frozen, no sodium added, the sodium content here isn't worth counting.

1 pound green beans, if fresh, trim them, but leave whole. Boiling takes out nutrition and cut beans just present more ways for the good stuff to leak out. Cook your beans. I steam them in a basket over boiling water that doesn't touch them. Won't take long, 8–9 minutes will make them crisp-tender. Then drain very quickly and drop into an ice water bath to stop the cooking. Now look how nice and green they are! If you have frozen, cook them per the instructions, but just till hot, not over cooked. Drain them well no matter what kind you're cooking.

While the beans finish draining, melt 2 tablespoons unsalted butter in a large skillet. Add a tablespoon of oil to keep the butter from burning. Toss in a couple tablespoons of thinly sliced shallots, about 1 good-sized shallot will due. If you don't have them, use green onions or finely chopped sweet onion. If you like it, toss in a clove of minced garlic. And if you're family likes nuts, this is the time to toss in a few, say thinly sliced almonds. Give it a stir and about 1 minute over medium heat. Now is the time to cut the beans into bite-sized pieces, not too small. Toss 'em into the skillet (stand back from the sputtering) and cook and stir over medium-high until the beans begin to get a little golden-brown color. Once they look delicious, they are delicious. Enjoy.

Grilled Rosemary Potatoes

10 milligrams sodium per potato

For each potato, slice lengthwise into ½- to ¾-inch slices. Place in saucepan with water to cover and bring to a boil. Reduce heat to simmer and cook about 8 minutes until almost tender but not falling apart. Drain. Brush with olive oil and sprinkle on as much minced, fresh rosemary as you like. Add a tiny bit of minced garlic, too, if that appeals to you.

Grill over medium-hot coals in a foil packet coated with cooking spray and folded and crimped around the edges to keep juices in. Grill 3–4 minutes per side till browned but not overly softened. Sprinkle on more fresh rosemary if you like. To do on the stove, just toss the almost tender slices into a skillet heated with a tablespoon or two of olive oil. Sprinkle on as much minced rosemary as you like (of course you can switch to another herb—bravo for thinking of that!) and sauté until golden; flip to finish. Yummy.

Broccolini with Garlic and Shallots

There's no sodium to count here. And, yes, my picky kid loves it!

None. Nadda. Zero. Zip.

1 bunch broccolini

1 large shallot, sliced thinly

1 tablespoon olive oil

1 tablespoon unsalted butter

2 cloves garlic, minced

2 teaspoons fresh lemon juice (Toss in a little grated peel from that lemon, too if you want.)

Bring a couple inches of water to the boil in a large saucepan. Trim away the thick ends of the broccolini. Cut off the bottom 2–3 inches of the stems and toss them into boiling water, setting aside tops for now. Boil stems for 4–5 minutes until not quite crisp-tender. Toss in the tops, cover, and steam well for another 2 minutes until all is crisp-tender and intensely green. Drain. Meantime, warm the oil and melt the butter in a large skillet. Stir in shallot and cook and stir 1 minute. Stir in garlic and cook and stir half a minute more. Add the broccolini, lemon juice and grated peel. Stir to combine and add a touch of color to the broccolini edges. Serve hot. If you have some toasted sesame seeds at hand, toss some on for garnish.

Parsleyed New Potatoes

This is especially nice in the spring when the new potatoes really are new. No reason you couldn't toss in some snipped chives, too. They come on in the spring like, well, weeds, so they would make a naturally ready addition.

Serves 4 at 10 milligrams sodium each

1 pound small new potatoes
3 tablespoons unsalted butter
3 tablespoons chopped fresh parsley
1 teaspoon lemon juice

Scrub potatoes. Peeling is ok if you really want the skins off. I leave them on because the nutrition hides just under the skin of a potato, and new potatoes generally have thin skins anyway. Red potatoes are especially pretty with the parsley.

Cook in boiling water until tender. That may take only 10 minutes depending on how small they are. Drain. Meanwhile, melt butter and stir in the parsley and lemon juice. Pour over hot potatoes and serve.

Corn Salad

I adapted this from a physical therapist friend from work, Pat Beach. It's so fresh and enticing, like summer on your plate. Made this way, it's 4 generous servings for 130 mg. sodium each, but you can change it to 30 mg. in each serving just by making your own mayo. See page 83 for recipe.

Serves 4 at 130 milligrams sodium each

1 carrot, small dice
1 rib celery, small dice
1/2 red pepper, small dice
1/2 green pepper, small dice
3–4 ears corn (you can substitute 1 1/2 cups frozen, thawed, patted dry)
3 scallions, thin sliced (I have substituted a couple slices red onion, small dice in a pinch)

Dressing

1/2 cup homemade mayo
2 tablespoons milk
2 tablespoons vinegar (pick your favorite; I use white wine or champagne)
2 tablespoons sugar (don't go up on this, it'll be too sweet, but at this amount it balances the vinegar and heightens other flavors perfectly)
Several grinds fresh black pepper

Here's the secret: grill the ears of corn. I shuck and remove silks, then put them directly on an outdoor or in-door grill at medium-high and keep turning a little at a time until you have good char all around. Let them cool till you can handle them, then stand them on the stalk end and cut off the kernels. Toss all the veggies then combine the dressing ingredients and pour over the veggies. Uh-huh.

Apple Cider Baked Beans

Slow cooked in a flavorful sauce, the wonderful aroma of these simmering beans will warm hour heart and your kitchen. Beans are winter comfort food. They are naturally low in fat and high in vegetable protein, vitamins, minerals, and fiber. Oh, and the main source of sodium here is the Dijon. So of course I set out to reduce that. And guess what? I was able to cut the Dijon in half to 4 teaspoons by adding a teaspoon of mustard powder (great in deviled eggs, too) and a couple teaspoons vinegar! Uh-huh! Remember that one cup dried beans will yield slightly more than 2 cups cooked (see my discussion of beans page 70).

Serves 8 at 100 milligrams sodium each

2 cups dried white navy beans
1 small onion, diced
4 tablespoons molasses
4 teaspoons Dijon mustard
2 tablespoons tomato paste
2 teaspoons black pepper
2 teaspoons dried thyme
1 teaspoon dry mustard powder
1 small bay leaf
2 teaspoons cider vinegar
4 teaspoons "No Soy Sauce" (see recipe page 142)
1 1/3 cups apple cider, boiling
Boiling water

Pour beans onto a flat surface (countertop) in a single layer. Pick out rocks, dirt balls, off colored and broken beans. Discard. Wash beans in two changes of cold water. Cover with 3 inches of water and allow beans to soak overnight or 8 to 10 hours. (Quick soak method: Cover cleaned beans with 3 inches cold water and bring to a boil over medium heat. Boil for 10 minutes, turn heat off and let stand for 2 hours or more. Proceed as directed below.)

Preheat oven to 250°. Drain beans, reserving liquid. Bring liquid to a boil. Pour beans into an oven-proof casserole or bean pot. Add all the ingredients, stir and add enough boiling reserved liquid to cover beans. Cover the casserole with foil or the lid. Bake 6 hours, adding a little more water or cider if necessary after 3 hours of baking.

Summer Garden Vegetables

Bumper crop of summer squash? Neighbor has a bumper crop and you've been bestowed with all you can eat? Try this. Most of the sodium here is from the cheese. And it's quick and easy. Cut the amounts in half to cook for two.

Serves 4 at 100 milligrams sodium each

1/2 pound fresh green beans, trimmed
1 pound fresh snap or snow peas
2 tablespoons olive oil
1 1/2 cups julienned zucchini
1 1/2 cups julienned yellow summer squash
1 to 1 1/2 teaspoons each (or according to taste): minced fresh rosemary, basil, parsley, and thyme
1/2 teaspoon red pepper flakes
1/4 cup grated Parmesan cheese

In a large skillet, cook beans and peas in oil about 3–4 minutes. Add zucchini, yellow squash, herbs and pepper flakes. Cook and stir 4–5 minutes more or until vegetables are crisp tender. Sprinkle with cheese and serve immediately.

Yam and Apple Bake

A yummy holiday side dish.

Serves 6 at 134 milligrams sodium each

3–4 large sweet potatoes (sometimes mistakenly called yams)
3–4 large golden Delicious apples
1/2 cup sugar
2 tablespoons cornstarch
1/4 teaspoon salt (be careful)
1 cup boiling water
1/4 cup unsalted butter (half a stick) cut into 4 pieces

Poke the skins of the sweets with a fork and pop them into the micro for 3–4 minutes on high to soften but not cook through. Peel and slice into 1- to 1 1/2-inch pieces. Peel apples and slice into 1/2-inch thick slices. Butter a 2-quart baking dish and arrange potatoes and apples in it. In medium saucepan, combine sugar with cornstarch and salt. Stir in boiling water, then add butter. Over medium high heat, stir and bring to a boil. Reduce heat to full simmer and cook and stir sauce 1–2 minutes to dissolve sugar and blend all ingredients. Pour over potatoes and apples and place dish in oven for 45–60 minutes at 350° until all is tender and sauce is thickened.

Roasted Vegetables

Since I discovered the great flavor that roasting brings out in so many vegetables, I use this method very often. I've been able to get my kids and finicky husband to eat more vegetables this way, too. If you don't sprinkle on salt (what the TV chefs refer to as "seasoning") there is only the natural sodium found in the veggie you prepare to worry about.

The key to doing more than one type of vegetable at a time in this way is cutting them into uniform-sized chunks. Keep in mind, wedges of tomato (plum tomatoes are meatiest and work best here) or onion will cook more quickly than dense potatoes or carrots. Don't turn away from those turnips, parsnips (oh, sooo sweet done this way), or other veggies you may not like when boiled to death. Remember—this is an adventure.

Typically, the best method I've found is to place cut-up veggies on a heavy rimmed baking sheet or roasting pan that you lined with foil (heavier pans withstand the higher heats and are less prone to letting the veggies burn). Drizzle on some olive oil and stir it all around with your hands so every bite gets lightly oiled, and so does the pan. Then sprinkle on pepper and any dried herb you like, and toss that around, too. Save fresh herbs till the veggies are just about tender as the fresh stuff will burn easily, so will garlic (a good way to add all herbs and garlic from the beginning is to roast in a tightly wrapped foil packet, best reserved for grilling as it does steam them more than roast the veggies. While it's delicious on the grill, there is much more flavor when open-roasted in the oven on high heat). Roast at 425–450°. Don't shy away from the high temp— that's how you get the browning and flavor development. Depending on the density of the vegetables and size of the pieces, it will take about 45–90 minutes in total. Add the tender veggies (tomatoes, especially) after half an hour. Stir the whole thing occasionally and keep an eye on it. They're done when you see crispy golden edges and the veggies yield easily to the point of a knife. You may want to drizzle just a tiny bit of honey over them for a change, 5 or 10 minutes before you take them out. When they are done, or nearly so, toss in nuts or seeds, or sprinkle with a citrus juice. Once you put them in the serving bowl or platter, sprinkle with minced fresh herbs or dot well with herb butter. If you go with cheeses, beware the sodium content—look it up to be safe.

Actual sodium will differ from veggie to veggie. Check the listings on page 22.

Lighter density (shorter cooking times)

- Eggplant, leave peels on, cut in thick slices then cross cut to make 2-inch pieces

- Green and yellow beans (slim ones are best) trim and leave whole

- Tomatoes, cherry and grape roasted whole, Romas in thick slices or quarters. Big summer tomatoes in thick slices—think about roasting slices of sweet onion at the same time (they'll need a little more time than the tomatoes), well oiled, and then dressing them all with a few shakes of balsamic vinegar and a few pinches of fresh thyme leaves as a salad.

- Zucchini and other summer squashes quartered lengthwise

Medium density (medium cooking times)

- Asparagus in 2- or 3-inch lengths

- Broccoli cut into little trees

- Cauliflower cut into little trees

- Onions, especially sweet or red, cut in thick wedges

- Peppers in bite-sized chunks

- Portabellos whole, thick-sliced, or chunked up

- Scallions trimmed but left whole

- Turnips peeled and in 1x2-inch chunks

High density (longer cooking times)

- Beets in thick slices or quartered if smaller in size

- Carrots in 1- or 2-inch chunks

- Garlic—uh huh. Nothin' like it. Slice the top off a whole head, no need to remove the papery peel. Leave the cloves intact. Be sure it's well-oiled and wrap snuggly in foil. They will need more time than the rest so plan for this when you have the oven heated for other things. When a knife through the packet and into the garlic slides in easily, remove from oven, loosen foil and let cool till you can handle it. Then press the pulp of the garlic cloves out. Use the pulp like butter on bread or to flavor anything you like that mellow garlicky goodness in.

- Parsnips, peeled and chunked like carrots

- Potatoes: cut-up or thick-sliced red or Yukon Gold are terrific (leave peels on)

- Sweet potatoes, peeled and chunked or thick sliced

- Winter squash, peeled and chunked or thickly sliced

Warmly Spiced Winter Squash

What a tasty side dish. Squash always seems to get buttered and mashed. How about baking it with warm spices and a little honey? Try different squashes and vary the spices and proportions to your taste.

Serves 2 at 8 milligrams sodium each

1 6- to 8-inch-diameter acorn squash or small similar winter squash such as Delicata or Buttercup
1 tablespoon honey, flavor of your choice (I like orange blossom here)
1/2 teaspoon coriander
1/2 teaspoon cumin
1/2 teaspoon garlic powder
1/2 teaspoon cardamom
1/2 teaspoon powdered ginger (you could grate fresh if you preferred)
1/2 teaspoon smoky paprika

Cut squash in half and clean out seeds. Level the bottoms so they will stand well in baking dish. Spray baking dish with cooking spray. Place squash halves, cut side up in dish and drizzle and spread honey over flesh of squash. Combine spices and herbs and sprinkle evenly over squash. Bake, uncovered in a 350° oven, 1¼ to 1½ hours until tender.

Parmesan Zucchini

Serves 2 at 95 milligrams sodium each.

2 very small or one medium zucchini, thinly sliced
1 small onion, chopped
1/2 teaspoon oregano
1/4 teaspoon basil
A few grinds of fresh pepper
1 tablespoon olive oil
2 tablespoons shredded Parmesan cheese

Sauté zucchini, onion and seasonings in oil about 5 minutes on medium high until crisp-tender. Reduce heat to medium and stir in cheese. Cook another couple minutes until cheese melts.

Harvard Beets

Here's proof fresh "beets" canned: scrumptious!

81 milligrams sodium for each of two servings

1 cup sliced fresh beets
2 tablespoons sugar
3/4 teaspoon flour
2 tablespoons white vinegar
2 teaspoons unsalted butter

Simmer beets covered by water in small saucepan 15–20 minutes or until tender. When you drain them, save 1 tablespoon of the cooking liquid. Set beets aside. Combine sugar, flour, vinegar, and reserved beet juice in the same saucepan. Cook over low until thickened. Stir in butter, add beets and simmer on low 5 minutes.

No-Fries with a Bite

Serves 2 at only 32 milligrams sodium per serving

2 tablespoons vegetable oil
1 teaspoon chili powder
1/4 teaspoon onion powder
1/4 teaspoon garlic powder
1/4 teaspoon sugar
1/4 teaspoon paprika
Tiny pinch cayenne pepper

2 large red-skinned potatoes, unpeeled and cut into wedges In a medium bowl, combine oil and seasonings. Toss potato wedges in and coat well. Arrange in a single layer on greased baking sheet. Bake at 400° about a half hour, turning once. Baking like this cuts down on the fat content but still gives you a crispy fry. Should be tender and golden brown.

No-Fries without a Bite

Made the same as the ones that bite, but with a change in seasonings, same sodium. Mix and match the herbs they way you like them. If you use fresh, remember that 1/4 teaspoon dried converts to 1/4 teaspoon fresh minced.

Serves 2 at only 32 milligrams sodium per serving

2 tablespoons vegetable oil
3/4 teaspoon dried parsley
1/4 teaspoon dried basil
1/4 teaspoon dried thyme
1/4 teaspoon dried rosemary
1/4 teaspoon garlic powder
Pinch or two paprika
Fresh ground pepper to taste
2 large red-skinned potatoes, unpeeled and cut into wedges

In a medium bowl, combine oil and herbs. Toss potato wedges in and coat well. Arrange in a single layer on greased baking sheet. Bake at 400° about a half hour, turning once. Should be tender and golden brown.

Cherry Tomato and Mozzarella Sauté

Makes 2 servings for 110 milligrams sodium each

2 tablespoons chopped shallots (about 2 little ones)
1 small clove garlic, minced
Pinch dried or 1/2 teaspoon fresh thyme
2 teaspoons olive oil
1 cup (half a pint basket) cherry tomatoes, halved

A grind or two of fresh pepper
2 ounces fresh mozzarella in half-inch cubes

Heat oil in medium skillet and stir in shallots, garlic and thyme. Stir a minute or two to soften, but not brown. Add tomatoes and pepper, cook on medium, stirring 3–4 minutes until heated through. Remove from heat; stir in cheese and serve 2 hearty and healthy sides.

Cucumbers in Sour Cream

Serves 2 at 20 milligrams sodium each because cucumbers don't have to be salted!

1 small cucumber, peeled if you like it better without it, thinly sliced
1/2 small purple onion sliced and separated into rings
1/4 cup vinegar
1 teaspoon sugar
1/2 cup water
1/4 cup dairy sour cream
1/4 teaspoon dill seeds
Dash of hot pepper sauce

Combine cucumber and onion slices in small bowl. Combine vinegar, sugar, and water; pour over cucumber mixture. Let stand at room temperature 1 hour and drain well. Combine sour cream, dill seeds, pepper sauce, and maybe a grind or two of pepper if you'd like. Toss with cucumber mixture and chill, covered, at least an hour.

Butternut Squash Casserole

Tasty anytime of year, but best when fresh squash is available

Serves 2 at 75 milligrams sodium per serving

1 small butternut squash, peeled and cut into chunks (Hate this process as much as I do? Look for the packages of it already prepared in the produce section. Just remember it won't last forever once cut up, so use it soon.)
3 tablespoons sugar
1 egg
1 1/2 tablespoons milk
1 tablespoon butter, softened
1/2 teaspoon vanilla
Pinch each of cinnamon and nutmeg

Stovetop method: Place squash into pan and cover with water; bring to a boil, reduce heat and simmer covered 12–15 minutes until tender. Drain.

Microwave method (less watery, more vitamins): Place squash into microwave-safe dish (no water). Cover with wet, not dripping, paper towel and micro on high 5–7 minutes until tender. Beat squash until smooth then beat in remaining ingredients. Transfer into small baking dish or casserole dish prepared by spraying with cooking spray first. Bake, covered at 350° about 25 to 30 minutes until cooked through.

Dressy Carrots

Pretty, and pretty easy

Serves 2 at only 20 milligrams of sodium each

2 tablespoons unsalted butter
One large carrot, peeled and sliced 1/4 inch thick
2 tablespoons golden raisins
2 tablespoons unsalted walnut pieces
1 tablespoon honey
2 teaspoons brown sugar
1/2 teaspoon lemon juice
2 grinds fresh pepper

Toast walnuts by putting them in a hot medium skillet with nothing else in the pan and stirring for a few minutes over medium-hot to just bring out the flavor. Remove and set aside. In same skillet, melt butter over medium-low. Add carrots and cook 2 minutes, stirring occasionally. Add remaining ingredients, stir and cover. Cook 20 minutes or until crisp-tender, stirring occasionally. Uncover and cook another couple minutes until sauce thickens, stirring constantly.

Dilly of a Pea Dish

Make as much or as little as you want using a bag of frozen peas so you can take one serving or many.

Serves 2 at about 20 milligrams of sodium. Pay attention to the label on your peas; the ones I buy with my grocer's own label have no sodium in them, same as fresh. Sour cream runs differently, too. The brand in my refrigerator right now runs 40 milligrams for 2 tablespoons, many are more or less.

1 cup frozen peas, cooked and drained
2 tablespoons sour cream
1 teaspoon dried dill or 1 tablespoon chopped, fresh

Combine and serve.

By now you must be tired of hearing me repeat myself about the high-sodium content of things in cans, jars, and otherwise-processed foods, and the importance of reading labels and thinking creatively. So I'll cut to the chase. A lot of food just cries out for something poured, scooped, drizzled or ladled onto it. Try these before you think about opening that forbidden container.

Barbecue Sauce #1

This is the one we consider standard at our house. Makes 2 cups.

3 milligrams sodium per tablespoon

2 tablespoons olive oil

1/3 cup chopped onion

1 clove garlic, minced

1/2 cup honey

1/2 cup no-sodium ketchup

1/2 cup vinegar (your choice, I use red wine vinegar)

2 teaspoons dry mustard

1/2 teaspoon dried basil

1/2 teaspoon dried oregano

1/4 teaspoon fresh ground pepper

Sauté onion and garlic in oil until tender but not brown in medium saucepan. Stir in remaining ingredients, bring to boil. Reduce heat and simmer 5 minutes to blend flavors. Store in refrigerator.

Barbecue Sauce #2

Makes 2 1/4 cups, be sure to use very low sodium ketchup so it will add up to only 10 milligrams sodium per tablespoon. Otherwise it's ten times that!

10 milligrams sodium per tablespoon

2 tablespoons olive oil

1 cup chopped onion

1 cup no-salt ketchup

1/2 cup water

1/2 cup red wine (you could substitute juice or broth, just be sure to adjust the sodium calculation)

2 tablespoons packed brown sugar

2 tablespoons red wine vinegar

1 tablespoon Worcestershire sauce

1 teaspoon mustard seed

1 teaspoon dried oregano

Heat oil in medium saucepan. Sauté onions until tender. Stir in remaining ingredients and bring to a boil. Reduce heat and simmer a few minutes until slightly thickened.

Marinade #1

Works great for beef and pork. Makes 2/3 cup, negligible sodium.

None. Nadda. Zero. Zip.

1/4 cup good olive oil

1/4 cup dry red wine

1 tablespoon lemon juice

2 tablespoons green onion or chives

2 tablespoons chopped fresh parsley

Pinch each: oregano, rosemary, and basil

2 shakes garlic powder

Combine right in a large zipper plastic bag and add meat to be marinated. Zip bag expressing all air out. Refrigerate at least a couple hours. Discard marinade. Grill, broil, or bake meat as you like it.

Marinade #2

Another tasty treat with negligible sodium content.

None. Nadda. Zero. Zip.

1 small onion, sliced and separated into rings

1/2 cup olive oil

1/2 cup dry white wine

1/4 cup lime or lemon juice

2 tablespoons chopped fresh parsley

1 tablespoon chopped fresh rosemary

Combine in zipper bag and add meat distributing onion rings evenly. Zip closed, expressing all the air. Refrigerate at least 2 hours or several more as desired. Discard all marinade and onions. Especially nice with lamb or poultry.

Vinegar-Cucumber Sauce

Makes about a cup and a quarter.

20 milligrams sodium per tablespoon

3/4 cup plain yogurt

1/2 medium cucumber, peeled, seeded, and chopped

2 tablespoons green onion slices, including tops, or fresh chives

2 tablespoons sour cream

1 teaspoon spicy brown mustard

1/4 teaspoon fresh ground pepper

Combine and refrigerate. Use with fish—especially salmon—or in pita sandwiches, especially with lamb.

Chili Sauce

Makes about 2 1/2 cups darn good chili sauce. Use it plain or in recipes. The whole thing will cost only 80 milligrams sodium. Enjoy.

2 milligrams sodium per tablespoon

2 tablespoons olive oil

1/2 cup finely chopped onion

1 clove garlic, minced

1 1/2 tablespoons chili powder

1/4 teaspoon dried oregano

1/4 teaspoon ground cumin

1 8-ounce can (1 cup) low-sodium tomato sauce
1¼ cups water

Heat oil in medium saucepan. Sauté onion and garlic until golden. Add remaining ingredients and bring to a boil. Reduce heat and simmer, uncovered for 15–20 minutes until slightly thickened.

Tomato Basil Sauce

This is the easiest, freshest-tasting pasta/vegetable sauce you could imagine. No long cooking. And it will only cost you the price of the sodium in the tomatoes. Carefully chosen, the whole recipe is less than 20 milligrams of sodium.

Entire recipe is less than 20 milligrams sodium

28-ounce can no-salt tomatoes (diced or whole) or use fresh
2–3 cloves garlic
¼ onion, no need to chop
1 small bunch of fresh basil, stems removed
½ teaspoon dried oregano
Pepper to taste

Mix all the ingredients together in a blender and season with pepper. Pour into a sauce pan and heat lightly until just heated through. Toss with hot pasta or vegetables. Makes about 2 cups.

Tartar Sauce

Makes 12 tablespoons at 34 milligrams sodium each unless you dig up low-sodium pickles (which are not easy to find, but do exist).

34 milligrams sodium per tablespoon

¼ cup plain yogurt
¼ cup homemade mayonnaise (see section on salads)
2 tablespoons chopped dill pickles, (try to locate those hard-to-find low-salt ones; they are a little lower than regular)
⅛ teaspoon onion powder
⅛ teaspoon fresh ground pepper

Combine and mix well. Refrigerate.

Poultry-Wine Sauce

Makes about 3 cups. Make this with your next turkey, chicken or goose, or use your frozen homemade stock to make this tasty sauce.

Serves 12 at 10 milligrams sodium each

Giblets and neck from roast
2½ cups water
1 celery stalk, cut up

1 medium onion, peeled and quartered
1 medium carrot, peeled and cut up
4 black peppercorns
1 bay leaf
Dry white wine, about a cup
2 tablespoons all-purpose flour

Simmer giblets, (except for liver), and neck with water, vegetables, peppercorns, and bay leaf in a large saucepan, covered, for 2½ hours while roast cooks. Add liver for last 15 minutes. Remove giblets and chop into small pieces discarding neck. Strain broth pressing vegetables to release juices into broth. Measure broth and add white wine to make 3 cups; set aside. Skim fat from drippings. Place 2 tablespoons drippings back into empty roasting pan and whisk in flour. Over very low heat, stirring constantly, cook flour until lightly browned. This improves flavor greatly. Remove from heat and whisk in giblet broth. Bring to a boil, reduce heat and simmer, stirring, 5 minutes until thick and smooth. Stir in giblets and simmer another 5 minutes to warm through.

Fresh Mint Sauce

None. Nadda. Zero. Zip.

I love this one for lamb, particularly since I have a lot of mint growing in my garden. I make it by taking big handfuls of mint (washed of course), stripping the leaves until I have enough to fill a 2-quart saucepan. Then I add enough water to cover but not drown them. It should be 3–4 cups, enough to simmer the leaves and steep them well. So now you bring the whole thing to a boil, reduce the heat and simmer a few minutes, then set aside to steep for 20–30 minutes. (As you can see, these are pretty loose instructions, but that's how I like to do things like this.) Once you're happy with the strength of the tea, strain it, pressing the leaves to return as much juice as possible to the brew. Return the liquid to high heat and boil down to 2 cups. Combine 2 tablespoons cornstarch with 2 tablespoons water, mixing till smooth. Add to mint liquid. Cook and stir over medium high until thickened and bubbly, about 2–3 minutes. Add a couple drops green food color if you want to. Cool and serve with lamb. Mmmmm. There's no sodium in the whole potful, either.

Horseradish

3 milligrams sodium per tablespoon

If you really love the stuff, or like to use it in homemade shrimp cocktail sauce, you can make it yourself just by grinding the horseradish root to a fine texture and stirring in white vinegar to taste. Start with ½ cup horseradish root to ½ cup white wine vinegar. A half cup will have about 25 milligrams sodium which is 3 milligrams per tablespoon. I make cocktail sauce by combining horseradish and ketchup in a 1:3 proportion. You can get fancy by stirring in a little lemon juice or adding other things as long as you're mindful of the sodium content of it all.

Dill Sauce

Nothing beats a dollop of this on sliced up cucumbers. Growing dill and cukes? Super!

5 milligrams sodium per tablespoon

½ cup sour cream
1 tablespoon onion, finely chopped
1 teaspoon lemon juice
½ to 1 teaspoon dried dill weed

Combine and **refrigerate**.

Lemon Butter Sauce for Fish

Are you eating more fish? This will dress any plain fillet up.

None. Nadda. Zero. Zip.

½ cup softened unsalted butter
¼ cup fresh lemon juice
1 teaspoon grated lemon rind
¼ teaspoon herbs, pick a favorite one or two; try thyme, dill, tarragon, basil or oregano
Pinch onion powder
Pinch garlic powder
Pinch cayenne pepper

Combine and serve with fish or shellfish or use to baste while grilling or baking.

Ketchup

This is the closest I can find to the flavor of processed ketchup without the salt. See what you think. It makes about 2 cups and can be frozen. It won't keep as long as store bought in the refrigerator, maybe 3–4 weeks. Made as described here, each batch adds up to 116 milligrams sodium. How it breaks down per tablespoon depends on how long you cook it down and what your final volume is.

116 milligrams sodium per batch

1 cup no-salt tomato paste
2 cups water
¼ cup chopped onion
¼ cup chopped celery
¼ cup cider vinegar
¼ cup granulated sugar

2 teaspoons brown sugar
1 tablespoon unsalted butter
Pinch each: ground cloves, basil, tarragon, black pepper, onion powder, garlic powder

Process all ingredients in food processor until smooth. Transfer to medium saucepan and simmer an hour until thick stirring occasionally. Change the proportions as you wish, just don't forget to calculate the sodium content when you're done.

"No Soy Sauce"

It took a long time to get a good substitute for the salty stuff. I think I nailed it!

Makes 1 cup at 7 milligrams sodium total

2 teaspoons sodium-free beef bouillon powder
2 tablespoons balsamic vinegar
2 teaspoons dark molasses
½ teaspoon ginger (fresh grated from the root itself is best)
¼ teaspoon white pepper
2 cloves garlic sliced
1½ cups water

Bring all ingredients to a boil. Reduce heat and simmer until reduced to about 1 cup. Remove ginger and garlic bits by pouring through a sieve. Refrigerate and keep on hand. Without the pounds of salt, it will go bad after a while. You can freeze it in cubes to keep longer.

Lemon-Herb Vinaigrette

A tasty dressing for veggies and salads with NO SODIUM to worry about. (Use a peeler to slice green and yellow zucchini into ribbons lengthwise working first on one side till you reach the seedy center, flip it over and repeat till you reach the seeds again. Toss out the seeds and toss the vinaigrette with the ribbons. Pretty and tasty. Or spill a little over sliced tomatoes, thinly sliced red onion, and match-stick slices of red peppers. Pretty and tasty. Or drizzle over seedless cucumber slices, thin slices of crunchy jicama, and chopped green onion. Pretty and . . . you get the point.) Makes 1 cup.

None. Nadda. Zero. Zip.

¾ cup extra virgin olive oil (yep, here's a good place for the good stuff)
¼ cup fresh lemon juice
2 teaspoons finely grated lemon zest (a microplane is so helpful here)
2 teaspoons minced basil
1 teaspoon minced oregano

Whisk it all together. Keep the extra in the chill box.

Marinade for Steak

Total sodium in this marinade? I can't calculate in numbers this small. Just enjoy!

None. Nadda. Zero. Zip.

3 tablespoons lime juice
2 cloves garlic, minced
1 jalapeño, rough chopped
1 teaspoon "No Soy Sauce" (see page 142)

Whirl in processor and spread over steak working over whole surface. One hour is usually long enough to sit in marinade before cooking.

Aunt Cathi's Plum Barbecue Sauce

This sauce packs a bunch of flavor and a little twist to standard barbecue sauce. It works very well on oven-baked meats, and keeps in the freezer well.

Serves 8 at 38 milligrams sodium each

1/4 cup unsalted butter
2/3 cup onion, minced
1 jalapeño pepper, seeded (unless you like the heat) and minced
2 envelopes Herbox or other no-salt chicken bouillon
2 envelopes Herbox or other no-salt beef bouillon
1 can purple plums, drained and well rinsed to get all the syrupy stuff off
1/2 cup brown sugar, packed
1/3 cup vinegar
1 tablespoon chile powder
1 teaspoon cinnamon
1 teaspoon dry mustard
1/2 can (5 level tablespoons) low-sodium tomato paste

Sauté onion and jalapeño pepper in butter until soft. Add remaining ingredients. Let simmer for 20 minutes. Wonderful spooned over chicken, pork, or shrimp. This recipe can be divided and frozen in plastic containers.

Cucumber-Yogurt Sauce

Makes about a cup and a quarter (20 tablespoons).

20 milligrams sodium per tablespoon

3/4 cup plain yogurt
1/2 medium cucumber, peeled, seeded, and chopped
2 tablespoons green onion slices, including tops, or fresh chives
2 tablespoons sour cream

1 teaspoon spicy brown mustard
1/4 teaspoon fresh ground pepper

Combine and refrigerate. Use with fish—especially salmon—or in pita sandwiches, especially with lamb.

Citrus, Garlic, and Herb Oil

Makes 3/4 cup. Enhances vegetables like fresh tomato slices or boiled potatoes; goes well on cooked meat and makes a good spread or dip for bread.

None. Nadda. Zero. Zip.

Zest peeled from 2 lemons, avoid the white, pithy, bitter stuff (refrigerate naked lemons in tightly sealed plastic bag, air removed, and you can juice them for another recipe later)
6 cloves garlic, minced
2 medium sprigs rosemary, more if you love it. Leave the leaves right on their stems for easy retrieval later.
3/4 cup olive oil (don't get out the expensive stuff; save it for when you want the light olive oil taste by itself, the garlic will keep you from appreciating it here.)
1/4 cup minced flat leaf parsley

Warm the zest, garlic, and rosemary in the oil over medium heat just till you see a few bubbles start coming up. Don't let it sizzle harder or the garlic will fry, burn, and taste bitter. Keep at just a bare simmer 4–5 minutes and remove from heat. Cool. Remove zest and rosemary, stir in parsley. Drizzle and dip. Hold leftovers tightly closed in the fridge.

Fruit Salsa

Goes so well with spicy or hot foods. Makes 2 cups with less than 20 mg. sodium in the whole thing! Maybe you should get your spoon . . .

20 milligrams sodium in the entire batch

2 cups chopped fresh pineapple
1/2 cup chopped cucumber
1/2 cup thinly sliced red onion
2 tablespoons chopped fresh cilantro
2 teaspoons cider vinegar

Stir it all together and enjoy. Will keep 3–4 days covered tightly in the refrigerator.

Honey-Mustard Dipping Sauce

Be careful: even though this is homemade (and incredibly delicious) and so it allows you control of the sodium content, it isn't without sodium. Makes 3/4 cup sauce. Each tablespoon contains 110 mg. sodium. (Using my home-

made mayo, page 83, reduces the sodium content to a mere 60 mg. per tablespoon). Try mixing 4 or 5 tablespoons of this sauce with 2 or 3 tablespoons of apricot preserves and brush it on a pork tenderloin over the grill. This is where it really sings!

110 milligrams sodium per tablespoon

8 tablespoons "real mayonnaise" (Kraft or Hellmann's contains the lowest sodium I've found available commercially)

2 tablespoons honey (any type you like, experiment with flavors like buckwheat, orange blossom, or wild flower, as just three of the many possibilities)

2 tablespoons prepared yellow mustard

1 tablespoon Dijon mustard

1/2 tablespoon lemon juice or apple cider vinegar

Combine thoroughly and store covered in the fridge.

Salsa #1

A few pulses in a food processor makes your job easier! Just be careful of the sodium content of whatever you eat this salsa with. Look for my easy "corn" chips recipe on page 64.

35 milligrams sodium in the entire batch

3 small tomatoes, seeded and coarsely chopped (1 1/2 cups)

1 small onion, coarsely chopped (1/3 cup)

1 or 2 fresh jalapeño peppers, to taste, seeded and finely chopped

2 tablespoons lime juice

1–2 tablespoons chopped cilantro, to taste

Pile it all in the processor and give it 3–4 pulses to bring it to the consistency you like. Makes a cup and will keep 3–4 days tightly covered in the fridge.

Salsa #2

Are you a salsa lover who thought your days of enjoying it were over because of the sodium restriction? Not so! This little baby has 4, yep, only 4 milligrams sodium per tablespoon. You can cut that even more if you search for canned chopped chili peppers that are really low in sodium. They're out there. For this recipe I did the calculations using Old El Paso chopped green chili peppers in a jar, 2 tablespoons contain 110 milligrams sodium.

4 milligrams sodium per tablespoon

4 medium ripe tomatoes, peeled and chopped

1/2 cup chopped onion

1/4 cup chopped green pepper

1/4 cup olive oil

2 tablespoons chopped green chili peppers (as above)

2 tablespoons red wine vinegar

1 teaspoon mustard seed

1 teaspoon cilantro

1 teaspoon coriander seed crushed

Dash fresh ground black pepper

Combine all ingredients. Cover and refrigerate several hours or overnight, stirring occasionally. Makes 3 cups of a relish to rival the best on the market.

Steak or Chop Sauce #1

The cream and Roquefort cheese add a level of elegance to a simple cut of meat that will almost make you want to light the candles. Actually, it works on veggies well, too.

38 milligrams sodium per tablespoon

1 1/2 cups heavy cream

2 ounces Roquefort cheese (Be careful, this is where all the sodium is)

1/4 teaspoon freshly ground pepper (think about white pepper here, it's prettier)

1 tablespoon minced chives

Warm cream and continue to heat to a simmer to reduce volume to about one cup. Stir in remaining ingredients and turn off heat. Allow cheese to melt; stir to blend.

Steak or Chop Sauce #2

All that flavor in the meat-cooking process just sticks to the bottom of the pan. Wine helps make it part of the sauce and the cream smoothes it all out. I love thyme in this.

2 milligrams sodium per tablespoon

1 cup dry red wine

1/2 teaspoon minced herb of your choice

2 tablespoons heavy cream

In the skillet or baking pan you used to cook the meat, while keeping meat warm, stir in wine and herbs. Boil and stir to get up all the flavorful brown bits chefs call "fond" (the whole process is called "deglazing the pan"). Cook and simmer 2–3 minutes to reduce slightly. Stir in cream and serve.

Red Wine and Mushroom Sauce

Makes about a cup

2 milligrams sodium per tablespoon

1 tablespoon olive oil

1/2 cup sliced mushrooms (double if you love 'em)

2 cloves garlic, minced

$1/2$ cup dry red wine (one you would like to drink—no skimping)

$1/3$ cup sodium-free beef broth

$1/3$ cup heavy cream (ever notice how often this ingredient comes up in sauces?)

$1/4$ teaspoon fresh ground pepper

Add oil to the skillet in which you just cooked a hearty meat (beef, pork, maybe lamb or game); heat over medium until hot. Add mushrooms and sauté 1–2 minutes. Add garlic; cook and stir 20–30 seconds—be careful not let it brown so it doesn't get bitter. Add wine to deglaze pan stirring as the wine gets hot to be sure you scrape up all the flavorful brown bits. Continue to simmer until reduced by half. Stir in broth and cream, season with pepper. Continue to cook and stir 5–7 minutes until sauce thickens. Spoon over meat.

Rub for Beef

This couldn't be easier. I keep a jar of chili powder made up ahead. While it enhances a nice steak, don't overlook a sprinkle or two on the ground beef as you make those patties!

None. Nadda. Zero. Zip.

Equal parts chili powder (see my recipe page 53) and ground coriander

Pepper to taste, if your tongue can take it!

Rub on all surfaces of the meat and lay on hot, oiled pan or grill.

Homemade Pesto

Makes 1$1/4$ cups. The sodium is in the cheese.

110 milligrams sodium per tablespoon

3 cups firmly packed basil leaves (about 3 oz. on your kitchen scale)

$2/3$ cup unsalted walnuts, toasted (toasting is important because it brings out so much flavor and beats the salt craving)

$2/3$ cup grated Parmesan cheese

$1/2$ cup olive oil

4 cloves garlic, smashed and peeled

Several grinds of fresh black pepper

Run all ingredients in a processor until smooth, scraping sides down frequently. Stores in fridge tightly covered a day or two. For longer storage, place 2-tablespoon amounts in each slot of a standard ice cube tray. Freeze and store pesto cubes up to 3 months.

Smoked Salmon Vodka Cream Sauce

This special occasion sauce will cost you. That's why you have to be very good before you reward yourself with this! Use it on pasta (boiled in unsalted water), fresh steamed (unsalted) vegetables, or a lovely piece of swordfish, tuna, or, yes, salmon.

Serves 2 at 250 milligrams sodium each

1 tablespoon unsalted butter

1 tablespoon finely minced shallots

$1/4$ cup (measure carefully) diced smoked salmon

$1/4$ cup vodka

$1/4$ cup heavy cream (must be the heavy stuff)

$1/4$ cup diced tomatoes

$1/2$ cup no-salt-added tomato sauce

Pinch freshly ground pepper, black, white, or pink will work here

Pinch freshly grated nutmeg

Pinch cayenne pepper

In a deep-sided saucepan, melt butter over medium-high. When it starts to foam and sizzle, stir in shallots and salmon. Cook 1 minute and REMOVE FROM STOVE to stir in vodka; don't set the kitchen on fire, please! Once it settles down, return to burner and stir in the heavy cream, tomatoes, and tomato sauce. Stir and just barely simmer on medium for 2 minutes—heavy cream can't handle boiling. Add seasonings. Heat through. If too thick, add a tablespoon of heavy cream and heat through.

Salsa with Black Beans

Great flavor and texture combination and the whole 2$1/2$ cups contains less than 80 mg sodium; what a deal. Just remember—canned beans are poison unless you can find them canned with NO SALT added. See my discussion page 70 (Black Bean Cowboy Chili).

Makes 2$1/2$ cups at 80 milligrams sodium total

1 large mango, peeled and diced

$3/4$ cup diced jícama (FYI: this veggie is high in fiber and vitamin C)

$3/4$ cup black beans, prepared from dried

1 teaspoon finely minced jalapeño

2 teaspoons finely minced fresh mint

$1/4$ cup finely chopped red onion

Juice and zest of 1 lime

1–2 teaspoons light vinegar, such as rice

Combine and chill till serving time. Keep covered tightly in refrigerator.

Cranberry-Raspberry Sauce

Makes about 2 cups.

22 milligrams sodium per ¼-cup serving

2 tablespoons sugar

1 tablespoon cornstarch

1¾ cup (about half a 16-ounce can) whole berry cranberry sauce

1 10- or 12-ounce package frozen raspberries in syrup, thawed

2 tablespoons orange flavored liqueur or brandy

In a medium saucepan, combine sugar and cornstarch. Stir in cranberry sauce and the juice from the thawed berries. Cook over medium heat until thickened and bubbly. Cook and stir another minute or two. Remove from heat and fold in berries and liqueur or brandy.

Try a couple spoonfuls in a tall glass alternating with pound cake or ice cream for an elegant parfait! Don't forget to count the sodium in the cake or ice cream.

Easy Marinara Sauce

Only takes 20 minutes or so to make, but delicious!. Don't forget to count the sodium in whatever you pour this over. Uncooked pasta starts out sodium-free; it's what you do to it that ratchets up the count. Makes a pasta meal with this sauce a good way to balance a heavier sodium intake from other meals in the day. Works great with eggplant or chicken, too. And measure any cheese you dump on— that's the sodium count killer!

Serves 4 at 30 milligrams sodium each

1 28-ounce can (about 3 cups) salt-free whole tomatoes; do not drain

¼ cup red wine, if desired

2 tablespoons chopped fresh basil (or a scant 2 teaspoons dried)

Several turns of the pepper mill

2 tablespoons olive oil

1 clove garlic, minced

Puree tomatoes and their juices in food processor or blender. Stir in wine, basil and pepper; set aside. Heat olive oil in large saucepan and cook garlic just a minute. Letting it brown will add bitterness to the sauce. Stir in tomatoes and bring just to boiling. Reduce heat and simmer, uncovered, for 10–15 minutes.

Sweet and Sour Sauce

Here's a great sauce for chicken nuggets, shrimp, or pork. Using the "No Soy Sauce" is the only way to make this work and keep the sodium under control while enjoying something you never knew was too salty! Makes about 1 cup and the whole thing is less than 5 mg. sodium. That's less than half a mg. of sodium per tablespoonful.

Makes 1 cup at less than 5 milligrams sodium total

2 tablespoons cornstarch

½ cup sugar

¼ cup white vinegar

¼ cup pineapple juice

2 teaspoons No Soy Sauce (page 142)

¼ cup water

Stir cornstarch into sugar in a medium saucepan. Whisk as you add remaining ingredients to keep sauce smooth. Bring to a boil; reduce heat and simmer gently for about 5 minutes until thickened. Serve immediately or chill until you need it. Use cold or warm on low power in the microwave, stirring every half minute or so.

Butters

Mix up the butter and seasonings, then transfer the combo to a sheet of wax paper. Scoop it all tightly together to make a roll 4 to 8 inches long depending on how much you want to store. Roll it snuggly in the paper. Store in the fridge 3–4 days or freeze for 3 months. Be sure to label and keep in a plastic bag for freezing. What are you going to put it on? Well, obviously vegetables, but how about baked potatoes, mashed potatoes, mashed sweet potatoes, grilled or broiled steak, baked or broiled fish, tossed with hot pasta, or spread on bread and broiled (think garlic and herb on thick slices Italian bread). In short, put it on anything you need more flavor on, especially if you are tempted to reach for the salt shaker.

Curry

Combine ½ cup (1 stick) softened, unsalted butter with 1½ teaspoons curry powder, ½ teaspoon ground cumin, and a small shake of cayenne powder.

Garlic and Chive

Combine ½ cup (1 stick) softened, unsalted butter with 2 cloves finely chopped garlic and 1 tablespoon finely chopped chives.

Garlic and Herb

Combine ½ cup ((1 stick) softened, unsalted butter with 3 cloves garlic, minced, and 1 tablespoon minced parsley, ½ teaspoon ground white pepper. Try that on your fettuccine.

Fresh Herb

Combine ½ cup ((1 stick) softened, unsalted butter with 1 teaspoon each chopped fresh basil, thyme, and parsley (or your favorite fresh herbs).

Lemon

Combine ½ cup (1 stick) softened, unsalted butter with 2 teaspoons freshly grated lemon zest (use 1 teaspoon dried if necessary, but let butter sit a few hours in fridge to rehydrate the lemon), 1 tablespoon fresh lemon juice, 2 teaspoons minced fresh parsley, and 2 teaspoons minced fresh chives. If you're putting this on swordfish, take my word and through in a couple teaspoons of minced fresh thyme, too.

Maple

Combine ½ cup (1 stick) softened, unsalted butter with 2 tablespoons maple syrup and 1 teaspoon minced parsley for corn on the cob. Switch out the parsley for 1 tablespoon ground walnuts for cornbread, oh, baby.

Parmesan and Pepper

Combine ½ cup (1 stick) softened, unsalted butter with 2 tablespoons grated Parmesan cheese and ⅛ teaspoon freshly ground black pepper. (do remember that Parmesan cheese is sodium heavy and be careful)

Rosemary

Combine ½ cup (1 stick) softened, unsalted butter with 2 tablespoons minced rosemary and 2 minced cloves garlic. Spread this between the skin and breast meat of a chicken or turkey breast before roasting. Switch out the rosemary for sage to get that traditional thanksgiving taste and aroma.

Mustard Sauce

Makes about a half cup and tastes great on fish and pork.

The whole recipe contains 147 milligrams sodium, so each tablespoon will run you about 18 milligrams.

¼ cup Greek or plain, full-fat yogurt
2 teaspoons honey, flavor of your choice
1 teaspoon Dijon mustard (careful, this is the higher
    sodium mustard)

Juice of one lemon (about 4 Tablespoons)
2 tablespoons chopped or snipped fresh chives
2 or 3 grinds of fresh black pepper

Whisk yogurt, honey, and Dijon until smooth. Whisk in remaining ingredients.

Steak Marinade

Makes a cup and a half. Because the sodium comes mostly from the Worcestershire sauce (360 mg.), and the expectation is that you will discard any marinade that is used with raw meat, it is difficult to determine how much sodium you will consume from this recipe.

Be aware of the total for the entire recipe (372 milligrams or about 16 milligrams sodium for each tablespoonful you eat) and act judiciously.

¾ cup red wine vinegar
½ cup olive oil
2 tablespoons Worcestershire sauce
2 cloves garlic, minced
1 teaspoon ground Cayenne pepper (vary to taste)
¼ cup packed brown sugar

Mix together, add to meat in zipper-closing plastic bag. Seal and refrigerate at least 30 minutes. Remove meat when ready to cook and reseal bag to discard marinade.

Bourbon Chicken Basting Sauce

Makes enough for a pound of chicken. Be sure to add the sodium of whatever meat you are eating.

The whole recipe contains 8 milligrams sodium.

2 tablespoons olive oil
¼ cup "No Soy Sauce" (see page 142)
2 tablespoons red wine vinegar
2 tablespoons bourbon
¼ cup packed brown sugar
1 green onion (scallion) chopped
2 thin slices fresh ginger
2 cloves garlic, roughly chopped

Combine all ingredients in a medium saucepan being sure to stay away from gas flame when pouring bourbon. Bring up to the simmer, cook covered for about 8 to 10 minutes, stirring occasionally, until thickened somewhat. Sauce your grilling chicken or cover the chicken with sauce and oven-bake.

Cardamom Custard Sauce

A delicate dessert sauce.

It makes about a cup of sauce; the entire recipe has 255 milligrams of sodium or 16 milligrams per tablespoon.

3/4 cup evaporated milk
3 large egg yolks
1 1/2 teaspoons vanilla extract
1/3 cup granulated sugar
1/8 teaspoon ground cardamom

Heat ¾ cup evaporated milk, egg yolks, sugar, vanilla extract, and cardamom in small saucepan over medium heat, stirring constantly, until sauce coats back of spoon. Do not boil. Remove from heat. Use to sauce pound cake, fruit, or whatever you like.

Cinnamon Butter Sauce

Makes about 2 cups of the most delicious sauce; you will want to eat it with a spoon.

The whole batch will cost you 110 milligrams sodium, about 3½ milligrams per tablespoon.

1 cup firmly packed brown sugar
1/2 cup (1 stick) unsalted butter
1/2 cup heavy cream
2 teaspoons cinnamon extract

Mix sugar, butter and cream in medium saucepan. Bring to boil on medium heat. Reduce heat and simmer 10 minutes or until slightly thickened, stirring occasionally. Stir in 2 teaspoons extract. Serve warm with apple desserts.

Savory Yogurt Sauce

Making a lamb sandwich? Pass this sauce for sure. Zippy and a very safe way to sauce up meats or veggies.

The whole recipe contains only 66 milligrams sodium

1/2 cup plain nonfat yogurt
2 teaspoons red onion, minced
1 teaspoon fresh cilantro, minced
1/4 teaspoon ground cumin
Dash ground Cayenne pepper

Combine all ingredients. Slobber it on!

This is probably the chapter you least expected to find in a low-sodium cooking guide. After all, dessert is an unlikely time to see anyone with a salt shaker. But, as I discussed earlier, there is plenty of sodium in baked goods, and dessert is no exception. You were introduced to a high-sodium cake recipe a while back. Let's see if we can't find some ways to enjoy dessert without getting into sodium trouble.

Pie Crust

This is a little different from the crust you're used to because it uses sugar in place of the salt. But filled with tasty fruit or other filling, you won't miss the salt. It's the same recipe my grandmother and mother used, except for dropping the salt. The recipe makes 2 crusts, and the whole thing is worth just 80 milligrams of sodium. If you only need pastry for a single crust pie you can approximate half of all the ingredients. It's easy as pie!

80 milligrams sodium in the entire recipe!

2 1/4 cups all purpose or unbleached flour
1/2 teaspoon sugar
1/3 cup cold milk
1/2 cup + 1 tablespoon olive oil

Sprinkle sugar over flour in a medium bowl. Add milk and oil all at once and stir with fork. Form into 2 equally sized, smooth balls without overworking or kneading the dough. Roll each ball out between 2 sheets parchment or waxed paper. (If you sprinkle a little water lightly on the surface where you are working, it will help keep the bottom paper from sliding around.) Roll out each ball into the size of the pie pan to be used. Fill and cover with second crust. I like to brush a teaspoon or two of milk on the surface and then sprinkle lightly with more sugar. It gives it an attractive golden look and makes the crust crisp-tender and delicious. Bake according to the fruit or other filling you're using.

Fruit Fillings

There's no mystery here, make your usual apple, blueberry, peach, rhubarb or whatever fruit filling you always do, just leave out the salt. It'll be just fine without it. If Eve had salted that apple, we might not be in this mess. But she didn't because fruit wasn't meant to be salted. It's just another eating habit we find hard to break. You will find that fruit pies are wonderfully flavorful without any added salt. Just for fun, here's a couple I use.

Apple Pie

The entire pie with the crust made according to the recipe above has only 90 milligrams of sodium. Therefore, a normal serving (1/6 of the pie) has a mere 15 milligrams.

3/4 cup sugar
1 tablespoon cornstarch
1 teaspoon cinnamon
1/2 teaspoon ground cloves
1 tablespoon lemon juice
6 cups apple slices
1 tablespoon unsalted butter

Combine all but butter and put into shell. Dot with butter and cover with remaining crust, vent, brush with milk, sprinkle with sugar. Bake at 425° for 50 minutes.

Rhubarb Pie

This one, including the crust from the recipe above, has only 17 milligrams sodium per one-sixth serving.

1 1/4 cups sugar
1/4 cup cornstarch
2 teaspoons orange rind
1 teaspoon cinnamon
5 cups rhubarb in 1-inch pieces
1 tablespoon unsalted butter

Combine all but butter and put in shell. Dot with butter and cover with remaining crust, vent, brush with milk, sprinkle with sugar. Bake 45 minutes at 425°.

Pumpkin Pie

This one is worth 622 milligrams for the filling. This pie uses only one crust, so that's 40 milligrams if you use the recipe on this page. That makes 662 milligrams total or 110 milligrams sodium for each one-sixth of the pie. Don't forget to add on for any whipped cream you use. Unwhipped heavy cream has 89 milligrams per cupful. The kind in a pressurized can has 0 milligrams. Now, the pie:

2 eggs, beaten
16 ounces (2 cups) pumpkin (I've used both canned and homegrown, home-prepared pumpkin puree with equal success. The home stuff is more work but better flavor and you can buy excellent pie pumpkins to prepare yourself, too)
1 cup brown sugar
1 teaspoon cinnamon
1/2 teaspoon nutmeg
1/2 teaspoon ginger
1/4 teaspoon cloves
1 tablespoon flour
13-ounce can evaporated milk
1 9-inch pie shell, unbaked, see recipe this page

Preheat oven to 425°. Combine eggs and pumpkin. Blend in sugar, spices and flour. Mix well. Add milk, mixing well. Pour into shell and bake in preheated oven at 425° for 15 minutes. Without opening oven, reduce heat to 350° and continue to bake another 35–40 minutes until set. Cool to room temperature then chill thoroughly before serving.

Lemon Meringue Pie

This is the pie I make when I want to do something special for my older son, Nathan. He absolutely loves this pie. This is exactly how I make it every time:

Serves 6 at 40 milligrams sodium each

1 1/2 cups sugar
1/3 cup + 1 tablespoon cornstarch
1 1/2 cups water
3 egg yolks, slightly beaten
3 tablespoons unsalted butter
2 teaspoons lemon peel
1/2 cup fresh lemon juice
2 drops yellow food coloring

Meringue

3 egg whites
1/4 teaspoon cream of tartar
6 tablespoons sugar
1/2 teaspoon vanilla

Prepare a one-crust pastry for 9-inch pie (see page 150) and pre-bake. Heat oven to 400°. Mix sugar and cornstarch in medium saucepan. Gradually stir in water. Cook over medium heat, stirring constantly, until mixture thickens and boils. Boil and stir one minute. Gradually stir at least half the hot mixture into egg yolks. Blend into hot mixture in pan. Boil and stir one minute. Remove from heat, stir in butter, lemon peel, juice and food color. Pour into baked pie shell. Prepare meringue: Beat egg whites and cream of tarter until foamy. Beat in sugar one tablespoon at a time. Continue beating until stiff and glossy. Do not underbeat. Beat in vanilla. Heap onto hot pie filling spreading to seal to crust edge. Bake 10 minutes or until a delicate brown.

Gramma Berry's Depression Chocolate Cake

Let's talk about this first. My mother says this cake originated in the depression years when eggs were scarce. It rises because of the interaction of the baking soda and vinegar. Remember those grade school science fair volcanoes? Same principle. But baking soda is sodium, so this isn't a perfect recipe for a very-low-sodium eater. It is about the best you can do with baked goods, so I share it here with you. One ninth of the cake, a 3-inch by 3-inch square, unfrosted, is worth 265 milligrams of sodium. Save it for special days when you've been very good (every day?). This is the cake my whole extended family always requests for their birthdays. The beauty of this cake is that you mix it right in the pan.

Serves 9 at 265 milligrams sodium each

1 1/2 cups flour
1 teaspoon baking soda
3 tablespoons cocoa
1 cup sugar
1/3 cup olive oil
1 tablespoon vinegar (I use white)
1 teaspoon vanilla
1 cup water

Combine dry ingredients thoroughly in 9-inch square pan. Combine well; mom used to sift it together, I never bother. Make 3 depressions, (another reason it may have earned the name "depression cake"), in flour mixture and place oil, vinegar, and vanilla each into its own depression. Pour water over all and mix well with fork. I've tried using wooden spoons, whisks, electric beaters; none work any better than the fork, it just dirties more utensils. Bake at 350° for 30 minutes or until toothpick comes out clean.

Spice Cake

This is so much better tasting than boxed mixes. You can vary the spice combinations and proportions to suit your taste. Instead of frosting, try serving with powdered sugar and a little Raspberry Sauce, page 157.

Serves 9 at 97 milligrams sodium each

2 cups all-purpose flour
1 teaspoon baking powder
1/2 teaspoon baking soda
1/2 teaspoon ground nutmeg
1/4 teaspoon ground cinnamon
1/4 teaspoon ground ginger
1/4 teaspoon ground cloves
1/2 cup sugar
1/2 cup honey
1/2 cup olive oil
1/2 cup strong, brewed coffee, room temperature
1 egg
Confectioner's sugar

Heat oven to 350°. Grease and flour a 9-inch square pan. In one medium bowl, stir together flour, baking powder, baking soda, nutmeg, cinnamon, cloves, and ginger. Next, stir in sugar, honey, oil, and coffee. With an electric beater at medium speed, beat batter for two minutes; add egg, and beat for one minute longer. Pour into prepared pan. Bake until a cake tester inserted in center comes out clean, about 45 minutes. Cool completely before serving, and then dust with a little confectioner's sugar. Enjoy!

Chocolate Frosting

This is the classic frosting everybody, especially the kids, wants on Gramma Berry's Depression Chocolate Cake. Generously frosts the cake with plenty for the beater- and bowl-lickers at your house.

None. Nadda. Zero. Zip.

3 tablespoons solid shortening
2 tablespoons unsalted butter or margarine
1/4 cup unsweetened baking cocoa
1 pound confectioner's sugar
4–5 tablespoons boiling water
1 teaspoon vanilla

Just beat it all with electric mixer until smooth and creamy. Adjust consistency by adding a little more powdered sugar or another dash or two of boiling water as needed.

Angel Frosting

This recipe earned its name because it's so light and airy. It's the one I like best. This makes enough for the cake above, but if you want more you can't just double it; for some reason I have yet to figure out, it just curdles when you try. It's not as big a deal as you might think to run through the recipe 2 or 3 times, I do it all the time.

60 milligrams sodium in the whole batch!

2 3/4 tablespoons all-purpose or unbleached flour
1/2 cup milk
3 3/4 tablespoons unsalted butter
3 3/4 tablespoons solid shortening
1/2 cup sugar
1/2 teaspoon vanilla

Pour milk into small saucepan and whisk in flour until well blended. Cook over medium high heat, stirring constantly until it thickens to a paste. Cool. Combine butter, shortening and sugar in small bowl of electric mixer. Beat at high speed 5 minutes until light. Stir in vanilla. Beat in flour-and-milk paste on high speed another 5 minutes until doubled in volume. Tint with a couple drops of your favorite food color, if you'd like.

Brownies

Here's another recipe I grew up on. Still have a chocolate craving? These will help. This recipe is meant for a 9x9-inch square pan. I purposely didn't calculate the calories or fat, but it doesn't take a rocket scientist to figure there's plenty of those.

Serves 12 at 26 milligrams sodium each

3/4 cup flour
1/2 teaspoon baking powder
6 tablespoons cocoa
2 eggs
1 cup sugar
1/3 cup + 1 1/3 tablespoons olive oil
1 teaspoon vanilla

Beat eggs, add sugar and beat well. Add oil and vanilla, beat well. Stir in dry ingredients, then beat thoroughly. Pour into lightly greased 9x9-inch pan and bake in preheated 350° oven for 30 minutes. Cool completely before trying to cut.

Apple Bars

Apple Bars are chewy, warmly spiced bites of autumn. Skip icing them; try sprinkling a blend of 1 teaspoon cinnamon and 2 tablespoons sugar over them hot out of the oven.

Serves 36 at 29 milligrams sodium each

1/2 cup shortening
1 1/3 cups packed brown sugar
1 egg
1/4 cup milk
1 teaspoon baking soda
2 cups all-purpose flour
1 teaspoon ground cinnamon
1/2 teaspoon ground cloves
1/2 teaspoon ground nutmeg
1 cup chopped walnuts
1 cup dates, pitted and chopped
1 cup chopped apples

Preheat oven to 350°. Cream the shortening and brown sugar together. Mix in the egg and milk. Stir in the apples. Add the flour, baking soda, ground cinnamon, ground cloves, ground nutmeg. Stir in the nuts and dates. Spread dough into a 13x18-inch lightly greased jelly roll pan. Bake for 20 to 25 minutes. Let cool, then ice, if desired.

Cinnamon Cookies

Ahh, can you smell these little nuggets? Takes me back to Grandma's kitchen. Plus, if you're careful about their size, the cost in sodium is small enough that you can have more than 1 or 2.

Serves 36 at 28 milligrams sodium each

1 cup unsalted butter, softened
1 1/2 cups white sugar
1 egg
1 1/2 tablespoons molasses

2 1/4 cups all-purpose flour
1 1/8 teaspoons baking soda
1 tablespoon ground cinnamon

Preheat oven to 350°. Cream together butter and sugar. Mix in egg and molasses, blending well. Mix flour, baking soda and cinnamon; add to creamed mixture, mixing well. Drop by teaspoonfuls onto ungreased cookie sheet. Bake for 10 to 12 minutes.

Soft Molasses Cookies

Mom used to keep these around when we were kids. She said the molasses and raisins were good for us. I just knew they were good—especially with a cup of cocoa.

Makes 36 at 32 milligrams sodium each

1 1/2 cups white sugar
1/2 cup shortening
3 eggs
1/2 cup molasses
2 3/4 cups all-purpose flour
1 teaspoon baking soda
1 teaspoon ground cinnamon
1 teaspoon ground allspice
1 teaspoon ground ginger
1 1/2 cups raisins

Preheat oven to 350°. Grease baking sheets. Cream together the sugar, shortening, eggs and molasses. Stir in the flour, baking soda, cinnamon, allspice and ginger. Add the raisins and stir to combine. Drop dough by tablespoonfuls onto the prepared baking sheets. Bake for 12 to 15 minutes. Watch carefully for doneness.

Oatmeal Cookies

Makes the best oaties you ever tasted!

Makes 42 at 44 milligrams sodium each

1 cup shortening
2 cups brown sugar
3 eggs
1 cup sour milk
1 teaspoon vanilla extract
3 cups all-purpose flour
1 teaspoon baking powder
1 teaspoon baking soda
1 teaspoon ground cinnamon
2 cups rolled oats
1 cup raisins
1 cup semisweet chocolate chips

Preheat oven to 350°. Grease cookie sheets. In a large bowl, cream together the shortening and sugar until light and fluffy. Add the eggs one at a time, beating well

with each addition, then stir in the vanilla and sour milk. Combine the flour, baking powder, baking soda, and cinnamon, gradually stir into the creamed mixture. Finally, stir in the rolled oats, raisins and chips. Of course you can choose between raisins and chips if you want. Drop by rounded spoonfuls onto the prepared cookie sheets. Bake 12–15 minutes in the preheated oven. Allow cookies to cool on baking sheet 5 minutes before removing to a wire rack to cool completely.

Peanut Butter Cookies

Using unsalted peanut butter makes these possible. I like to roll the raw cookie dough balls in sugar to bake then press a chocolate Kiss or Hug into the hot cookie right out of the oven.

Makes 36 at 15 milligrams sodium each

1 3/4 cups flour
1 1/4 teaspoons baking powder
1/2 cup sugar
1/2 cup packed brown sugar
1/2 cup solid shortening
1/2 cup unsalted peanut butter
1 egg
2 tablespoons milk
1 teaspoon vanilla

Combine all ingredients and mix on low speed of electric mixer. Shape into balls. Press dough with fork and sprinkle with sugar. Bake on ungreased cookie sheets at 375° for 10 minutes or till lightly golden around the edges but still soft.

Raspberry Walnut Cheesecake

This is easy and fancy. Nice for a party or holiday meal.

Serves 16 at 208 milligrams sodium each

Walnut Crust

1 1/2 cups unsalted walnuts, finely chopped
1/2 cup flour
2 tablespoons unsalted butter, softened

Cake

4 8-oz packages cream cheese, softened
1 1/2 cups sugar
1 tablespoon flour
1 teaspoon vanilla
2 eggs
1 cup raspberries, fresh or frozen
Chopped walnuts for garnish
Fresh raspberries for garnish

Mix ingredients for walnut crust until dough forms. Press in bottom of ungreased 9-inch springform pan. Bake at 400° for 10–12 minutes or until edge is golden brown. Cool. Set aside. Reduce oven temp to 325°. Beat cream cheese, sugar, flour and vanilla in large bowl with electric mixer on low speed until fluffy. Beat in eggs on low. Beat on medium one minute, scraping bowl occasionally. Coarsely chop raspberries and fold into cheese mixture Do this gently or the juices will muddy the appearance of the filling especially if using frozen. Some swirling of the pink juices is pretty. Spread into prepared pan. Bake 55 minutes or until center is set. Cool in pan on wire rack 30 minutes. Refrigerate at least 3 hours but no longer than 48. Run metal spatula along edge of cheesecake to loosen; remove side of pan. Garnish with walnuts and raspberries.

Gingerbread

This is a great seasonal favorite that's easy on the sodium.

Serves 9 at 107 milligrams sodium each

2 1/4 cups flour
1/3 cup sugar
1 cup dark molasses
3/4 cup hot water
1/2 cup shortening
1 egg
1 teaspoon baking soda
1 teaspoon cinnamon
1 teaspoon ginger

Heat oven to 325°. Grease and flour a 9x9-inch pan. Measure all ingredients into large mixer bowl. Blend 1/2 minute on medium scraping bowl constantly. Beat 3 minutes on medium scraping bowl occasionally. Pour into pan. Bake 50 minutes or until toothpick comes out clean. Serve warm with whipped cream or applesauce.

Lemon Pudding Cake

This is Grampa Berry's favorite. Makes four delicate, tasty servings.

Serves 4 at 52 milligrams sodium each

2 eggs separated
1 cup sugar, divided
1 teaspoon grated lemon peel
1/4 cup lemon juice
2/3 cup milk
1/4 cup flour

Preheat oven to 350°. In small mixer bowl, beat egg whites until soft peaks form, about a minute. Gradually beat in 1/4 cup sugar beating on high until stiff peaks form, about 2 minutes more. Set aside. In another small

bowl, beat egg yolks on high speed until foamy, another minute or so. Reduce speed to low and blend in lemon peel, lemon juice, and milk. Beat in remaining sugar and the flour until blended. Gently fold lemon juice mixture into egg whites. Pour into a 1-quart casserole dish with high sides. Set in 8- or 9-inch baking pan and fill pan with hot water to about one inch deep. Set into center of preheated oven and bake 45–50 minutes until toothpick inserted only half its length comes out clean. Deeper layer is the pudding layer and will remain moist. Remove from pan of water and cool a half hour or so before serving. Yummy.

Chocolate Sauce

One last way to beat the chocolate craving. This makes 1 1/4 cups of sauce. It's not the sauce that will get you, it's what you put it on. Enjoy.

6 milligrams sodium per tablespoon

2/3 cup semisweet chocolate chips
1/3 cup sugar
1/2 cup evaporated milk
1 teaspoon unsalted butter or margarine

Heat chips, sugar and milk in small saucepan over medium heat until chocolate melts and mixture comes to a boil. Stir constantly, using a whisk if you have one. Once full boil is achieved, remove from heat and stir in butter. You could stir in a couple drops of almond or peppermint extract here for a variation, if you want. Use hot or chilled.

Fruit & Nut Snickerdoodles

Mix and match the nuts, fruit, and spices to make it your own signature cookie!

Makes 18 at 38 milligrams sodium each

3 tablespoons unsalted butter, softened
2 tablespoons shortening
1/3 cup plus 2 tablespoons sugar
1 egg, beaten
1 cup flour
1/2 teaspoon cream of tartar
1/2 teaspoon baking soda
1/4 cup finely chopped nuts (I love it with hazelnuts)
1/4 cup dried fruit (don't be boring, branch out and try blueberries or chopped mangoes. I like the combination of dried cranberries with the hazelnuts)
1/2 teaspoon spice such as cinnamon, or nutmeg. Cardamom goes well with hazelnuts and cranberries!

In large bowl, cream butter, shortening and 1/3 cup sugar until light and fluffy. Beat in egg. In separate bowl (or just on a sheet of paper towel if you hate washing dishes), combine flour, cream of tartar, and baking soda. Gradually add flour to butter mixture. Stir in fruit and nuts. Combine the spice with the remaining 2 tablespoons of sugar. Roll dough into 18 balls about 1½ inches in diameter. Roll in the sugar-spice and place 2 inches apart on baking sheet coated lightly with cooking spray. Bake in 350°, preheated oven 10–12 minutes until golden around the edges. Cool and ice the tops if you want.

On the Top

You can skip the icing since they get rolled in spiced-up sugar, or mix a little milk into some confectioner's sugar and drizzle a little on each cookie. My favorite Cranberry/Hazelnut/Cardamom combo is divine with a tiny drizzle of melted white chocolate. Uhhh huh.

Cinnamon Toffee Crisps

So good with a mid-morning cup-o-java!

Makes 48 at 25 milligrams sodium each

2 cups all-purpose flour
³/₄ teaspoon baking powder
2 teaspoons good ground cinnamon, divided
10 oz (2¹/₂ sticks) unsalted butter, softened
3 tablespoons instant espresso powder
1 cup confectioner's sugar
¹/₂ cup packed brown sugar
1 8-oz bag (1¹/₃ cups) English toffee bits
¹/₄ cup granulated sugar

Combine flour, baking powder, and 1½ teaspoons cinnamon; set aside. Beat the butter and espresso powder thoroughly (it won't completely dissolve). Beat in both confectioner's and brown sugar. Gradually stir in flour; fold in toffee bits.

Combine granulated sugar with remaining half-teaspoon cinnamon. Using scant tablespoons (yes, you better use a real measuring tablespoon to keep it even, so the sodium content doesn't vary from cookie to cookie) roll dough into balls. Place on ungreased cookie sheets a good 2 inches apart—they will spread out some (I figure a dozen to a standard-sized sheet). Tap the bottom of a glass or something with a flat bottom on the dough in the bowl to make it a little sticky, then into the sugar cinnamon mixture. Press gently down on cookie balls to flatten some and leave plenty of cinnamon sugar. Bake in preheated 350° oven.

Now here's the trick—start watching them after ten minutes. They may need as much as another 4–5 minutes, depending on your cookie sheet type, oven, and personal taste for cookies that are softer and a little chewy or more crispy-edged. Cool only a couple minutes then move to rack to finish. As they set they will

want to stick on the cookie sheet because of the toffee. Greasing the sheet just makes a slimy mess and doesn't help. Boy, are these worth it. People who don't eat low sodium won't even notice that these are only 25 milligrams of sodium each, most of which comes from the toffee. Share with your friends!

Pumped-Up Filled Chocolate Cupcakes

OK, they take a little time, but they wowed the whole security department at work when I presented them with a basket full of these—totally worth it.

Serves 12 at 115 milligrams sodium each

Cupcakes

¹/₃ cup cocoa
¹/₃ cup semisweet chocolate chips
1 tablespoon espresso powder
¹/₂ cup boiling water
³/₄ cup sugar
¹/₂ cup sour cream
¹/₂ cup vegetable oil
2 large eggs
1¹/₂ teaspoons pure vanilla
1¹/₄ cup flour
1 teaspoon baking powder
¹/₂ teaspoon baking soda

Filling

4 tablespoons unsalted butter, at room temperature
1 cup powdered sugar
2 teaspoons pure vanilla
3 tablespoons heavy cream
1 cup marshmallow crème

Glaze

2 tablespoons heavy cream
2 tablespoons unsalted butter
4 ounces unsweetened chocolate, chopped
2 teaspoons pure vanilla

For Cupcakes

Preheat oven to 325°. Prepare muffin pan by greasing and flouring cups (you can flour with cocoa powder if you prefer). Combine cocoa, semisweet chips, espresso powder, and boiling water; stir to melt and whisk smooth. Add sugar, sour cream, oil, eggs and vanilla and whisk in well. Combine flour, baking powder, and baking soda; stir into chocolate. Pour or spoon into prepared muffin pan. Bake 18–22 minutes. Cool on rack; don't be alarmed if they sink a bit in the middle—we're going to fix that shortly with the filling.

For Filling

In electric mixer, cream butter until light; beat in half the sugar, then the vanilla and 1 tablespoon heavy cream. When smooth, beat in remaining sugar and heavy cream. Warm marshmallow crème in micro only 15 seconds just to soften—do not let melt at all. Beat into filling. Reserve ⅓ cup. Chill.

Prepare cooled cupcakes by removing a cone of the cake from the top. As you do so leave a rim of cake around the edge—don't slice the top off. The rim will help stabilize filled cup and give you an edge to set the top back into. Cut off the lower half or ⅔ of each cone; reserve cut away cake for some other use. Divide filling among the cupcakes, filling the divot created. Recap by placing tops back over the filling and adjusting gently.

For Glaze

In small, microwave-safe bowl, warm heavy cream and butter just till butter melts. Sprinkle chopped chocolate over hot mixture; let stand 2–3 minutes, then stir till melted and smooth. Let stand again just a minute or two till barely warm. Beat in vanilla. Spread over tops of cupcakes. Allow to cool completely. Place reserved crème filling into small plastic bag and snip the corner to make a small hole. Squeeze filling out onto cupcakes making traditional squiggly line or decorate as desired.

Lemon Curd Bars

I won a prize for these—didn't think I should tell them that there's so little sodium in each bar. What do you think?

Makes 32 at 20 milligrams sodium each

1 cup unsalted butter, softened
1 cup sugar
2 cups flour
½ teaspoon baking powder
1 11-ounce jar (or there about) lemon curd
¾ cup sweetened coconut flakes
¾ cup chopped nuts; pick your favorite—mine is hazelnut, but almonds work well, too. Toast them lightly before you add them to help bring out the flavor. You can do that easily while preheating your oven and prepping other ingredients by spreading them in the cookie pan in a single layer and baking 5–10 minutes just until lightly browned.

Cover your rimmed 13x9-inch cookie sheet or baking pan with greased parchment or foil that extends beyond the edges by several inches. Once baked and cooled you can lift them out with this, making cutting much easier. Beat butter until light in large bowl. Beat in sugar until fluffy. Add flour and baking powder, mixing until resembles coarse crumbs, don't be overzealous. Set aside about ⅔ cup of the crumb mixture and press the rest into prepared pan. Bake crust 5–8 minutes at 375° until top is golden. Remove and spread with the lemon curd (it spreads easier if you loosen it up first by stirring a minute or so). Spread almost to the edges of the crust. Combine coconut and nuts with reserved crumb mixture. Sprinkle evenly over lemon curd. Return to oven and bake another 18–20 minutes until top is golden. Cool in pan 10–15 minutes, then remove using prepared foil or parchment. Cut into 32 bars. Store airtight. Keep best in fridge, that is if you have any left to store!

Islands of Love

All the ingredients for a love-island vacation!

Makes 48 at 30 milligrams sodium each

2½ cups all-purpose flour
1 teaspoon baking powder
10 oz (2½ sticks) unsalted butter, softened
2 tablespoons coconut milk
   (remember, it looks kinda solid when you open the can, but stir it and it smoothes out. Look for other low-sodium coconut milk recipes since you've opened the can)
3 tablespoons grated frozen fresh ginger (see my discussion on page 131)
1 teaspoon rum flavoring
1 cup confectioner's sugar
½ cup packed brown sugar
6 ounce bag dehydrated pineapple pieces (near the dried cranberries, blueberries, apricots, etc.—does this stir thoughts of your own creativity?), diced up
2 cups toasted sweetened coconut (easily done just like nuts, in a baking pan in a 400° oven, stirred at the 4-minute mark, then every 2 minutes after that until they are toasty but not burned.
1 cup macadamia nuts, toasted then finely chopped (or run in a grinder or processor till coarsely ground. Watch closely! It only takes a very short time to over-grind into sticky meal)
½ cup granulated sugar
1½ teaspoons ground cardamom

Combine flour and baking powder; set aside. Beat the butter and coconut milk thoroughly. Beat in ginger and rum flavoring, then both confectioner's and brown sugar; beat well till light and fluffy. Gradually stir in flour; fold in pineapple, coconut flakes, and macadamia nuts.

Combine granulated sugar with cardamom. Using tablespoonfuls of dough (yes, you better scoop with a real measuring tablespoon to keep it even so the sodium content doesn't vary from cookie to cookie) roll dough into balls then roll in the cardamom-sugar. Place on ungreased cookie sheets 2 inches apart—they will spread out some. Press gently down on cookie balls to flatten just a bit. Bake in preheated 350° oven.

Start watching them after ten minutes. They may need as much as another 4–5 depending on your cookie sheet type, oven, and personal taste for cookies. Cool only a couple minutes then move to rack to finish. You may want to drizzle some melted white chocolate on them once they've cooled or mix confectioner's sugar with coconut milk and maybe a drop or two of lime juice to drizzle. Oh, baby!

Brownie Pie

It only takes a tiny slice to satisfy that chocolate craving—take it from a true chocoholic. If you add ice cream or whipped cream, don't forget to add the sodium for those into the total per serving (Cool Whip and Reddi Whip labels say there's no sodium in one serving).

Serves 8 at 224 milligrams sodium each

1 crust from a 2-crust packaged, prepared pie crust (should be at room temp to use)
1/2 cup unsalted butter
3 ounces unsweetened baking chocolate, chopped up
3 eggs
1 1/2 cups sugar
1/2 cup flour
1 teaspoon vanilla
1 cup unsalted chopped walnuts

Unroll pie crust and place in 9-inch pie dish. Fold and crimp edges; set aside. In heavy saucepan, warm and melt butter and chocolate over low heat, stirring often. Let cool to room temp (20 minutes—oh, it's well worth the wait). Preheat oven to 350°. In a large bowl beat eggs. Beat in sugar; stir in flour and vanilla. Stir in cooled chocolate-butter mixture and then the nuts. Pour into unbaked prepared piecrust. Bake 50 to 55 minutes until knife inserted into center comes out clean. Don't overbake! Let cool an hour or so on a rack (if you can!). It will cut easier when cooled some.

Apple Brownies

I make this small batch to keep from eating a whole pan myself!

Makes 12 at 75 milligrams sodium each

1 stick unsalted butter
1 cup sugar
1 egg, beaten
1/2 cup chopped (unsalted) nuts
2 medium apples, peeled, cored, and finely chopped
1 cup flour
1 teaspoon baking powder
1/2 teaspoon baking soda
1/2 teaspoon cinnamon

Cream butter and add sugar gradually, beating until smooth. Beat egg separately until light & fluffy, then add to butter mixture. Stir in nuts & chopped apples. Sift together dry ingredients & fold into batter with a spoon. Turn batter into a greased 7x11-inch baking pan. Bake 40 minutes at 350°. Cool & cut into squares. Recipe may be doubled for a 9x13-inch pan.

Fresh Raspberry Sauce

Of course this is great on pound cake, spice cake, ice cream, waffles, (all low-sodium, of course) and don't forget to lick the spoon! Try switching out the berries and liqueur to build this sauce to your own taste. Try blackberries and blackberry brandy. Very elegant.

Makes about 2 cups for 10 milligrams of sodium in the whole thing.

3 1/2 cups fresh raspberries or 1 12-oz. package frozen
1/3 to 1/2 cups sugar depending on sweetness of berries
1 cup water
1 1/2 tablespoons cornstarch
2 tablespoons raspberry liqueur

Thaw raspberries if frozen. Puree raspberries in food processor or blender with water until smooth. Strain into small saucepan, pressing puree through a mesh strainer. Whisk 1/3 cup sugar, cornstarch, and liqueur into sauce. Cook all ingredients together over medium-high heat until thickened and clear.

Remove from heat, taste, and add remaining sugar if necessary. Set aside to cool slightly before serving, or transfer sauce to a nonmetallic container, cover, and chill until ready to use.

Peanut Butter Brownies

Craving chocolate decadence? For 31 milligrams of sodium each, you can tame the craving 16 times. And yes, well wrapped you can freeze a stash for another day of need.

If you find the peanut butter made without salt, each one of these morsels goes down to just 8 milligrams a piece. Oh, yeah!

1/4 cup unsalted butter
2 squares (2 ounces) unsweetened chocolate
1 cup sugar
1/4 cup (measure carefully) chunky-style Skippy peanut butter or, preferably a brand made without added salt; they do exist.
1/2 teaspoon vanilla
2 eggs
1/2 cup flour

Melt butter and chocolate over low heat or in microwave; cool. Blend in sugar, peanut butter, and vanilla. Beat in eggs, one at a time. Stir in flour. Spread in 8x8x2-inch baking pan and bake at 350° about 25 minutes. Cool before cutting or you'll have crumbs. You can hold out a little while longer!

Maple Shortbread Bars

A tasty change of pace, shortbread doesn't have to puff up like regular cookies, so there is no need to put sodium-laden leavening agents in the mix!

Without baking powder, baking soda or salt, one of these 2-square-inch cookies is only 4 milligrams of sodium. You'll have 16 cookies to savor.

1$^{1}/_{4}$ cups flour
$^{1}/_{4}$ cup sugar
$^{1}/_{2}$ cup unsalted butter
$^{2}/_{3}$ cup maple syrup—just the real stuff, remember
1$^{1}/_{3}$ cups flaked, unsweetened coconut

Combine flour and sugar, cut in butter until mixture resembles fine crumbs. Press into 8x8x2-inch baking pan. Bake at 350° 15–20 minutes; don't let them get brown. Meantime, combine syrup and coconut in small saucepan. Cook over medium until coconut absorbs most of the syrup. Spread over hot bars and bake another 10 minutes. Cut into 16 bars. Ooooo.

Peach Melba

Only 64 milligrams sodium and pretty enough for company

1 scoop vanilla ice cream
1 small fresh peach, sliced
1 tablespoon raspberry jam, warmed to just melting in the micro, 20 seconds should do it
2 tablespoons thawed whipped topping
1 vanilla wafer cookie, crushed

Assemble in bowl in order given and grab a spoon!

Lime Cooler Bars

One of my personal favorites, it always gets rave reviews.

Each of 18 bars contains 32 mg. sodium. Enjoy!

2$^{1}/_{2}$ cups all-purpose flour
$^{1}/_{2}$ cup confectioners' sugar
$^{3}/_{4}$ cup cold, unsalted butter
4 eggs
scant 1$^{3}/_{4}$ cups sugar
$^{1}/_{2}$ cup lime juice (best if you can use fresh)
1 teaspoon grated fresh lime peel

$^{1}/_{2}$ teaspoon baking powder
Additional confectioners' sugar

In a large bowl, combine 2 cups flour and confectioners' sugar; cut in butter until mixture resembles coarse crumbs. Pat into a greased 13-in. x 9-in. baking pan. Bake at 350° for 20 minutes or until lightly browned.

In a large bowl, whisk the eggs, sugar, lime juice and peel until frothy. Combine the baking powder and remaining flour; whisk in egg mixture. Pour over hot crust.

Bake for 20–25 minutes or until light golden brown. Cool on a wire rack. Dust with confectioners' sugar. Cut into squares.

Ooey Gooey Coconut Bars

These will taste sinfully delicious!

Only 36 milligrams sodium in each of 12 bars

For crust
$^{1}/_{2}$ cup unsalted butter
$^{1}/_{2}$ cup brown sugar
1 cup unbleached all-purpose flour

For topping
2 large eggs
1 cup packed brown sugar
1 teaspoon pure vanilla extract
1 cup chopped walnuts
$^{1}/_{2}$ cup shredded sweetened coconut
2 tablespoons flour

Preheat oven to 375°. Line an 8-inch square baking pan with foil and spray with nonstick cooking spray. Set aside.

For Crust

Cream ½ cup butter till fluffy. Gradually add ½ cup brown sugar and beat until smooth. Stir in flour. Press this mixture into bottom of prepared pan; bake at 375° for 20 minutes or until golden.

For topping

While crust is baking, beat eggs with 1 cup brown sugar until smooth. Stir in vanilla and walnuts. Toss coconut with flour and add to egg mixture. Stir till combined. Pour this topping mixture over hot baked crust and smooth with a spatula. Return pan to oven and bake for an additional 20 minutes or until topping set and golden brown. Cool pan on rack. When completely cool, lift foil sling out of pan and place on cutting board. Gently peel away from sides and use a spatula to separate from bottom. Discard foil. Cut into bars using a large chef's knife. Store in an airtight container.

Menus for All Occasions

Now you have an abundance of new recipes with the sodium content calculated per serving and tables to refer to as you redesign your old recipes. Just for fun, let's put some new and old food ideas together and see what a few days might look like for the sodium minded. Of course you would cook all the "oldies" without salt. An asterisk (*) indicates that the recipe is provided in this cookbook.

Twelve Great Ways to Start the Day

Notice that the high sodium standards such as bacon, sausage, ham and cheese are conspicuously absent. Some breakfasts might go like this:

1. Breakfast Smoothie*
    2 slices toasted Spice Swirl Bread*
    Unsalted butter mixed with a little grated
      lemon zest
    Total: 295 milligrams sodium

2. Old Fashioned Hot Cocoa*
    Peanut Butter and Jelly Muffin*
    Banana
    Total: 206 milligrams sodium

3. Raspberry Peach Cooler*
    Fresh Peach Muffin*
    1 egg, scrambled, peppered, not salted
    Total: 238 milligrams sodium

4. Fresh fruit slices, your choice
    2 tablespoons Fruit Dressing*
    8 ounce glass skim milk
    1 slice toasted Oat Bran Bread*
    Unsalted butter mixed with a little honey
      and orange juice or orange extract
    Total: 241 milligrams sodium

5. Hot oatmeal (instant plain, 1 envelope)
      sprinkled with a tablespoon of brown sugar
    2 tablespoons raisins
    ½ cup skim milk
    Creamy Strawberry Sipper made with White
      Grape Juice*
    Total: 176 milligrams sodium

6. 1 poached egg, pepper as desired, no salt
    My Favorite Blueberry Muffin*
    6 ounces orange juice with calcium added
    Total: 163 milligrams sodium

7. 2-egg omelet made with thyme and lightly
      sautéed, chopped bell peppers, onions and
      mushrooms
    1 slice toasted Honey Whole Wheat Bread* with
      Unsalted Herb Butter*
    6 ounces grapefruit juice
    Total: 244 milligrams sodium

8. Apple Fritters*
    Real maple syrup
    8 ounce glass of an all real juice blend
    Total: 61 milligrams sodium (a good breakfast
      when you have a day ahead where there may
      be trouble, like a party or a holiday meal)

9. 1 slice Pumpkin Bread*
   1 cup applesauce
   8 ounces cranberry juice
   Total: 285 milligrams sodium

10. 1 egg, fried in unsalted butter
    1 slice toasted Potato Bread*
    1 tablespoon strawberry jam
    8 ounces apple juice
    Total: 198 milligrams sodium

11. 2 large pieces Nabisco Shredded Wheat
    ½ cup milk
    ½ banana
    This is for days you know you need to start out being good. This is only 65 milligrams sodium.

12. 2 slices French toast, made with low-sodium bread
    ¼ cup real maple syrup
    ½ cup fresh berries
    This is for days you know you need to be very, very good. Made with low-sodium, store-bought bread, this will only cost you 30 milligrams sodium! And it makes great French toast, too. I promise.

Munchable Lunchables

There's always last night's leftovers. You can also try some combinations of an old favorite, soup and bread. Here are some couples I think work especially well together (most leave room in the sodium count for seconds):

Vegetable Soup* and Oat Bran Bread*, *175 milligrams sodium*

Colorful Corn Chowder* and Honey Whole Wheat Bread*, *176 milligrams sodium*

Best Cream of Broccoli Soup* and Herb Bread*, *208 milligrams sodium*

Chicken and Rice Soup* and Lemon Loaves*, *177 milligrams sodium*

Asparagus Soup* and Potato Bread*, *180 milligrams sodium*

Winter Warmer Soup* and Pumpkin Bread*, *287 milligrams sodium*

Beef Soup Made Your Way (use your homemade no-salt broth, leftover beef roast, chopped up, some noodles or barley, a few handfuls of leftover vegetables and maybe a fresh chopped tomato or two. Toss

in a teaspoon of your favorite herb for the last 15 minutes of simmering. Mmmm good.) Serve with Seasoned Croutons* and you'll probably run *between 150 and 180 milligrams sodium per serving.*

If soup and bread doesn't fill you up, add a few slices tomato, pepper strips, baby carrots, and cucumber slices drizzled with regular or Raspberry Vinegarette Dressing*.

Too hot for soup today? Why not have a scoop of Waldorf Salad* or make a broccoli slaw by chopping fresh or lightly blanched broccoli, well chilled. Toss with a few raisins and top with Cole Slaw Dressing*.

Make Salsa* or Onion Salsa* and dip fresh veggies or homemade Potato Chips* or "Corn Chips"*.

Boil some angel hair pasta (no salt in the water) and buzz together some Tomato Basil Sauce* to top it. The sauce keeps well in the refrigerator a couple days and in the freezer several weeks.

Mix some low-sodium tuna with chopped onion and Coleen's Mayonnaise*. Serve on your favorite low-sodium bread with fresh lettuce leaves. Use one slice of bread instead of two to reduce the sodium count, if things are tight in the sodium budget.

Try Chicken Fingers with Honey Mustard Sauce* and a tossed salad with Italian* or Farmstead Dressing*.

Dice up cold leftover beef, lamb, pork, or chicken and roll it into a corn tortilla, or tuck into a pita bread (be wary of the sodium content on the label). Top with some Cucumber-Yogurt Sauce*.

In the Brief Case

Are you a brown-bagger? As long as you choose your bread carefully, you can still make your basic sandwich. Watch out for what you dress it with and please don't use deli meats. By all means, pack some fresh fruits and vegetables and a homemade cookie or two, but skip the pickle, chips, and pretzels.

What Will I Make for Dinner Tonight?

Dinners and suppers can be a big challenge to the sodium dodger so let's look at several ways to put together an evening meal. Often you'll see where the sodium content allows for seconds and many are so light in sodium content that you can fit in snacks or desserts. Just be sure to be conservative and keep within your prescribed daily sodium intake parameters.

The Handbook of Practical Low-Salt Living

Many of these meals can be put on the table in a short time and some cook in the crockpot all day to set you free, so dust off the slow cooker and get ready to cook:

Slow Cooker Country-Style Spareribs*
Frozen corn cooked with a dash of chili powder
Waldorf Salad*
Total: 245 milligrams
Bowtie Chicken and Vegetables*
Tossed Salad with Vinegarette Dressing*
Total: 168 milligrams sodium, seconds are in order here!

Curried Turkey Breast*
Sour Cream Blueberry Muffin*
Dilled Peas and Cauliflower*
Total: 264 milligrams

Beef Stroganoff*
Peas and onions
Herb Bread*
Total: 345 milligrams sodium

Trout Almondine*
Snow Peas and Water Chestnuts*
Fresh Peach Muffin*
Total: 344 milligrams sodium

Baked Ziti*
White Bread Rolls*
Tossed Salad with Italian Dressing*
Total: 310 milligrams sodium

Chicken with Tomatoes and Mushrooms for the Crockpot*
Boiled noodles
Steamed green beans with almonds
Total: 224 milligrams sodium

Fresh haddock, 4-ounce serving sautéed in a little sesame oil and fresh lemon
Dill Sauce*
Snow Peas and Water Chestnuts*
Winter Fruit Salad*
Total: 157 milligrams sodium (for those days you've been very bad)

Sirloin steak, 4-ounce portion tenderized in Marinade #1*
Baked potato with sour cream and chives
Steamed mixed vegetables
Tossed Salad with Farmstead Dressing*
Total: 258 milligrams sodium

Stuffed Mushrooms*
Chicken breasts poached in equal parts homemade no-salt Chicken Stock* and white wine with chopped fresh chives and sage

Steamed fresh beets
My Favorite Blueberry Muffin*
Total: 367 milligrams sodium

Broiled lamb chop with rosemary
Fadge*
Oven Tomatoes*
Honey Whole Wheat Bread made as rolls*
Total: 195 milligrams sodium

Crunchy Oven "Fried" Fish*
Tartar Sauce, 2 tablespoons*
Herb Bread*
Steamed zucchini
Total: 228 milligrams sodium

South Seas Chicken and Vegetables*
Honey Sweet Potato Biscuit*
Cooked noodles or rice
Total: 245 milligrams sodium

Winey Pork Chops*
Shredded fresh potatoes sautéed with onions and green peppers
Steamed spinach
Applesauce
Total: 180 milligrams sodium, and you won't believe it was possible when you're done!

Favorite Swordfish Steaks*
Lemon Butter Sauce*
Mashed potatoes with a dash of milk, sour cream and garlic
Steamed broccoli
Total: 221 milligrams sodium

Spaghetti with Sauce*
White Bread*, sliced, lightly spread with unsalted butter, sprinkled with a little garlic powder and 2 teaspoons grated Parmesan cheese for each slice, then broiled until golden
Mixed greens with Italian Dressing*
Total: 247 milligrams sodium

Chicken in Creamy Herb Sauce*
Brown rice
Sour Cream Blueberry Muffin*
Glazed Carrots*
Total: 201 milligrams sodium

Jason's Fish Fry*
Diced leftover cooked potatoes sautéed with onion and herbs
Cabbage Salad with Cole Slaw Dressing*
Total: 171 milligrams sodium, hard to believe but it can be done.

Apricot Sauced Pork Chops*
Baked potato
Winter Fruit Salad*
Total: 142 milligrams sodium, isn't it amazing?

Crockpot Stuffed Peppers*
Couscous made with homemade no-salt Chicken
    Stock* and chopped zucchini
Chilled canned pears
Total: 98 milligrams sodium, a most astonishing
feat.

Turkey tenderloins lightly browned then simmered
    until done in a sauce made of apricot marme-
    lade, white wine, grated gingerroot and minced
    garlic
Rice with parsley
Oat Bran Bread* made as rolls
Mixed greens with Raspberry Vinegarette Dressing*
Total: 174 milligrams sodium

Grilling, It's Not Just for Summer Anymore

Let's look at some outdoor eating ideas. Of course anything you can do on a barbecue you can do in a broiler,
too.

Grilled Chicken in Marinade #2*
Packet Potatoes*
Sliced fresh vegetables in Raspberry Vinaigrette*
4 Peanut Butter Cookies*
Total: 191 milligrams sodium

Lean Country-Style Pork Ribs with Barbecue
    Sauce #2*
Grilled Corn*
Honey Sweet Potato Biscuits*
Tomato slices drizzled with a teaspoon of olive oil
    and sprinkled with chopped fresh basil
Total: 279 milligrams sodium

Grilled Halibut*
Grilled Vegetables*
Lemon Loaves*
Chopped cabbage and carrots with Cole Slaw
    Dressing*
Total: 166 milligrams sodium, would you have be-
lieved you could go away from the table full of good
tasting food for so little sodium if you didn't see it
with your own eyes?

Chicken breast in 1½ inch bites in marinade #2*
    then skewered with pineapple chunks, red and
    green bell peppers, and cherry tomatoes and
    grilled

Rice cooked with a little chopped parsley and sage
Honey Whole Wheat Bread* made as rolls
Total: 198 milligrams sodium

Grilled Herbed Fresh Catch*
Baked potatoes wrapped in foil, tossed into the hot
    coals, and turned every now and then for about
    an hour or until done
Zucchini and summer squash sautéed lightly in a
    tablespoon of unsalted butter and a tablespoon
    of olive oil with chopped fresh dill
Brownie*
Total: 222 milligrams sodium

Shrimp on the Barby:
Skewer raw, unshelled shrimp or toss them in a
    grilling basket. Brush often with a mixture
    of 2 tablespoons melted unsalted butter and
    1 tablespoon lemon juice while turning and
    grilling. This is a real favorite at our house.
Italian Pasta Salad*
Chilled canned pears
Herb Bread*
Total: 323 milligrams sodium

Company's Coming: Springtime Get-Together
Marinated Leg of Lamb on the Grill*
Fresh Mint Sauce*
Old Fashioned Potato Salad*
Fresh asparagus steamed with a squirt of lemon
    juice in the water
White Bread Rolls* with Herb Butter*
Rhubarb Pie*
Total: 293 tasty, filling milligrams of sodium!

The Weather Outside is Frightful:
Suppers to Warm Your Tummy

Of course a hearty soup with salad and a slice of homemade bread is always a great warmer-upper at supper
as well as lunchtime. Look back through the soup offerings and see what tickles your tummy, or create
your own low-sodium soup recipe with salt-conscious
ingredients you especially like. Here are some other
hearthside hearty ideas:

Old Fashioned Rump Roast*
Boiled potatoes and carrots
Oat Bran Bread*
Depression Chocolate Cake* with Angel Frosting*
Total: 538 milligrams sodium, still less than a quar-
ter of the American Heart Association recommenda-
tion for daily sodium intake.

Easy Burgandy Stew*
Tossed salad with low-sodium French Dressing*

Honey Whole Wheat Bread*
Apple Bars*
Total: 260 milligrams sodium (with 2 apple bars for dessert!)

Macaroni and Cheese*
Canned or fresh fruit with Fruit Dressing*
Fresh tomato slices with Vinaigrette Dressing*
Angelfood cake with Chocolate Sauce*
Total: 570 milligrams sodium

Sweetly Spiced Pork*
Shredded cabbage with Vinegar-Cucumber Sauce*
Applesauce
2 Oatmeal Cookies*
Total: 196 milligrams sodium

Chicken Cacciatore*
White Bread*
Mixed greens with Italian Dressing*
Apple Pie*
Total: 242 milligrams sodium

Swiss Steak for the Crockpot*
Mashed potatoes made with a little milk and
    unsalted butter
Lemon Broccoli*
Spice Cake* dusted with powdered sugar
Total: 273 milligrams sodium, incredible!

Lamb Rosemary*
Sliced carrots steamed with mint
Wild Rice with Leeks and Mushrooms*
2 Soft Molasses Cookies*
Total: 215 milligrams sodium

Thanksgiving

The quintessential feasting holiday is demonstrated here in two ways. First you will see a typical dinner at a Norman Rockwell table, delicious with all the trimmings. Then you will be treated to another equally delicious meal, but this one has been significantly reduced in sodium content. I believe you will not feel the least bit deprived with the second menu, but I know you will be healthier and much less likely to put in an appearance at the local emergency room before dessert.

The Old Way:

5 butter crackers (135 milligrams sodium)

2 tablespoons onion dip (230 milligrams sodium)

Eggnog, ½ cup (80 milligrams sodium)

Pre-basted turkey, 8 ounces, white meat (540 milligrams sodium)

Stuffing from mix, 1 cup (880 milligrams sodium)

Mashed potatoes made with butter and milk, 1 cup (141 milligrams sodium)

Gravy, ½ cup, from turkey drippings (660 milligrams sodium)

Candied yams, 5 ounces frozen (130 milligrams sodium)

Dinner roll, 1 (120 milligrams sodium)

Butter, 2 teaspoons (78 milligrams sodium)

Pumpkin bread, a ½-inch thick slice (190 milligrams sodium)

Green bean bake made with creamed soup and canned French-fried onion rings, ½ cup (435 milligrams sodium)

Creamed peas and onions, canned ½ cup (720 milligrams sodium)

Cranberry sauce, canned ¼ cup (15 milligrams sodium)

Pumpkin pie with whipped cream—only ½ of the pie with 3 level tablespoons whipped cream (295 milligrams sodium)

Apple pie with vanilla ice cream—only ½ of the pie with ¼ cup vanilla ice cream (310 milligrams sodium)

A Grand Old-Fashioned Thanksgiving Meal: 4959 milligrams sodium!

The New Way:

5 "Corn" Chips* (25 milligrams sodium)

2 tablespoons Garlic Dip* (180 milligrams sodium)

Gramma Balch's Fruit Punch*, 1 cup (30 milligrams sodium)

Fresh or frozen non-prebasted Roast Turkey*, white meat, 8 ounces (158 milligrams sodium)

Homemade Stuffing*, 1 cup (48 milligrams sodium)

Mashed potatoes made with unsalted butter and milk, 1 cup (26 milligrams sodium)

Poultry Wine Sauce*, ½ cup (20 milligrams sodium)

Sweet potatoes mashed with unsalted butter, brown sugar, and walnuts, ½ cup (48 milligrams sodium)

Honey Whole Wheat Roll*, 1 (94 milligrams sodium)

Herb Butter*, 2 teaspoons (0 milligrams sodium)

Pumpkin Bread* a 1-inch thick slice (180 milligrams sodium)

Steamed green beans and almonds, ½ cup (3 milligrams sodium)

Saucy Brussels Sprouts*, ½ cup (44 milligrams sodium)

Cranberry Orange Mold*, ½ cup (52 milligrams sodium)

Pumpkin Pie*, ¹⁄₁₂ of pie with 3 level tablespoons whipped cream (55 milligrams sodium)

Apple Pie*, ¹⁄₁₂ of pie with ¼ cup vanilla ice cream (33 milligrams sodium)

This is an equally Grand Old Fashioned Meal but a much healthier one at an extremely delicious 996 milligrams sodium. You will go away stuffed and satisfied at one-fifth the sodium of the "old way" and less than half your daily allowance besides. Plus you still get a big helping of turkey and you get to try both pies, no agonizing decisions here. Leftovers?

Winter Holidays

The holiday season often brings people together to celebrate and where there are celebrations, usually there is food. If you've been invited to a bring-a-dish-to-pass party, bring something you love and can fill up on without fear. Then choose carefully among the other offerings to avoid a salt load that could spell trouble. Of course giving the party yourself can be a lot of work but it gives you a chance to gather friends and family close to you and control the salt on the table. If you're planning a menu for an open house, for example, consider including some of these (*indicates recipe provided):

Hot Spiced Wassail*

Gramma Balch's Fruit Punch*

Garden Mousse*

Stuffed Mushrooms*

Garlic Dip*

"Corn" Chips*

Cold cooked shrimp with cocktail sauce made from homemade low-salt ketchup* and home-prepared horseradish*

Gingerbread*

Cinnamon Cookies*

Of course, you can add saltier foods for your guests who aren't restricted, but look at the variety you have to enjoy for yourself!

Conclusion

The whole focus of this handbook has been to offer you ways to keep to the low-salt diet your heart needs without eating tasteless, boring foods while learning to create your own low-sodium dishes and menus. An important point to make is that you taste first with your eyes. If the food is appealing to look at then you've won half the battle.

So get out the good dishes and a table cloth from time to time. Light candles and put flowers on the table. Use little touches to decorate your plate. Put your serving of potato salad on a pretty lettuce leaf. Sprinkle some poppy seeds on your noodles. Use edible flowers.

One of my favorite ways to present deviled eggs is with a fresh, well washed johnny jump-up blossom on the stuffing. You can candy pansies and decorate a cake with them. Nasturtium flowers are a challenge to clean well but pretty in a salad and they add a peppery flavor. Chive blossoms add a nice taste boost and color to a plate, too.

Think about the colors on your plate—broiled chicken breast, boiled noodles, yellow beans, and applesauce are good for you but very blah to look at all on the same plate. Mix your colors and your flavors to tease your taste buds.

Here's How It All Shakes Out

Salt is part of our lives, but it doesn't have to shape or control our lives. Living with heart failure is a real challenge but not an insermountable one. Taking your medications and keeping your doctor's appointments are vital parts of the management of your heart problem, but keeping salt out of your diet is equally important. The more salt you consume, the more medication you need to counteract it. Eventually you face side effects from such high doses or the medications begin to lose their effectiveness. You can take control. Pass on the salt, read the labels, cook low-sodium foods with low-sodium recipes, and advocate for yourself.

Epilogue

This guide is only the beginning. Look at that collection of recipes you have. Dust off the old cookbooks and find ways to adjust the sodium content. Inventory your cupboards, pantry, and fridge. Toss out or give to a food bank everything that could hurt you. Change your style as well as the attitudes of those around you. Now you have all the tools to move forward on your journey into low-sodium living.

A final few words of encouragement: Never waste time worrying about what's gone on before. Devote yourself to the future, not the past. Don't become discouraged if it seems difficult at first. Just keep going and never look back, lest you become a pillar of that white stuff. Eat well, live well, stay well. The health of your heart is in your hands. Handle with care.

Index

The Handbook of Practical Low-Salt Living